JOHN MACDONALD   A Philosophy of Education

A

Philosophy

of Education

JOHN MACDONALD

University of Alberta

Scott, Foresman and Company

Library of Congress Catalog Card No. 67-22559
© W. J. Gage Limited 1965. All rights reserved.
Published in the United States of America by Scott, Foresman and Company,
Glenview, Illinois 60025. Printed in the United States of America.
Regional offices of Scott, Foresman and Company are located in
Atlanta, Dallas, Glenview, Palo Alto, and Oakland, N.J.

Contents

64077

Foreword

This book makes no claim to originality in any strict sense of the word. The philosophy of education has engaged the attention of too many keen minds for too long a time to leave much scope for that. *A Philosophy of Education* is an essay in synthesis rather than in fresh exploration, and, as such, it may lay claim to a certain novelty of conception and development. It possesses, moreover, several specific features to which I should like to draw the reader's attention.

The philosophy of education is treated as a subject of study in its own right. It is not regarded as a practical application of, or deduction from, any system of general philosophy. Here and there the argument commits itself to positions representative of the stand of one or another school of philosophy, such as those of pragmatism, idealism, realism, or existentialism. This method does not, however, imply eclecticism, in the sense of deliberate concentration on such features of each philosophic system as appear suggestive for a philosophy of education. On the contrary, the argument is developed without advance regard for the tenets of any particular philosophic system.

In viewing the philosophy of education as a study in its own right, one is committed to placing certain limitations on the meaning of education. It is possible, and indeed very common, to start with so broad a definition of education that a philosophy of education becomes, in effect, an aspect of a general philosophy. For example, the writer who begins by defining education as the sum total of influences, conscious and unconscious, material and spiritual, that affects the individual's development throughout the entire course of his life, commits himself to a concept of education applicable to all organisms whatsoever.

A parallel situation exists in the field of ethics or moral philosophy, as borne out by the writings of men like Herbert Spencer and Leslie Stephen in the nineteenth century, Julian Huxley in the present century, and many others who have sought to place moral philosophy in the framework of the general theory of evolution. However legitimate this broad approach may be, it is not likely to shed much direct light on what the ordinary man means by morality.

The term education, as it is used in this book, is not taken to mean something that is happening to everyone all the time. Rather it is considered to mean something formal and specific, namely, the deliberate effort on the part of the mature members of society to mould the development of the immature. The philosophy of education then becomes a matter of setting forth the values by which this effort should be directed.

The scope of this inquiry is limited still further to a consideration of the most important agency of formal education, the school. The influence of educational agencies operating outside the school is assessed, in so far as it can be assessed at all, with respect to the manner in which these agencies further or thwart the purposes of the school.

A philosophy of education developed from this point of view is a philosophy of values, but not a general philosophy of values—it concentrates on values with direct and basic significance for the school. The essential purpose of this book is, therefore, to present a coherent, systematic account of those values that should serve as guideposts both to the practical teacher and to the educational administrator, and that should enable the intelligent layman to pass informed judgment on what the schools, colleges, and universities are doing.

One feature of this volume that will be at once evident to the reader who is already knowledgeable in the field of educational philosophy is the avoidance of the use of classifications or captions such as "traditionalist," "essentialist," "reconstructionist," "progressivist," and others. Labels of this nature are no doubt useful as indications of a writer's general outlook on education, but they can easily lead one to render less than justice to that person's thinking. The contribution of one "essentialist," for example, may be very different from that of another. Undergraduates in particular, the author has observed, frequently derive a curious satisfaction from being able to "label" a writer. One suspects that the label, instead of serving as a guide to a more perceptive study of the particular author, becomes merely a pretext for summary disposal of him. For the hard-pressed student, the label may be all that he knows, and all that he believes he needs to know. In this study such captions are regarded as manifestations of a fundamental and permanent tension in educational thought and practice, the nature and causes of which are explicitly explored.

A Philosophy of Education is divided into three sections. Part 1 presents an account of what the author regards as the universals or constants of educational philosophy. It is of this timeless aspect of educational values that the author presented a schematic account in an earlier publication.[1] In the present volume that account is expanded, and practical applications of its tenets are explored.

The second section examines these basic values of educational philosophy in the context of the twentieth century. Considered in this light, they suggest new problems, or rather, old problems that have acquired new significance and urgency. In addition, these universal values focus attention upon the source of a confusion that is all too common in current controversy, the failure to discriminate the contemporary—the significant contemporary—from the ephemeral.

The third part contains notes on some of the philosophical systems mentioned in the other sections of the book. The object of these comments is to give the student who is without background in the history of philosophy an idea of the essential tenets of these systems and to draw his attention to certain of their facets that are of special interest from an educational point of view.

[1]See John Macdonald, *Mind, School, and Civilization* (Chicago: University of Chicago Press, 1952).

Part I:

The Universals of Educational Philosophy

1 *The Meaning of Education*

The need for formulating an acceptable philosophy of education has given rise to one of the most baffling inquiries to which philosophers and other thinkers have addressed themselves. Yet the term "education" can denote something that raises no philosophical problem at all. Let us begin by considering this simpler meaning of education.

At the primitive level of society, one meaning of education was vocational training, as we would call it today. The young had to be taught how to use tribal tools and weapons, how to fish and fight, so that in due course they could carry their weight in maintaining the economy of the tribe. Because the aim or object of this task was quite definite, it raised no questions pertinent to the philosophy of education. It could and no doubt did pose the problem of the best way of attaining the desired result, but this was not a question for philosophy. The philosophy of education is concerned not with the *how* but with the *what*, and at that unsophisticated level there was never any question about the "what."

In addition to learning practical skills, the young had to be trained in the acquisition of something further, something that also created no philosophical problem at this primitive level. They had to learn the mores of the tribe, the body of custom, belief, ritual, and taboo by which the tribe regulated its daily behavior. A large part of this training was acquired incidentally, as the result of constant association with the adults, but much of it also had to be directly and deliberately taught. For this purpose, as well as for instruction in the skills already mentioned, the tribe might have had a teacher as well as something corresponding to our school. But the tribe depended on incidental and direct instruction as imparted by the elders. Whatever the situation, the family played an important part in the education of the young.

At the civilized level, the level with which we are concerned in this book, the picture appears to be a very different one, but basically it remains the same. The young must master the knowledge and "skills" (one of the more useful words adopted by recent writers on education) that their elders consider essential. They must also acquire the mores of the group to which they belong. Here, as on the primitive level, this process is accomplished to a considerable extent incidentally, as the result of day-to-day living, although direct teaching plays a relatively much greater part at the civilized level than it does at the primitive level.

Several important factors greatly complicate the picture at the civilized level. The family can no longer adequately cope with the knowledge and skills that must be imparted to the young, and the professional teacher therefore becomes an integral part of the picture. No simple, clearly marked group like the tribe, with its very definite mores, exists on the civilized plane. It is true that for a long time civilized society did not differ greatly from the primitive tribe in this respect, since the primitive tribe was replaced, in so far as education was concerned, by the social class. Born into a certain social class, the young used to be trained to take their place in it by learning not only its manners, modes of speech, and other such externals of conduct, but also its distinctive ways of thinking and feeling—in a word, its ideology. In a well-established social class, this ideology was usually definite enough to be inculcated in the young both by indirect influence and by explicit teaching.

This specific kind of education applied to the lower as well as to the upper classes. In so far as the lower classes received any education at all, it took the form of vocational training (vocations themselves being a matter of class) and training "to know their place," which meant training in the mores of their particular class.

It is in the upper classes, however, that we find the clearest examples of class education. Let us examine a few of these illustrations by way of presenting a background for the very different situation that confronts the educationist of today.

In the Middle Ages, one important side of education was directly vocational in character. This was the education that aimed at producing the men of letters, or the clerks, as they were called. They were taught to read and write, and this meant reading and writing Latin, because Latin was the language in which written communication was, for the most part, carried on.

Turning to the education of the medieval knight, we come upon a pertinent illustration of class education. The product of such an education carried the unmistakable stamp of his knightly class. Edmund Spenser, in his poem *The Faerie Queene*, composed in the days of Elizabeth I, refers to the distinctive characteristic of the medieval knight:

> There is I know not what great difference
> Between the vulgar and the noble seed,
> Which unto things of valorous pretense
> Seems to be borne by native influence,
> As feates of arms, and love to entertaine,
> But chiefly skill to ride seems a science
> Proper to gentle bloud.[1]

And everything else about the knight was as "classy" as his seat in the saddle. His singular traits were usually attributed to heredity, to blood, and to breeding, a sure sign that education had done its work well.

Throughout the eighteenth and nineteenth centuries, education in the so-called Public Schools of England—Eton, Harrow, St. Paul's, Winchester, and the rest—was largely of this same character. A good part of this education, and indeed for the parents probably the most important part, was expressly and very successfully aimed at turning out an individual whose speech, manners, and general mental outlook were those of his class. A few discerning persons claimed that they could even identify an individual as the product

[1] *The Faerie Queene*, II. IV. 1.

of a particular school, but in any case nobody could mistake his being a Public School boy. Although some of the qualities of this product were undoubtedly of high calibre, others were of much more dubious worth. The class itself, however, harbored no serious doubt as to the value of the product of this education. Any such doubt on the part of the class would have meant questioning its own value in the scheme of things, and a well-established class never does that.

With the passing of time and the further development of civilization, a new factor came into play. Philosophers hit upon a question which, once it had found its way into the thinking of the ordinary person, was to put an end to the smugly simple ideas of education that we have been referring to. The philosophers' query carried within itself a direct challenge both to vocational and class education. Should the human being not be trained to be something more than a competent worker and a member of a particular social class? Is there not something in the nature of man as man that should set a goal for education, for the education of all men?

The Greek philosophers had discovered this question, as they had most of the important problems in philosophy. Aristotle returned an answer to it that would be difficult to improve upon had he but developed its implications with something of the same creative genius that he brought to the topics of ethics, politics, and literary criticism. "Human excellence" was his formula for the aim of education, and by this term he meant the bringing to fruition of those traits that are distinctive to man and in virtue of which man stands supreme in the animal world. What Aristotle did, however, was to give the civilized world still another formula, or rather two other formulas, for class education.

Aristotle held that the highest form of human life is that of *theoria*, or the scholarly life, to give the word its approximate modern equivalent. The life of *theoria* is one devoted to the pursuit and contemplation of knowledge, the life which, according to Aristotle, is the true expression of Reason, the highest of the human faculties. During the Middle Ages and the Renaissance, when the universities were looking principally to Aristotle for the answers to all important *secular* questions (in matters of religion and theology they looked to the Medieval Church), they saw in this idea of the scholarly life confirmation of what they themselves were actually doing. The road to knowledge—secular knowledge—was to be found, they believed, in a study of the literatures of Greece and Rome. Such study was of course confined to a small class, but then Aristotle himself had said that only a limited number of persons possessed the capacity for the scholarly life.

For the ordinary run of freeman (the worker and the slave did not figure in these considerations at all) Aristotle posited an alternative ideal, the life according to *moral* virtue. (Intellectual virtue meant *theoria*, the aforementioned higher kind of life.) The moral level of the good life possesses its own kind of perfection, illustrated by Aristotle in his famous picture of "the high-minded man," in which he sets forth the traits that he evidently considered to constitute the ideal Athenian.[2] Too long to quote here, the passage contains a picture that the reader will find rewarding to examine and to ponder on his own. There can be little doubt that Aristotle's description of the high-minded man contributed much towards the creation of that concept in which the English Public School and Oxford itself found a congenial educational goal for the great majority of their students, namely, the idea of "the English gentleman." This goal was, however, a class concept through and through, really only a later version of "the perfect knight" of the Middle Ages, and had no more relevance to the situation of the ordinary man than the medieval view.

In his *Republic*, Plato presented a systematic treatment of the whole problem of education, and many of his observations and ideas are still well worth our attention. Plato's plan, however, was specifically designed as one of class education, with one kind of education for the guardians, another for the soldiers, and yet another for the masses. While he perceived the importance of education as clearly as any philosopher ever has, Plato was by no means thinking of education of the people for the people, as we mean it today.

[2]Nicomachaean Ethics, IV. 3.

Greek philosophy, then, was not as important a factor as it might have been in challenging vocational and class education. Any significant alteration in outlook, any new idea, such as the change in the goal of education already noted, is likely to be gradual in appearing, and due to the operation of many causes. One would not be far wrong in seeing a very important source of change in the work of certain early educational reformers who were primarily practitioners of education rather than theorists.

Comenius and Pestalozzi are two cases in point. These men possessed a profoundly religious outlook on education, and no person with such an attitude is content to have his educational vision circumscribed by the requirements of a job or the standards of a social class. Pestalozzi in particular reveals by his pre-occupation with the famous plant metaphor that he feels, if he does not clearly see, that the concept of education must mean something more than merely vocational and class education. The plant metaphor likens the relationship of teacher and pupil to that of gardener and flower, with the skilful gardener providing the nurture that in due course leads the plant to blossom and bear fruit. We shall encounter this same concept later on in a more up-to-date form.

The idea of something mysterious and precious accomplished by education had become widely accepted as early as the period of the Renaissance. One would logically expect two developments to have followed: first, that people would ask what that something precious might be; and second, that they would inquire whether the schools and colleges were likely to attain it by what they were doing. A few thinkers did raise these very questions, but another kind of reaction occurred, one that historians of education tend to overlook, and one that was much more general and more typical of the way in which a new idea is apt to be received. The precious something remained for the public a mysterious something. People did not ask what it was, or if they did, they found an answer in some vague metaphor, such as "opening the windows of the mind." Yet they did not doubt that education made a man different and that this difference was of great importance.

Furthermore, it was simply taken for granted that this difference in man came about by way of the traditional curriculum of the schools and colleges. Anyone duly exposed to that curriculum was initiated into the world of knowledge, and knowledge somehow meant wisdom. This same thought lies at the root of the widely held view that evil living is more reprehensible in the educated man—the theory being that he should know better. The adage that "knowledge comes but wisdom lingers" would be regarded by persons of this opinion as a curious paradox.

To illustrate this attitude towards knowledge, one could cite at random almost anything said or written "in praise of education." When the poet Thomas Gray wrote of the humble folk buried in the country churchyard:

> But Knowledge to their eyes her ample page,
> Rich with the spoils of time, did ne'er unroll,[3]

the "Knowledge" to which he referred was the literary and classical education of which he himself was an accomplished product. Gray was reminding us that the underprivileged peasants had to get along in the world without benefit of the riches that this education bestowed. A more recent example of this viewpoint is contained in the following passage from J. M. Barrie's play *Mary Rose*:

MARY ROSE: Is your father a crofter in the village?

CAMERON: Yes, ma'am, when he is not at the University of Aberdeen.

SIMON: My stars, does he go there too?

CAMERON: He does so. We share a verry small room between us.

SIMON: Father and son. Is he going into the ministry also?

CAMERON: Such iss not his purpose. When he has taken his degree, he will return and be a crofter again.

SIMON: In that case I don't see what he is getting out of it.

CAMERON: He iss getting the grandest thing in the world out of it; he iss getting education.[4]

[3]*Elegy Written in a Country Church Yard.*
[4]*Mary Rose*, Act II.

One is reminded of the carrying out of ritual, for basically this form of education appears to be just that. The important part that ritual plays in human living and the curiously strong appeal that ritualistic behavior holds for human beings have often been stressed by social psychologists. The psychological origin of ritual is clear enough. The human being finds himself faced with a situation where he must do something. The situation is not one that can be dealt with in a logical or instinctive way, as his more common practical problems can be, and yet he realizes that he must deal with it.

Ritual provides the way out. A certain definite form of behavior comes to be prescribed and, if rigidly observed, it will serve the purpose. The purpose may be quite specific, as in a pre-hunting ritual, or it may be conceived in the vaguest manner, but in both instances it is keenly felt to be important. Moreover, there is no idea of how the series of acts that constitutes the ritual brings about the result, but there are few doubts among those who follow the ritual that it does so.

The attitude to education that we have been discussing, the belief that exposure to the traditional curriculum of education inevitably yields wisdom, seems to have developed in this same fashion. The public perceived the idea of an objective to be achieved, in this case, a change in the human being. However vaguely this change was conceived, it was felt to be profoundly important. The attainment of it came to be connected with what the schools were doing. The training provided by the schools might have vocational value, just as it might have value for fitting the individual into a social class, but this other potency was also attributed to it. It might not make the pupil "better off," but it certainly made him better. It achieved the status of ritual, which meant that nobody questioned its efficacy and that any departure from it was "viewed with alarm."

We have stressed this aspect of educational history not only because it is interesting as a phase in the general history of ideas, but also because it is most relevant to our own quest for a philosophy of education. It helps us to understand the opposition encountered by educational reformers who have questioned the value of the traditional curriculum. Historians of education have usually attributed this resistance to vested interest, especially, as we have seen, to vested interest in the classics. Teachers whose training was expressly designed to enable them to teach the traditional subjects were not likely to welcome any innovation which implied that their training had been along the wrong lines. Those whom they had taught would naturally share their feeling in this respect.

Vested interest, with the prejudices it inspires, is unquestionably always an important factor in the opposition to social change of any kind. But vested interest is hardly enough to account for the stubborn and prolonged resistance encountered by those who advocated any substantial change in the traditional ideas and practices of education. Back of this opposition there lay something more difficult to deal with and also more deserving of respect than mere selfishness or stupidity. The reformers were touching one of the most sensitive nerves in the human psyche—devotion to ritual.

Two further observations are appropriate at this point. First, it should be kept in mind that ritual may include elements that have a logical relationship to the end in view. Primitive ritual in connection with the treatment of disease, for example, is not uncommonly found to contain (hidden in the elaborate proceedings that make no scientific sense) elements that are recognizable as good medical practice. Second, with respect to *what* education should do to the individual, the reformers seemed to be almost as much at a loss as those whose ideas they were trying to change. Even the most radical of the reformers, Rousseau himself, notable pioneer though he was in the *how* of education, left no clear picture of the *what* of the product that education should turn out, beyond telling us that this product is not to be soldier, magistrate, or priest, but a man.

The efforts of subsequent thinkers to make good this all-important omission have been unremitting, but the overall result seems, on the surface at any rate, to be little more than a vast maze of "argument about it and about." Let us enter this maze to see whether, by way of it, we can arrive at a valid answer to our question, and consequently at an acceptable philosophy of education.

2 *Education and Human Nature*

Our inquiry into the philosophy of education will be concerned with certain fundamental concepts or ideas that have exercised a profound influence on both educational thought and practice. They are: first, the concept of human excellence, which was clearly formulated by Aristotle but not developed by him in a manner acceptable to present-day thinking; second, the idea of formal mental training, one that has long influenced educational thought and practice; third, the concept of growth, a reflection of the influence of the biological sciences on educational thinking; fourth, the notion of social adjustment; and fifth, the understanding of personality and its development.

Educational thinkers have been inclined to select *one* of these basic notions and to define education in terms of it. Thus they might state that the aim of education is human excellence, or mental discipline, or growth, or social adjustment, or the development of personality. We shall proceed differently. Beginning with one of the five concepts that we have mentioned—it matters not which one—we shall examine that concept in such a way as not only to bring out its own basic meaning and importance, but also to show how it inevitably leads us to each of the other four ideas. None of these five concepts is in itself adequate to present a complete picture of the nature and purpose of education; each of them is, however, an essential facet of the total picture. Our investigation thus aims at showing, not that these ideas basically amount to the same thing, for they do not, but rather that they are mutually compatible and complementary. We are not called upon to choose among these concepts; we are required to find a place for all of them in what reveals itself as a complete picture.

We shall select as our starting-point the first concept mentioned, that of human excellence. To say that human excellence is the aim of education implies that one is *deducing* the meaning of education from a study of human nature. Through all the differences of race, class, and training that divide men, there runs a common core of humanity, and the capacities and traits that make up this core give us the clue to what education ought to accomplish. Education should foster and develop these capacities, for they are the universals or constants that we can detect behind the great and ever-changing diversity that constitutes human nature as we actually find it.

Clearly, one qualification must be made forthwith: human nature possesses bad as well as good traits. Cruelty, for instance, seems to be just as universal as kindness. We are compelled to say, then, that education must aim at developing those traits that are considered good or desirable, *worthy* of being developed. To revert to Aristotle's idea, it is the traits that are *distinctive* of man (the good ones, of course) that we must discover if we are to set a goal for education.

We learn the nature of man (as we learn the nature of any other animal) by observing how he behaves. Human nature is what human nature does. Behavior in this connection, however, includes the reasons, motives, or needs that make the human being behave in a certain way. Our interest, then, lies in those traits that have resulted in the permanent standards or values by which man lives, in so far as he is expressing what is good or worthy in his nature.

Man is *homo cognoscens,* a creature striving to know and understand the world in which he finds himself. The acquisition of knowledge springs partly from the necessity of coping with the problems of everyday living, and partly from the need to know for the sake of knowing. Under the spur of these two demands, man has built up an extensive body of knowledge, ranging all the way from the practical insights that enable him to deal with matters of daily life—the unsifted gleanings of experience passed on from one generation to the next—to the highly systematized and well-tested body of knowledge which is modern science.

But man does more than simply try to know his world; he responds in another way, in a way indicated by the word "aesthetic." He is *homo sentiens* as well as *homo cognoscens*. Certain combinations of colors, sounds, and forms are felt to be in themselves interesting and pleasing. The feelings associated with this aesthetic experience are not merely pleasure, pain, and instinctive emotions like anger and curiosity, all of which man shares with the animals. They are more complex and, presumably at any rate, distinctively human.

Man is also *homo socius*. He is concerned with his fellow humans in a manner very different from the animal's consciousness of kind. First and foremost, he is involved with them morally and politically —he strives for better, more satisfying ways of living with them. In the course of his evolution, man has developed standards to regulate the relationships of individual to individual, group to group, and individual to group. Terms like "social science" and "political science" remind us of the fact that man is also interested in his fellow humans from a scientific point of view, since they are part of the world he needs to understand. Man is concerned with them aesthetically, finding their behavior and their ways of thinking and feeling interesting to contemplate on their own account. Drama and fiction are the fruits of this latter interest.

It remains to mention two values that hold a special position with respect to education. The first of these is the religious value, and here we shall consider only the basic need that religion claims to satisfy. Some thinkers have held that this need is not really permanent or basic, but rather one that is peculiar to the lower levels of human mental development. Considering the extent to which religion has been a formative agency in the development of great civilizations in the past, including our own, the burden of proof certainly rests upon those who would dismiss it merely as a passing phase of human history. On the civilized level at least, the underlying motive of the religious need appears to be complex.

The religious value expresses the need for finality, for some ultimate illumination in a world which ordinary human knowledge, however deeply it penetrates, still leaves shrouded in ultimate mystery. This is the stark fact that always confronts *homo cognoscens*, however sophisticated a level of knowledge and understanding he may attain. Again, man perceives himself to be an infinitesimally small something in an infinite universe. His feeling of personal significance is depressed, as is his sense of the ultimate significance of the values he lives by. Moreover, during his more reflective moments he cannot escape the awareness of ultimate loneliness or isolation that dwells in the inmost core of his personality. Matthew Arnold characterizes this sense of human desolation in the well-known lines:

> Yes, in the sea of life enisled,
> With echoing straits between us thrown,
> Dotting the shoreless watery wild,
> We mortal millions live *alone*.[1]

A sense of impenetrable mystery, a feeling of personal near-nonentity, the desolation of aloneness—religion has its roots in the need to find a way of feeling at home in this kind of world.

The second of these values that hold a special position with regard to education is the material or economic value. We may define this value in terms of man's interest in avoiding physical suffering on the one hand and enjoying the comforts, amenities, and luxuries made available by our civilization on the other. The material or economic value is the one implied in the common phrase "a high standard of living." The outlook of our civilization has changed radically with regard to this aspect of life. In the past, the attitude to physical suffering was to regard it as inevitable for large sections of the population, and even, indirectly, as a possible blessing—a discipline valuable as training in the moral virtues. Today, it is common to look on physical suffering, in any of its manifold forms—poverty, disease, high rate of premature mortality, economic insecurity, and the like—as evil. Suffering is considered a physical evil, as distinct from the moral evil inherent in the flouting of basic social values discussed earlier.

The spectacular manner in which Western civilization has coped with physical evil and raised the general level of material well-being is probably the main reason for the penetrations that our

[1] "To Marguerite," from *Poems*, (Macmillan & Co., London, 1908) p. 197.

Western civilization has made into so many other civilizations. The Marxian philosophy, as the West is nervously aware, lends itself to presentation as a special gospel for the ultimate removal of physical evil. The bearing of this situation on education is indirect, but, as we shall see later, nevertheless of first importance.

Let us now turn from the basic values with which education must concern itself to the matter of skills, the most fundamental and pervasive of which is language. Two questions require analysis in this regard: the nature of language, that is, the kind of mental capacity that makes language possible; and the use of language as a tool, as a skill strictly so-called, in human communication. The solution to the first of these problems bears significantly on the issue of general mental training. The topic of language as a tool in human communication will be examined in detail in another section of this study.

The use of language sets man apart from the rest of the animal world. Those who claim that some animals can learn to use language are merely using the world "language" in a vague and inexact fashion. They take it to mean communication by any sort of sign whatsoever, and it is, of course, a well-known fact that human beings do communicate with animals and that animals communicate with one another. But the reader should satisfy himself that in all such cases the signs are either (a) sounds or gestures instinctively produced and instinctively reacted to, as when a dog snarls to "warn" another dog to keep away, or when a bird calls to its mate, or (b) sounds or gestures mechanically reacted to as a matter of training or habit, as in the case of a sheep-dog and its master. The fact that some animals are more intelligent than others can be accounted for without introducing any new factor into the argument.

Admittedly, there are instances of communication between animal and animal and between man and animal that have about them an appearance of mystery, and that may indeed involve some phenomenon that is without parallel or analogy in human experience. Yet one consideration must always lead us to draw a firm line at attributing language to animals, namely, if animals are capable of using language in any significant way at all, it is impossible to see why then they should not have developed a social life com-

parable to that of man. Animal life has not achieved this development, the ant-hill, the bee-hive, and similar examples of animal
society not being analogous in any important way.

The language sign, or "symbol," as it is more correctly called,
possesses several noteworthy characteristics. It has a more or less
permanent core of meaning, as opposed to the changeable one of
the knot in a handkerchief or the counters in a game of poker.
The meaning of the language symbol, unlike that of the mathematical symbol, is always in some degree affected by the context
in which it appears. At the civilized level in particular, the language symbol is usually conventional or arbitrary—there is no
natural connection between the sign and the thing signified. "A
rose by any other name would smell as sweet"; the connection
between the symbol and the object symbolized must be taught
and learned.

For our purpose, the most important fact to note is that the
ability to apprehend and use language presupposes a basic mental
capacity, the capacity to generalize and abstract. Abstraction and
generalization are fundamentally one process, since they both rest
on the ability to detect the common element in different objects
and situations. We "abstract" this common element, that is, we
select it for attention, and this process we may refer to either as
abstraction *or* generalization, or as abstraction *and* generalization.

The individual who learns the word "book," for example, has
given evidence that he is capable of forming some idea of the
characteristics common to the objects thus called, and of discounting other characteristics such as color, size, and weight. To
arrive at the meaning of the word "steal," the individual must
grasp the general idea of taking what belongs to another without
that other person's consent. If he cannot comprehend this general
idea (as happens with low-grade imbeciles), all that can be done
is to condition him to behave correctly with respect to the property
of his brother, his sister, his friend, and in any other specific
relationship or situation that he may be expected to encounter.
This latter conditioning is obviously the type that can be successfully communicated to animals.

The capacity of abstraction and generalization is the basis of all
thinking, including that elaborate, highly-controlled thinking called

"reasoning." The question is frequently asked, which comes first in human development, thinking or language? Unlike the poser about the chicken and the egg, this question has point and can be answered. Language presupposes thinking, but without language, thinking would remain very rudimentary and simple. Furthermore, it is always well to bear in mind that an idea has not become a permanent possession of mankind until some form of expression in language has been found for it.

There is yet another distinctively human skill which education must take into account. Man is not only *cognoscens, sentiens,* and *socius,* he is also *faber.* Like the animals, he must adjust himself to a natural environment, and, again like the animals, he inherits reflexes and instincts which form the basis of such adaptation. But, as *faber,* man goes far beyond the animals in the way of actively changing the environment to meet his needs. He progressively creates a non-natural environment of houses, roads, bridges, ships, planes, and so forth. This technological environment, as we may call it, not only satisfies specific needs; it gives rise to new needs, and moreover, to major new problems of adaptation, as we shall see more fully in a subsequent chapter.

But it is not only in connection with man's material interests or values that this creative, manipulative faculty has found significant expression; it has also played a notable part in the furtherance of his spiritual values.

Man as a knower would not have progressed very far without experiment, that manipulation of environment which yields a clear and reliable answer to a question. Without the manipulative impulse, moreover, *homo sentiens* would be limited to passive acceptance of what nature has to offer. He would never have set about the impressive project of reproducing beautiful objects in the form of works of art, thereby not only giving them permanence, but also throwing into clear relief those qualities in them that aroused his aesthetic feelings.

3 *Knowledge as a Basic Value: The Kinds of Knowledge*

The universal values that are to be considered, theoretically and practically, in Chapters Three through Eight, are traditionally referred to as truth, beauty, and goodness. Instead of using the philosophically difficult term "truth," we shall employ the term "knowledge"; for "truth" implies not only correct knowledge, but adequate and even final knowledge (except of course for the pragmatist), whereas the term "knowledge" presumes no such claim. Wrong knowledge or error, for example, might be considered an advance on ignorance, in the sense that ignorance implies simple unawareness not only of an answer but even of a question. From our present point of view, the most important consideration is the fact that there are different levels or kinds of knowledge.

First, there is merely factual or informational knowledge. The height of Mount Everest, the day of the week on which Abraham Lincoln was assassinated, the name of Shakespeare's wife, and similar facts, are illustrations of this kind of knowledge. The acquisition of such knowledge depends on the basic fact underlying all memory—sheer native retentiveness—and individuals differ greatly with respect to this ability. At one extreme is the leaky memory that holds nothing for long, and at the other the fly-paper memory that retains anything that touches it. In neither instance can any reason be asserted for the fact that a particular piece of knowledge remains or fails to remain in the memory.

Educationists have belittled the factual form of knowledge, and with good reason. The temptation is strong for the teacher to see in it a shortcut to achieving the goal of making his pupils knowledgeable creatures. The method employed is simple repetition or rote learning, one that demands no special effort on the teacher's part. The temptation on the part of the teacher (as the history of education vividly portrays) is to lay the unction to his soul that in proceeding thus he is training the memory and increasing its native retentiveness, a result that, were it a reality, would indeed be most desirable. For, abuses apart, a mind well stocked with even this kind of knowledge is better than a vacuous one.

On a plane above mere factual knowledge or information is organized knowledge, in which facts are linked to form a unified whole. When we say that we have knowledge of the American Civil War, we recall what we happen to remember about the slavery issue and the movement of the South towards secession. The facts that we possess are regarded as part of the cause of the conflict. Names like Lincoln, Davis, Stanton, and Johnson we link by the idea of political leadership. Lee, Grant, Sherman, and Jackson we associate with military operations. All of these individuals and ideas combine to constitute a total picture, along with its emotional overtones, of what we mean by the Civil War.

Clearly, two principles of organization are at work here. One of these is mechanical organization, based on spatio-temporal connections: individuals and places recalled belong to a particular region and to a particular period. The other principle is logical organization, by which no memory fact is included unless it fits into the meaningful whole. Matters of foreign policy, such as colonial expansion, are excluded from the picture of a conflict that was purely internal. True, we include Lord Palmerston and the British government of that time in our portrait, but only because we remember their secret hope for a Confederate victory. So, too, we may add the feelings of the British people, because of the prevalence of strong anti-slavery feelings in England. We form a selective picture, and in so far as the selection is determined by what will and will not fit into the total image, it is a logical or meaningful, not a mechanical picture.

It is noteworthy, also, that this overall picture contains elements inserted as the result of unconscious inference; no person or book reveals to us that these facts are part of the whole—we infer, more or less unconsciously, that they must be so. Memory-training schemes are based largely on this same principle of getting the student to link an isolated fact with a constellation of other facts, so that he has not one, but a number of associative connections, to help him in his effort at recall.

Organized knowledge is the knowledge that we depend upon to a great extent in our day-to-day dealings with people and situations. Our memories and general experience build up a picture of what men and affairs are like, and we keep on adding to this picture, partly from new experiences and partly from reflection on old experiences. The philosopher John Locke called this type of knowledge "probable knowledge," by way of reminding us that it possesses a lesser degree of *certainty* than the other forms of knowledge that will presently be discussed. Locke gives the following very sound account of the factors upon which we more or less consciously depend in assessing the reliability of organized knowledge:

> First, the conformity of anything with our own knowledge, obser-vation and experience. Secondly, the testimony of others, vouching their observation and experience. In this is to be considered (1) the number, (2) the integrity, (3) the skill of the witnesses, (4) the de-sign of the author, when it is a testimony of a book cited, (5) the consistency of the parts, and circumstances of the relation, (6) con-trary testimonies.[1]

A very large part of our understanding of the world is acquired in terms of this knowledge—factual knowledge with the facts more or less permeated by spatio-temporal and logical or rational connections. A judge, for example, uses this knowledge when he reviews the facts of a case, making one fact support another, and reaching a reasoned verdict. It is organized knowledge which serves as the basis of literary criticism and appreciation, when we say, for instance, that such and such a character is or is not "true to life." Organized knowledge, as Locke's analysis shows, is the

[1] *Essay Concerning Human Understanding*, IX. xv. 4.

kind of knowledge represented, for example, by history and by political philosophy. Indeed a large part of what we mean by the humanities exemplifies this type of knowledge, a fact that is of great significance in education, since the humanities are concerned with the drawing of a clear distinction between this form of organized knowledge and scientific knowledge, strictly so called.

The oft-cited principle of the unity of knowledge can be accepted in the sense that knowledge, of whatever kind, consists in correct judgments about reality. But if we leave the matter there, we are ignoring differences that make all the difference, certainly where education is concerned. The reader may make up his mind on this point after considering those characteristics that appear to be a *sine qua non* of science in the strictest sense of the word.

Let us examine the realm of modern science. We say "modern" because the word "science" has commonly been used to mean all kinds of knowledge. The scientist commonly uses the word in this comprehensive sense, when he states that there is only one kind of knowledge, scientific knowledge, and that other forms are merely science in the making. There is, he claims, merely a difference in the penumbra of certainty that is attached to the various kinds of knowledge.

Science is systematized knowledge. Isolated pieces of information, however numerous, interesting, or even important, do not qualify as science. Knowledge with the status of science is knowledge that has its place in a system.

Science is progressive. The systems which constitute science are being continuously expanded, modified, and revised—there is nothing final about them. A discovery may have all the appearance of being final, of something having been made once and for all, but it is tentative or provisional nonetheless. Scientists in the century and a half following Newton regarded the Law of Gravitation as having been definitely formulated for all time, bedrock on which they could confidently build. Yet even Newton's basic law has undergone revision and restatement.

Science is tested knowledge, the test being of a particular kind. Usually this test is called the test of experiment, but this term of reference is not a wholly satisfactory one. The mystic also claims to have experimental proof of the validity of his insights, and the believer in Bahai insists that he has verified by experiment that his is a completely satisfying way of life. Scientific experiment is a totally different kind of experiment. Of its essence is: (1) that the procedure by which any particular conclusion is reached can be described and therefore repeated, and (2) that anyone who does repeat the procedure will arrive at the same result. Both requirements are summed up by saying that scientific knowledge is *public*.

The test of scientific knowledge is more usually defined as the power to control and predict events. This definition is a correct one, but one that is simply incidental to what is perhaps the most important characteristic of science, its "objective" outlook or viewpoint. The external world exists in its own right, independent of human wishes and aspirations. Events in the world occur in accordance with laws that human beings can discover, and the discovery of these laws in turn enables man to predict events and often to use them for the furtherance of human purposes. These *laws of nature*, as they are called, are uniform or fixed; there is no place for caprice in any form in the world that they govern.

Because of our civilized sophistication, we are apt to find the idea of a *natural event* quite simple and obvious. Far from being obvious, however, this concept is a late discovery in human mental history, and even now many people find it an idea difficult to accept. The explanation that commends itself to the primitive mind is rather different. Events occur because of the actions of psychical creatures that we may call "spirits." Such creatures are thought of as similar in nature to human beings, activated by feelings like love, hate, sympathy, resentment, jealousy, and the rest. For example, the idea of death resulting from natural causes is simply not part of the mental equipment of truly primitive man. In his view, death is due to the action of some malevolent spirit. This way of looking at the world is called animistic or anthropomorphic, and the objective outlook can be achieved only through its complete abandonment. The abandonment of this conception required a very long period of history. Science, therefore, simply because the objective outlook is so essential to it, is a late-comer on the human scene. In point of fact, science is an achievement of our own Western civilization.

The distinction between science and what we have called organized knowledge should now be clear, as should the importance of the distinction. Science is organized and logical knowledge, but it is not the *only* knowledge that possesses these characteristics. Science is a species of a genus that includes "probable knowledge," to revert to Locke's phrase. From the proposition that "all scientific thinking is logical thinking," the scientist is apt to infer that all logical thinking is scientific thinking—a fallacy familiar to the student of elementary logic.

In this same connection, the term "objective" is often used ambiguously. The word is broadly used to mean the absence of prejudice or prepossession, open-mindedness of outlook. All thinking that is to yield any real knowledge must be objective in this sense. The objective viewpoint of science goes beyond this, however, to imply the positive belief that events occur in accordance with fixed laws that are discoverable, and that make prediction possible.

The scientist sometimes means the objective outlook to be applied to human behavior as well as to other spheres, and the science of psychology reminds us that he is to a certain extent right in this attitude. But if the scientist means that there is no valid knowledge of human behavior except scientific knowledge of it, then he goes too far. He assumes (and often states) that if we knew enough about human behavior, and all the factors involved in it, then it, too, would exemplify the rigid, mechanistic sequences established by science in other fields. At this point in his reasoning, the scientist should be reminded that it is one thing to proceed on his assumption as a working scientific hypothesis, but quite another thing to assert ultimate philosophic justification for it. Human experience does not indicate that reality is of this mechanistic nature, and, lacking omniscience, man must come to terms with reality as he encounters it in daily life.

Yet another type of knowledge that merits our consideration is purely logical or deductive knowledge, knowledge that develops the necessary or logical implications of concepts or ideas. In the past, philosophers were accustomed to point to mathematics, especially to Euclidean geometry, as the clear example of logical knowledge, or demonstrative knowledge, as Locke and other philosophers called it. Since it possessed the quality of absolute certainty, purely logical knowledge was held up as the ideal to which all knowledge should aspire.

In our own century, a rethinking of the question of the nature of mathematics, in particular by Alfred North Whitehead and Bertrand Russell, has shown that mathematics is only a special case or branch of formal logic, the application of formal logic to the purely quantitative aspect of reality. Thinking in the field of formal logic concentrates exclusively on abstract logical relationships as such, and excludes from the outset the possibility (always present in scientific knowledge) that some new fact of experience will contradict its findings.

Closely allied with formal logic, and indeed an outcome of it, is philosophy. The need that philosophy aims at satisfying is clear enough, and appears, moreover, to be a need or interest that is permanent in human beings, the need for a comprehensive intelligible picture of reality as a whole.

What do the different kinds of knowledge, with their illumination of diverse fields of experience, finally add up to? To appreciate the significance of this question, let us adopt, and rather freely adapt, an allegory used by Theodore Greene in another connection.[2] Imagine a high mountain surrounded by territory that presents very different topographical features from one vantage point to another. A number of individuals ascend the mountain by different paths and observe the view below. As each person moves upward, his view becomes more and more extensive, but it is always limited by his particular position on the mountainside.

Each of these individuals is in communication with a person at the foot of the mountain, to whom he reports from time to time a picture of the surrounding country. The task of the person at the foot of the mountain is to construct from the various reports a picture of what the country all around the mountain really looks

[2] See "*Religion and the Philosophies of Education,*" *Religious Education,* New York Religious Education Association (March-April, 1954).

like. The climbers paint very diverse pictures, and they suspect one another of inaccurate reporting. One is accused, for example, of using glasses that distort the picture. His answer is that without glasses, and particularly without the kind that he is using, no true view is possible.

The man at the base of the mountain is, of course, the philosopher, and the climbers are scientists representing various sciences. To compound the confusion, artists and moralists are also working their way up the mountainside. Through it all, one fact is clear: no one will ever get to the top and settle the matter once and for all in that manner.

The allegory of the mountain climbers provides a vivid reminder that the experimental test is not available to the philosopher. His study is not another science, and his account is subject to two tests only. The first of these is the logical test. Is his report logically coherent? Can it be shown to use logically incompatible ideas? The second test is that of completeness. An account might be logically coherent, but it might be so as a result of having omitted important facts. The creation of a picture that is beyond suspicion on both of these counts is a goal as yet unachieved by any philosopher, and one that will presumably never be accomplished. But the attempt to portray a totally accurate image will continue, for every advance in knowledge acts as a fresh stimulus to it.

Two further kinds of knowledge require brief comment, intuition and mysticism. Philosophers have attached different meanings to the term "intuition." Some have said that man possesses intuitive knowledge of the existence of God. Henri Bergson argued that instinct represents a form of knowledge (he called it "intuition") entailing a direct insight into reality that is not given by human reason. We shall employ the word "intuition" in a less recondite sense than Bergson, namely, to denote the familiar fact that an individual may judge correctly in a very complex situation and yet be quite unable to give any reasonable ground for his judgment. The individual simply has a very strong "hunch" in a given matter. The juryman who has a definite conviction with regard to the question of guilt or innocence after listening to a long and confusing presentation of evidence *pro* and *con* is a case in point. He finds it hard to produce even one convincing reason for his stand, which no doubt means that his judgment is rooted broadly in his general experience. We shall have occasion to return later to this way of knowing.

Mysticism is the final type of knowledge that we wish to characterize. Mystical experience, according to the mystic himself, brings illumination of a direct and compelling character, which is not mediated by the ordinary avenues of knowledge. In the course of history it has not been unusual to discount such knowledge as an instance of simple hallucination, but more recently philosophers have shown a tendency to take the claim of the mystic more seriously. From either point of view, mysticism has no bearing on our present inquiry. "Ineffable" is apt to be the mystic's own word for describing his experience, a term that means something so purely, incommunicably personal that education can have no concern with it.

4 *Kinds of Knowledge: The Educational Problem*

Practical applications of the kind of knowledge properly called "science" present themselves on every side to the child of today. These applications range all the way from the spectacular, such as space exploration, to the numerous gadgets and gimmicks of science that have become integral parts of daily living. In no sphere of education is it as easy for the teacher to tap the interest of the pupil as in that of science. The psychological approach, as distinct from the logical approach, is clearly indicated as the right one for awakening this interest in the pupil, and teachers have been making effective use of it.

The psychological approach to teaching belongs, however, to the primary levels of education, and no matter how well it is practised, cannot, if used by itself, accomplish the essential purpose of education, namely, a true appreciation of science, a clear understanding of the fundamental meaning of science, what it does, and how it does it. It is this comprehension, rathe than an awareness of far-reaching practical impacts, that is the important element from the standpoint of the philosophy of education. How should we proceed in order to attain this comprehension?

The pupil should be introduced to a few typical cases of scientific system, or in other words, to a few typical special sciences. We say a *few*, because the day is long past when education meant a doughty effort to cope with the whole sphere of knowledge, scientific and non-scientific. We say *typical* cases, because the scientific method, while always basically the same, reveals characteristic variations in different fields of inquiry. Physics and chemistry, which are concerned with the inorganic world, illustrate the scientific method in its purest form. In the biological sciences, such as botany and zoology, procedure must be adjusted to cope with the world of organisms. The social sciences represent a region that the scientific method has indeed entered, but one in which the method is as yet without the sure sense of direction that has marked its progress in other fields. Another very important reason for variety in the science curriculum is the relationship between aptitude and interest in the learner. Students who are apathetic to what physics and chemistry have to offer may respond with enthusiasm and alertness to botany or zoology.

Education should convey to the individual an appreciation of the scientific method. To the uneducated person, scientific discoveries and their application are apt to be vaguely thought of as a form of magic, and scientists looked upon as latter-day magicians. The person with training in the scientific method will, however, regard the familiar phrase "marvels of science" as a misnomer. There is nothing magical in science, and indeed it may be described as a matter of observing the rules of the game with patience and uncompromising conscientiousness.

This is not to say that the growth of scientific knowledge is merely a matter of painstaking effort on the part of persons versed in scientific method. Nothing could be further from the truth. The great advances in the sciences have originated and always will originate with the individual who is endowed with that special kind of intelligence and imaginative flair called "scientific genius." Francis Bacon, who provided the first clear formulation of the scientific method, failed to give a place to scientific genius in his speculations about science. He ignored the factor of hypothesis, the intelligent and often inspired guess that sees facts as manifestations of a single principle which links them together and in effect explains them.

The ancients had observed planetary movements, and Kepler had described them accurately in modern times. People had always known, too, that apples fall from trees in a certain way. Yet it needed the inspired mind of Isaac Newton to make the connection between the two well-known natural happenings. The omission of this idea of genius in his formulation of the scientific method led Bacon to make the curious suggestion that a great central bureau be set up for the purpose of receiving, examining, and collating facts submitted by a large number of observers. His belief was that the facts would, in this way, inevitably yield the answers to the problems that they provided, a fallacious notion not without parallel in our own time.

Genius is always marvellous in whatever connection it appears. The point that we wish to make, however, is that the genius must be prepared to show his fellow scientists, and anyone else capable of following his demonstration, that the hypothesis underlying his discovery is the one that best explains the facts. To impart an appreciation of the scientific method means nothing more than to provide the student with the correct perspective on this sort of situation. The communication of this understanding does not call for any special intellectual gift, or for a protracted period of scientific training. Even one good laboratory course, under the guidance of the right kind of teacher, would contribute significantly towards achieving this desired goal.

As noted in the previous chapter, an accurate understanding of the general outlook or standpoint of science is of prime importance. The scientific point of view is objective, implying belief in the existence of an independent, external world, one operating in accordance with uniform laws. The facts concerning this external world that science claims to discover must be tested and so made public before they can be accepted as discoveries. The test may be purely logical, as in mathematics; it may be experimental, as in the natural sciences, which ultimately means an appeal to the senses ("look and see for yourself"); or it may also be the test of prediction and control, which, in the last analysis, also means an appeal to the senses.

Not all features of reality lend themselves to these tests, and science concerns itself only with those that do. This is what is meant by the statement that scientific knowledge is always more or less abstract; it abstracts those facts or features capable of being verified by one or another of its own tests. We might say that science concerns itself exclusively with "things," if we define "thing" (philosophically a very defensible definition) as the kind of entity that lends itself to being manipulated in the manner implied in scientific testing. The sciences of zoology and psychology deal with "things" in this sense; their investigations are limited to those features of the living object that lend themselves to scientific testing. We will be able to reason clearly and logically if we remember that the social sciences are in precisely the same category, in so far as they are sciences, strictly so called.

Once the picture of what science is and tries to accomplish has been clarified, we may accept the claim of science that no region of reality is outside its province. Science has right-of-way into all fields of human experience, and personal, social, as well as natural phenomena are within its domain. Its right-of-way is subject only to the following conditions. First, science must not claim that its findings are necessarily the whole story, or that there is no other kind of knowledge or insight except the type that it has to offer. Second, it must strictly enforce its own test of truth and refuse its hallmark to anything that fails to satisfy that test. Reference has already been made to the common practice of using the term "scientific" as equivalent to open-minded, free from conscious bias. The immense prestige that has gathered around the word "scientific" has led to very vague and perverse use of it.

General education properly performs its function in the realm of science if it results in the following personal achievements: (1) a certain background of scientific knowledge; (2) an appreciation of the systematic and progressive character of scientific inquiry; (3) a grasp of the scientific point of view and its significance for human living; (4) an understanding of scientific method sufficient to enable the individual to recognize it when he sees it, and especially to detect spurious imitations trading on the prestige of science; and (5) a sense of the limitations inherent in the scientific point of view sufficient to leave the mind of the individual receptive to other ways of looking at reality and other kinds of insight into its meaning. Add to these benefits that education furnishes a basis for detecting the special individual aptitude upon the development of which scientific advancement depends.

These aims for general education may perhaps appear pretentious or bombastic, but they must be accomplished if the particular "excellence" of human nature represented by science is to gain and maintain its rightful place in the educational picture as a whole. One does not claim too much in stating that science teaching at its best has attained this very goal. Science teaching has, however, often fallen far short of the best, notably because teachers themselves are frequently not clear as to what they should try to do, or, as is more likely at the higher levels where the teachers are specialists, because they are wrong-headed about it. These teachers seek to imbue the student with the specialist's reverence for exact knowledge and technical competence as ends in themselves.

Not less important from the standpoint of education are the other forms of knowledge that we called purely informational or factual knowledge, and logical or organized knowledge. For most people, indeed, it might well be argued that these forms of knowledge pose a more important problem with regard to education than does scientific knowledge. As asserted in the preceding chapter, geographical and historical knowledge take the form of purely factual knowledge to a great extent, as does much of our knowledge of the world around us. From the point of view of education, only one comment about this way of knowing appears necessary, namely, that it is a mistake to suppose that exercising the mind on the task of acquiring factual knowledge results in a general increase in retentiveness and a greater power of acquiring it. If there really is any gain in these cases, it is such an insignificant one that it is not worth the time and effort required to obtain it.

Organized, non-scientific knowledge, presents education with a task as interesting as it is complex. Before we consider this kind of knowledge, however, we must first take account of a special form of factual knowledge that seldom receives attention, but that is nevertheless of great practical interest and importance. This is the way of knowing represented by what Walter Lippmann calls the "mental stereotype." The mental stereotype is a relatively simple image that tends to oversimplify and in other ways falsify thinking.

The word "negro," for instance, may evoke an image of a black man toiling in the cotton fields or giving a white man a shoeshine. "Turk" may conjure up the image of a barbarous-looking peasant in balloon trousers and a flower-pot hat. The author never hears the word "bolshevist" without seeing the fleeting image of a rough, bearded man in the act of throwing a stone at a church window. Although the mental stereotype may be purely personal, a whole group may share a common stereotype—an important point to remember.

Whether personal or social, the mental stereotype represents a "fact," a supposed picture of a section of the world, which the fly-paper part of memory has caught from one source or another and will hold for an indefinite period, perhaps even permanently. If the mental stereotype meant no more than this, it would have no interest except as a minor psychological curiosity. But the mental stereotype can influence the individual's thinking, and therefore his knowledge, in a most important way. The individual may make the mental stereotype, more or less consciously, the basis of logical thinking about the object or situation that it represents, and a piece of reasoning that sets out from such an irrational starting point is clearly vitiated.

Social psychologists have investigated the mental stereotype and have shown how powerfully it can operate to distort thinking. For example, psychologists have traced college students' attitudes to policies of immigration—the question of which national and ethnic groups should be given preference in immigration—to the kind of mental stereotypes that these students happen to possess of the various groups. Psychologists have also shown that the influence of the stereotype on the student is in inverse ratio to the amount of knowledge and experience of the particular object that the student possesses. The mental image of the Turk, for instance, is likely to be clear-cut and stable, and that of the American vague and shifting. The student, in other words, would need to think carefully about the meaning of "American," but not about the word "Turk."

Education must strive to put the individual on guard against formulating mental stereotypes, an especially important aim in these times, when society expects the individual to hold opinions about peoples and cultures of which he has no direct experience. This function of education is also of significance for the individual's understanding of his own social milieu. The implanting of suitable stereotypes is one of the most familiar devices of the propagandist, and the individual must come to realize this. Politicians stress the importance of creating a good "image" of the party leader, and the same technique is widely used in advertising, industry, and many other fields. Unfortunately, there is no simple prophylactic against the spread of the mental stereotype.

Those who think of a school or college "course" as the solution whenever a question of learning something important arises would probably prescribe a suitable course in psychology in order to combat the mental stereotype. For young adolescents, in particular, there are aspects of psychology (and this would be one of them) likely to produce an unhealthy preoccupation with one's own mental states, a situation not at all conducive to clear and effective thinking. The only certain route to our goal is the long one—training in good thinking throughout the school career as a whole, with this training properly adjusted to the different stages of growth.

Let us beware, however, of any misunderstanding on this topic. Semanticists remind us, and rightly so, that pictures constitute not only a very effective but also a very valuable form of communication. These semanticists mislead us, however, whenever they fail to make clear that the effectiveness of a picture depends in large part upon the kind of picture presented. Rubens' "Descent from the Cross," Shakespeare's Iago, Dickens' Pecksniff, to cite a few random illustrations, are pictures, but they are not stereotypes. These pictures are unique because they embody the insight or perceptiveness peculiar to the artist, as opposed to the stereotyped pictures that appear irrelevant and trivial in so far as real understanding is concerned. The former merit and reward the viewer's contemplation purely on their own accounts, while the latter offer little of value in these respects.

Focusing once again upon the general problem of knowledge, we can state that purely logical knowledge, represented by mathematics and formal logic, possesses the quality of certainty. Scientific knowledge has provisional certainty; everybody accepts it until a better hypothesis or explanation is forthcoming. Organized, non-scientific knowledge—Locke's "probable knowledge"—is a blend of logic, science, factual information, and intuition. We can best think of it, not necessarily as "probable," for that term applies only to part of this blended knowledge, but rather as ranging from practical certainty through varying degrees of probability all the way to bare possibility, to mere guessing, or perhaps even to simple suspension of judgment. This kind of knowledge poses a different and more complex problem for education than does scientific knowledge.

In training the individual to acquire and effectively use this type of organized knowledge, one must take account of *growth*. This is also true of both purely logical knowledge and scientific knowledge, but one important difference exists with regard to the kind of knowledge with which we are now concerned. We know that understanding logical and scientific knowledge depends on intellectual growth in the strict sense. It depends on what the psychologists call "maturation"; one might say that it depends on the I.Q. Piaget,[1] for example, shows us, in his account of the growth of reasoning power, how the young child is unable to grasp the idea of cause, a basic concept of science. The child's thinking is "syncretistic": cause simply means the attendant circumstances. Trees become green in spring because birds are building nests in them. Good teaching must then await the appearance of requisite intellectual capacity in the child before it can take full effect.

Training in the blended form of knowledge that we are now discussing must take account not only of maturation in the strict sense, but also of *experience*. The student is able to master the binomial theorem provided that he has reached a certain stage in his mathematical thinking. Knowledge of men and affairs is not a requirement for understanding the binomial theorem; indeed, the student may be completely innocent in respect of both men and affairs. The comprehension of history, on the other hand, is a matter of degree, the degree to which the learner has a background of general experience that he can bring to bear on the topics with which history is concerned.

In this field also, the media of communication—language, the movies, radio, and television—lend themselves all too easily to sabotaging clear and informed thinking. Concerned as it is here with matters of everyday living, with social, political, and inter-

[1] *Judgment and Reasoning in the Child*: esp. chapters 1-5 (London, Kegan Paul, 1928).

national issues, thinking is peculiarly liable to distortion by self-interest, prejudice, emotionalism, and wishful attitudes generally. How this comes about will become clearer from our examination of the mechanisms of communication in a later chapter.

Education should foster respect, not for age as such, but for experience. This attitude is obviously desirable in matters such as marriage and vocational choice, where the lesson of the individual's own experience (the proverbial teacher of the foolish) may come too late to bring anything but regret. Parents are the natural advisors in such matters, although it is always something of a fine art for parents or other mature advisors to bestow upon the young the benefit of their more experienced counsel without appearing to be "giving a lecture"—the adolescent's formula for the sort of counselling that arouses his resentment and contempt.

Respect for experience is but a special facet of a more general attitude, respect for authority. Scientific knowledge, on the level at which the young are concerned with it, is itself a matter of authority, in so far as experiment is not used. The "right" answer is at the back of the book, clear and uncompromising, and its authority is accepted by the youngster as above suspicion. This cannot be said of organized, non-scientific knowledge, for it is always in some degree a matter of "opinion." Answers are not right or wrong, but rather good or bad, better or worse.

The training of the individual to make discriminating use of authority is an important part of education, and the media of mass communication are not always helpful in this. On the contrary, preoccupied as these media so often are with "celebrities" of the many kinds that society throws up before the public from time to time, these media are quite capable of quoting a celebrated crooner or "rock'n roller" on the subject of South African *apartheid.*

Underlying this discriminating use of authority, there should be a deeper, more pervasive attitude, respect for truth itself, and the type of thinking that seems to bring one closer to it. To tell the young person that he is "entitled to his opinion," whatever that opinion or the topic under discussion happens to be, is to give him false counsel. One is entitled to an opinion only if he is reasonably well equipped to form an opinion on the matter in question.

What is implied in being "reasonably well equipped" may itself of course be a matter of opinion, but there are certainly numerous instances where persons are not sufficiently well prepared to present a coherent opinion on a given matter. The author recalls, for example, how one educationist described with enthusiasm the manner in which a group of high school students used the method of committee discussion to cope with the assignment of deciding whether the United States should enter the war in 1940.

Nor is this attitude of respect for authority intended as an approval of the old custom of expecting the young to look, listen, and hold their peace in the presence of their elders. Teachers who saw in this approach a denial of the claims of personality, and who regarded subjects like social studies as means of encouraging the young person to think for himself and to express himself on important current issues were in large measure correct. They were wrong only in so far as they failed to exploit the situation in order to foster a sense of standards that would tend to make the student an intelligent and responsible critic of all thinking, including both his own opinions and those of other persons.

This attitude of critical alertness will itself occasionally lead the young person into ultimate difficulty. He will enter into the confines of that twilight region where the perennial issues of philosophy and religion—the existence of God, immortality, freedom, the ultimate meaning of good and evil—begin to take shape for him and demand that he come to terms with them in one way or another. But even in this realm, the ability to think clearly and to draw distinctions where distinctions are needed in order to avoid mental confusion will stand him in good stead.

For example, consider the case in which the youngster has heard a good deal about wishful thinking, and has also seen and heard religious faith referred to as merely a variation on wishful thinking. Should he not draw a distinction, and ask himself whether there is not an important difference between wishful thinking and religious faith?

Wishful thinking occurs when the individual accepts an idea because he finds it attractive and does not take the trouble to examine the evidence for or against it. It also occurs when, in examining the evidence, he allows his feelings to affect his assess-ment of the evidence. In the case of wishful thinking, evidence *is* available. Faith, on the other hand, pertains to matters in which, by the very nature of the situation, logical evidence is ultimately ruled out.

Philosophers and theologians have filled many books with logical reasoning—often extraordinary acute reasoning—directed at such matters. What we are saying, however, is that logical reasoning never was and never could be of the sort to command general agree-ment and acceptance with regard to questions of philosophy and religion. The individual who feels that he must come to terms with these ultimate issues in order to live a satisfying life must arrive at his settlement either on the basis of feeling (Pascal's "reasons of the heart that the reason does not understand")[2] and/or revelation. Neither of these bases is accessible to ordinary logic, and yet to dismiss them as "wishful thinking" would be superficial and foolish.

The school has special means available for the explicit teaching of responsible, intelligent, clear thinking in the field of organized knowledge. Social studies has already been mentioned as one realm in which this attitude of critical alertness can be fostered in the individual. Any area of the humanities that is directly concerned with human beings in action—history, fiction, and drama are obvious examples — provides limitless opportunities for the resourceful teacher who is clearly aware of the values that should govern his teaching.

At the high school and college levels in particular, the fact that the historical narrative is being constantly revised and rewritten in light of modern scholarship and changing perspectives brings fresh vitality and pertinence to the study of the past. Anyone who has come to appreciate the feelings and general mental outlook of both sides in the American Civil War will not only sense the depth of the tragedy of that conflict, but will also experience an exercise in sympathetic imagination and caution in judgment that can be very pertinent to the contemporary scene. So it is with literature— the study of literature is surely one of the important ways of foster-ing the responsible, individual thinking that results in a deeper and more comprehensive knowledge of one's fellow creatures.

[2]*Pensées* (Pensée 277 "Le coeur a ses raisons que la raison ne connaît point").

5 *Art as a Basic Value*

Science is the expression of man's interest in knowing and understanding his environment. Art is the expression of his interest in objects that appeal to what is vaguely called his sense of the beautiful. For most purposes this method of distinguishing between the two interests of science and art suffices, but in our study we must attempt to make the distinction clearer and more precise.

Consider a natural event, such as a thunderstorm. As scientist, man seeks to understand the thunderstorm. This means two things. First, he tries to discover its causes, connecting the storm to other events without which it would not have happened. He relates the storm to a long spell of hot weather that has resulted in the accumulation of moisture and the occurrence of electrical discharges. The scientist's primitive counterpart probably would have related the thunderstorm to some god or spirit who had been offended and was venting his anger in this noisy manner. This primitive explanation is also science, on its own primordial level.

The second point that interests the scientist is the effect of the event. The storm may have cleared the air and produced a change in the weather; and the lightning may have caused loss of life and damage to property. Thus, the scientist tries to place the event in a chain of cause and effect, and when this end has been achieved, he has then explained the event.

An artistic attitude is a fundamentally different one. It implies interest in the event for its own sake, as a natural occurrence, an interest usually expressed by saying that the artist is concerned not with explanation but with contemplation. The object considered arouses sensations and emotions that are interesting simply as experiences. The object may also, of course, arouse ideas, but these too are enjoyed for their own sakes. Philosophers sometimes use the word "enjoyment" instead of "contemplation" to describe this attitude as it pertains to art, and "enjoyment" is perhaps the better word, for it reminds us that feeling, rather than thinking, forms the core of the experience.

Man discovered that he could create for himself objects for enjoyment or contemplation. He felt the need to reproduce an interesting object so that he could contemplate it when it was no longer present before him. This was the beginning of creative art —the desire to continue or to recover an interesting experience. Moreover, the reproduction of the object would tend to throw into relief those of its features that prompted men to conserve or recover it. This is the reason why a purely mechanical reproduction, however exact, is not art. The product of the camera is art only to the extent that a photographer, *qua artist*, determines what his machine will do.

Different means or media were used in the creative work of reproduction undertaken by man. Music developed out of his interest in sound effects, pictorial art out of his interest in form and color, and literature out of his discovery that language could be used to furnish the mind with interesting objects for its contemplation. Such was the origin and motive of art, or of the "fine arts," as they are sometimes called.

The familiar distinction between the fine arts and the so-called "practical arts" should be noted here. Some writers have seen an unnecessary mystery in this distinction. The basis of the distinction is clear enough: man is a practical creature who constantly adjusts his environment to his needs, invents tools, erects shelters, and finds that he can make these tools and shelters pleasing to look at— by using bright colors, for example. In so far as he derives enjoyment from such decorations, man is an artist; the fact that the enjoyment happens in connection with practical projects makes no difference. Man can, however, be an artist in a more subtle way. The tool or shelter may present a neat, economical, and effective adjustment of means to an end that is interesting in its own right. To the extent that man's satisfaction with the efficient tool is purely practical, purely bound up with the fact that it does its job easily and well, he is, of course, *not* an artist.

The practical arts are frequently regarded as including all practical activity. From this point of view, everything from digging a ditch to setting up apparatus for a scientific experiment would be considered a manifestation of the practical arts. The practical arts are taken to include every expression of *homo faber*: artist is equated with maker. According to this line of reasoning, the creation must be deliberate or intelligent, not instinctive, as with the ant or the beaver. Except for this latter qualification, all activity that creates objects or makes changes in environment is judged to be practical art.

No objection should be raised to this mode of thought, provided that one recognizes that it gives the word "art" a meaning distinctly different from the one that we have given it above. When the practical arts are considered to include all practical activity, art is equated with skill; the element of enjoyable contemplation *per se* is no longer believed essential to art. Any pleasure or satisfaction derived is simply that which accompanies successful activity, namely, the pleasure of overcoming obstacles. The difficulty caused by this concept of art is that it leaves us without a word to denote the kind of experience in which the element of enjoyable contemplation *is* essential.

At the same time, this broadening of the term "art" serves to remind us that the human being is not an aggregate of different interests or attitudes that occur in separation from one another. Presumably the whole nature of the human being is in some measure expressed in every piece of his behavior. John Dewey no doubt had this fact in mind when he described art as "a quality of living." Dewey was probably also expressing his characteristic distrust of "dualisms," in this case the dualism of the practical arts and the fine arts. But may we not ask whether this dualism is not both a valid and important one, an outcome of the fact that human beings learned to isolate, develop, and exploit this particular quality purely for its own sake?

In this study, we shall regard the practical arts as meaning those activities in which the *primary* object is practical—that is, utility of one sort or another—and the artistic interest secondary or incidental. The fine arts are the activities in which the primary object, and for the most part, the sole object, is artistic creation. Let us beware of talking of the fine arts as "useful" in their own way. This manner of thinking deprives the word "useful" of any serviceable meaning whatever. The distinction between the practical arts and the fine arts is a clear one, and of much significance for education.

The meaning that we attach to art education depends on the answer that we return to another question. In relation to the knowledge value, one employs terms such as "true" and "false," and the thinking that yields knowledge is said to be "logical" or "illogical," "valid" or "invalid"—in other words, objective standards are available. The question arises whether such objective standards are valid in relation to art. Or are we concerned in the realm of art with something purely personal and subjective? If the answer to this question is in the affirmative, then it is difficult to see what significant meaning one can attach to art education.

It seems clear, in any case, that the "public" quality possessed by scientific knowledge cannot be claimed for aesthetic judgments. We do not think of aesthetic judgments as revealing facts or relationships that belong to an order of reality independent of us, one existing in its own right. It is true that some thinkers have gone so far as to argue that beauty no less than truth has its roots in the very nature of things, that words such as "beautiful" and "ugly," "fine" and "tawdry," "impressive" and "trivial"—the vocabulary of our basic aesthetic judgments—would still have meaning if man were to disappear altogether. At this point we need not attempt to come to terms with this extreme form of realism. But nevertheless we must ask whether there is any sort of objectivity at all in this region of experience. Let us consider the view that there are no truly objective standards with regard to aesthetic judgments, that everything is personal, subjective.

The out-and-out philistine voices this view when he says: "I don't know what is good or bad but I do know what I like and what I don't like, and that's all there is to it." Is there any sense in telling this man that he *ought* to like something that he does not like? Try to fall back on the "public" test, and it seems to fail you badly. The philistine is probably knowledgeable enough to remind us of how little agreement there is among the creative artists themselves as to what is "good" or "bad" art. Not only are the artists often at loggerheads with the general public, which is understandable, but among themselves they can present a babel of opinion, frequently with regard to points on which the ordinary man would conceivably expect agreement.

In this view of artists and their work, the philistine is right, so much so indeed that one could formulate a rule almost without exception that no great artist has escaped denigration at the hands of some other great artist. Even Shakespeare, of whom Matthew Arnold wrote: "Others abide our question, thou art free," is no exception, for Tolstoi discounted the bard as a bourgeois who lacked true insight into human character. Without entering into any general discussion of this issue, two observations may be made which bear out the fact that in this region of value objectivity is a matter of degree. Aesthetic judgment is not a matter of "either–or," with pure subjectivity (a chaos of personal opinion) on the one hand, and the complete objectivity claimed by science on the other hand.

The first of these observations is that the philistine who insists that his own liking or disliking is decisive is in large measure correct. *One* of the essential functions of art is to give pleasure. If the individual does not find the work of art, be it a picture, a piece of music, a statue, or a poem, interesting and worth contemplating on its own account, then for him that work is not functioning as art. Protagoras' formula is thus far applicable: man (the individual man) is the measure of all things. The individual who does not find a particular piece of art pleasing moves on to another work that he does find rewarding. The pleasure-giving quality is therefore one criterion or test in the formulation of aesthetic judgments.

It is, however, not the sole criterion in this regard. A second, most important quality is the significance or depth of the work of art in question. What is the effect of the piece on the individual, beyond merely giving him pleasure? Does it leave him with his capacity for feeling deepened, broadened, and refined? When he has contemplated the object—a painting, let us say, of "a primrose by the river's brim"—has he seen something in the way of fine coloring, delicacy or strength of line, that will mean that the painting will never again be for him a simple primrose and nothing more, but rather something that will tend to make not only primroses but the world around him more interesting, more deserving of contemplative observation? How far, moreover, have his higher human faculties been called upon to participate in the enjoyment of the object?

This last question is very important. One might say that there are two extremes of artistic enjoyment. At the one extreme, enjoyment is immediate or direct; the object has but to be presented and the response is forthcoming. The sensational picture or story, and the simple, rousing melody are enjoyed in this way. At the other extreme, imagination, reflection, and often specialized knowledge are required if enjoyment is to occur at all.

In the first case, the individual is mentally passive, while in the second he is intensely active. All artistic enjoyment falls somewhere between these two extremes. If the enjoyment inclines to the former extreme, we say it is on the sensational level, if to the latter, that it is on the spiritual level. "Sensational" literature is aptly named, for it implies that the intellectual faculties are not noticeably involved, just as they are not involved in the experience of sensations of color, taste, smell, and the like.

There are, then, two additional criteria of aesthetic judgments that are closely connected with one another, namely, the significance of the work of art for life in general, and the extent to which appreciation of the work involves the higher intellectual faculties. The first of these, the work's significance, supplies an answer to the much debated question of the role of the subject in art. Artists have often argued that the subject in itself has no importance, that everything depends on how it is treated. In painting, for instance, the subject may be a man smoking a pipe, a back lane with a garbage pail in the foreground, a tree on a hillside, an entire landscape, or one of the numerous historical or religious themes that have figured so prominently in Western painting. This is art for art's sake—the subject is an irrelevant consideration.

It should be kept in mind, however, that the doctrine "art for art's sake" protests against the idea that the artist should be a teacher and that his freedom with respect to topic and expression should be cramped by the proprieties expected of a teacher. As directed against this form of didacticism, the protest was unquestionably valid. But it is one thing to state that the artist should have no specific aim before him beyond making the most of the artistic possibilities of his subject; it is quite another thing to say that the general moral or ethical import of his creation is a matter of indifference. On the contrary, art should make life and the world we live in more meaningful, more interesting. In this fundamental sense the ethical criterion is inescapable. When Wordsworth tells us that "the meanest flower that blows" can give him "thoughts that do often lie too deep for tears," he reminds us that very ordinary things in our world repay attention and contemplation. If the artist penetrates further, and finds expression for those thoughts that make it possible for the rest of us to share them, then that meanest flower is indeed a worthy subject for his art.

The matter of the significance of the work of art suggests an explanation of a fact mentioned previously, the frequent disagreement among artists on what constitutes "good" or "bad" art. There are many different ways in which art can be significant. One artist may be preoccupied with a type of significance in which another artist has little or no interest. Tolstoi, for example, was obsessed with social-political issues and the application to them of the standards of Christianity, strictly and literally interpreted. Shakespeare's interests lay with quite different but equally significant issues. Jane Austen concerned herself with the day-to-day life of the English "county people," and she did so with consummate art. Another artist might well regard Miss Austen's themes with indifference or contempt, refusing to put on Miss Austen's "blinkers." In all such cases, what one artist might fittingly state about another is: "He is a great artist, but I am not interested in the subjects that he finds significant, or (perhaps) in his general outlook on them."

Being an artist, however, he may well have recourse to words such as "stupid," "shallow," or "rubbish"—a temperamental manner of expressing himself that cannot be taken seriously.

Some subjects are in themselves more "significant" (in the sense in which we have been using this term) than others. The Christian narrative supplied medieval painters with themes deeply significant for all who would view their work. The great personalities and events of secular history have likewise provided important material for the artist to work on. But whether the artist is occupied in rendering the significant more significant or in providing significance for the insignificant, the measure in which his work possesses the quality of significance yields a standard, and by no means a purely personal standard, for assessing the value of his product. This means in effect that the "public" test is applicable, though not of course with the clarity and finality attaching to it in the sphere of science.

Although some artists would insist that their creations need not contribute significantly to general living, we must realize that, when art is considered in the special context of education, our concern is with personality, the whole personality, and not just that part of it that is responsive to the appeal of art.

6 *The Art Value in Education*

The educational aim in the realm of art may be stated simply as the cultivation of good taste. The word "taste" conveys a suggestion of superficiality or dilettantism, but it is intended here in its fundamental sense of a development of the individual's aesthetic sensibilities that will equip him to recognize a good product when he meets it and to prefer it to an inferior work. To know and prefer the better—this idea takes us back to the question raised in the preceding chapter, that of standards in art.

We suggested that there are two basic standards of aesthetic judgment: the significance of the work of art, in the sense of the degree to which appreciation of it tends to expand and enrich experience, and the degree to which appreciation involves the exercise of the higher mental faculties, imagination, reflection, critical judgment, and the like. The professional artist would no doubt have much more to say about what constitutes excellence in his own special art. Here we are concerned with something implicit in all art as such, manifested in each particular art in its own peculiar way, due to the special nature of its medium. One may assume that the products that constitute our artistic heritage possess this quality of excellence, for without it they would not have withstood the test of time. Art education therefore should be especially directed towards an appreciation of this legacy from the past.

We also noticed, in the previous chapter, that the two standards referred to are, to a certain extent, objective: they are true standards. A third criterion already mentioned is the pleasure-giving quality of the artistic object. This latter quality is not, like the other two, normative in character; it does not imply judgments of "good" or "bad," "better" or "worse," "higher" or "lower." Any object meant to appeal to our aesthetic sensibilities must be interesting and enjoyable in and for itself; otherwise it is not functioning as art. Some teachers have inferred that the purely subjective test is the only valid one. Recognition of this purely subjective test has led these enterprising teachers into fallacy.

Art education becomes for them a matter of providing material—pictures, music, poems, stories, and the like—from which the pupil selects whatever happens to be of direct interest to him. It is assumed that with maturation and experience, with growth, in other words, his interests will change, and he will put away childish things and find his enjoyment in things of better quality. The essential requirement, these teachers feel, is that the pupil be interested, and it is this prerequisite that has led some teachers to lay special emphasis on the appeal of the contemporary—music that happens to be in vogue at the moment, stories that deal with matters of current interest, contemporary artists whose names are familiar from the newspaper, radio, television, and the other channels of daily communication.

These teachers are of course right in making interest a *sine qua non* of guiding the child's taste for higher standards. Their judgment is also accurate when they assume that interest will change as growth proceeds. But are they correct in concluding that this interest will necessarily be altered in a desirable direction, that taste will automatically improve with changing interest? The underlying fallacy of their standpoint is their belief that because interest is essential, it must always be immediate and direct. If true education is to take place, the teacher must be prepared to face the task of arousing interest in things which may be by no means directly and immediately interesting. This task, too, calls for recognition of growth and of the changing needs of the different stages in growth.

Education is a matter not only of growth, but also of *directed* growth, and in this connection the direction is indicated by the other two criteria mentioned. The individual who has grown up amid mean and ugly surroundings becomes accustomed to these surroundings if nothing happens to disturb his acquiescence in them. This is also the case with the man who has been left to regale himself with the tawdry and the shoddy, the merely exciting and sensational. If such a man feels the need for a change, it is usually only in the direction of more potent concoctions of the same ingredients.

This is not to say that artistic products of a high order, capable of making a direct appeal to the pupil at different stages in his growth, are not available. On the contrary, they are in plentiful supply, and the modern channels of communication are making them increasingly accessible. This good grain must, however, be sifted from the chaff that these same channels provide in such abundance, and someone has to help the pupil to carry out this process of sifting. Here, as in other fields of education, two requisites are essential: skilful teaching and interested, conscientious learning.

It might be objected that emphasis on effortful exercise of the higher faculties is rather unrealistic when applied to art appreciation. Such emphasis seems to make hard work of something commonly viewed as a legitimate form of enjoyment. Is it reasonable to expect any individual, child or adult, to attain and maintain such an austere level of art appreciation? Two observations must be added in this regard. First, appreciation of the higher forms of art will itself become increasingly pleasurable: interest will tend to dominate, and conscious effort will recede. The pleasure, moreover, will be of the rewarding, self-perpetuating kind that does not lose its savor with repetition—that is, indeed, enhanced by repetition. Second, the forms of art that make little or no demand on the higher faculties have their own place and function, namely, relaxation. It is important to distinguish between that part of living that we call "leisure" and that part given over to relaxation.

In the mental, as in the physical sphere, relaxation implies cessation of activity in order to recuperate tired faculties of body or mind. Leisure, on the other hand, is an opportunity to exercise faculties that are fresh and vigorous. The "whodunit" may be, and often is, a very humble level of art, with no significance of consequence, but it too has its legitimate function of relaxation or recreation, in the strict meaning of these words. The choice of the means for recreation is left to the individual. The school performs its complex task if it leaves the individual with a clear awareness that there *are* standards in the light of which he can view not only his own ideas of what is valuable and truly significant in the field of art, but also the ideas of others, whether of his elders or his peers.

On which of the fine arts should emphasis be placed, keeping in mind the more basic aims of education? Traditionally, as Dewey noted in a sarcastic aside,[1] literature has occupied the head of the table. This circumstance may have been due merely to considerations of convenience, good books having been heretofore much more easily accessible than good painting or good music. Whatever the reason, a strong case could be made for laying very great emphasis upon literature.

The overall aim of art education is usually and rightly said to be the "humanizing" of the individual, the broadening and deepening of his insights into the thoughts, feelings, purposes, and aspirations of his fellow man. Literature accomplishes this end in its own way, which is not the way of psychology, sociology, and the other social sciences. In these latter disciplines, the interest is not in the human individual as such, but in generalizations arrived at by the methods of science.

Literature presents human beings *directly*, as objects interesting in themselves. Its medium is language, which possesses unique range and flexibility. The literary artist, moreover, can turn the light of his creative imagination on the past and bring it to life with a penetration possible only through the medium of language. The writing of history can be literary art, as it is, for example, in biographies that recreate historical personalities on the basis of well-documented historical data. Every art holds a mirror up to nature, but it is human nature that literature strives to capture in its own particular mirror.

[1] *Democracy and Education* (N.Y. Macmillan Co., 1916), p. 288.

Perhaps the right inference is not that literature should be accorded a dominant role as compared with the other fine arts (a thesis which the painter and the musician would no doubt balk at), but that it is an *indispensable* part of the curriculum of general education. Self-expression and communication by way of language are universal tendencies or needs; they are distinctive of human beings, and indeed they are of the essence of the individual's humanity. The curriculum must, we should add, take account of a person's native aptitude and of the spontaneous interests arising out of it, especially in the realm of art, where native aptitude is often present in a very marked degree. Variety of offering is needed, as much of it as happens to be practicable in any particular case.

The need for variety is very clear in connection with yet another aspect of art education: development of the individual's creative powers. The individual is not only a "consumer," he is also a potential "producer." Teachers today stress the importance of encouraging the young person to express himself in a creative way, in painting, music, literature, and in other arts. Abundant grounds for this approach are found in the very nature of the young person. What individual has not, at one stage or another of his growth, tried himself in the role of painter, poet, or story-writer? Even if his efforts at creation are such that he cannot now recall them without some shame, they are at least evidence that art possessed the power to move him, a power that he may now discover (as Darwin did) to be lost on him because of the passage of the years. In art, as in science, education should aim at detecting and fostering native talent of a high order. The early signs of an exceptional artistic gift may not be at all clear to the ordinary observer; they may require the artist to read them aright. In all art, however, there is need and scope for direct teaching. With regard to painting, for example, many teachers attach such importance to spontaneous self-expression on the part of the pupil that they have largely, if not entirely, abjured the teaching of the ordinary drawing skills that it was the aim of the traditional drawing lesson to impart. The child then has *carte blanche*, literally and figuratively, to produce his own lines and colors, and to interpret the result in his own way, an activity in which his lively imagination will certainly never leave him at a loss.

As a method of engaging the young child's interest, this procedure is all to the good. But it is surely a mistake not to provide for the more or less systematic teaching of the teachable drawing skills, such as perspective, proportion, shading, and color-mixing. These skills, far from interfering with the child's freedom, open up new and fascinating vistas for him. Without these skills, the child sooner or later encounters frustration, for he comes to want something more by which to judge his production than merely his own purely subjective standards. To expect the child to achieve real quality by way of *laissez faire* is as mistaken as expecting an individual to write like Gertrude Stein or James Joyce when he has not yet even learned to write.

Skill in designing is often a most practical accomplishment. The student in the science laboratory, for example, finds it very helpful to be able to sketch quickly and accurately. This observation recalls the distinction drawn in the preceding chapter between the fine arts and the practical arts. In the fine arts, the object or result produced is worthy of contemplation on its own account, while in the practical arts there is an ulterior object or result that is the primary purpose of the activity. If this ulterior result were its sole purpose, then the activity would not be art at all, in the strict sense of the term. However, we saw that, incidentally or secondarily, such an activity may arouse feelings of the aesthetic kind. As *faber*, man manipulates objects to attain a variety of desired ulterior results, but he may do so in a way that appeals to him as *sentiens.* Representative drawing or painting is a practical art in so far as its purpose is to equip the individual with a useful accomplishment or skill. The traditional drawing lesson in the school was to some extent training in a practical art. The general role of the practical arts in this age of rapidly advancing automation poses a special problem that shall be considered later. There is, however, one form of practical art that has unique importance and should be discussed at this point.

This form of practical art is the use of language as a tool to achieve a specific result. It may take the form of imparting knowledge—instruction—as when a scientist reports the results of an investigation, or a lawyer explains the law as it pertains to particular issues. Or it may also be the communication of ideas in such a way as to secure their acceptance, the art that is commonly called "persuasion." Whatever this object may be, the activity is art in so far as it is performed in a manner that compels admiration on its own account. Remaining within the conditions laid down by the rules of grammar and syntax, the argument can show a fine economy of means, with nothing redundant or irrelevant, the use of interesting and telling illustrations, language adjusted to the nature of the topic and of the reader or audience to which it is addressed, emphasis falling where it belongs, and above all, a fine sense of the value of words—in short, it can be a model of what is ordinarily called "composition."

To illustrate this distinction and contrast between the practical and the fine arts, let us consider for a moment the plays of George Bernard Shaw, where the two kinds of art are juxtaposed in a manner that clearly indicates the difference between them. There are the plays themselves—*The Doctor's Dilemma, John Bull's Other Island, Back to Methuselah,* for example—and the famous prefaces to the plays. The Shaw play creates a picture that is interesting in itself as a segment of human living. In so far as argument occurs in the play, the argument is indirect, tied up with characterization and the dramatic needs of incident and situation. In the preface, however, the master of dramatic art is now the master of clear and persuasive exposition. Play and preface are both examples of literary art, each of its own kind.

One need not labor the importance of an art, the essence of which is the exercise of the most potent skill that the human being has devised, language. The engineer trying to "sell" a project to the public requires language no less than the salesman attempting to sell a brand of soap. Still more important is the fact that the individual who has learned to appreciate and enjoy the fine points of this practical art is no longer limited to the region of *belles-lettres,* for he now has access to a rich literary heritage representing a combination of instruction and admirable exposition, of utility in the broad sense and beauty in the special sense under consideration here. Classics like John Stuart `Mill's *Essay on Liberty*, Darwin's *Origin of Species*, Milton's *Areopagitica*, have their place in a program of education in literary art. Even technical philosophy has its classics available for the same purpose: Plato among the ancients, and Berkeley and Hume among the moderns, are obvious examples. Teachers who have fallen into the habit of considering *belles-lettres* as the only medium of education in literary art are apt to be left with an uneasy feeling that they are ignoring part of the literary heritage. The foregoing observations will, it is hoped, show reason for including this kind of writing in educational programs.

How far and by what means can education equip the individual for the competent practice of the language art? What can education do towards producing a good craftsman in language? With reference to literature as a fine art, with poetry as its pure form, we have suggested that all the school can do is to provide the young with opportunity and encouragement to give expression to whatever measure of creative impulse is in them. Literature as a practical art, on the other hand, is to a certain degree teachable. Some of the qualities that we have already mentioned as constituting effective composition can be pointed out by the teacher and learned by the pupil. Writing of a quality that deserves the name "art" cannot, however, be achieved through any such process of learning the "tricks of the trade." Nothing can take the place of direct, continuous experience of the best that has been written.

It may seem paradoxical and far-fetched to suggest that poetry is of particular value in this connection. Yet, the more one considers the matter, the clearer it becomes that the art that above all others explores and exploits the value of words bears directly upon the practical art in which the medium is language. The rare experience of meeting what Tennyson tells us he found in Virgil, "all the charm of all the muses often flowering in a lonely word," leaves a permanent imprint on the individual.

Great poets have on occasion turned from poetry to prose for purposes of instruction and persuasion, and have excelled in the use of the latter medium. The names of John Milton, Samuel Taylor Coleridge, William Wordsworth, and Thomas Hardy come most readily to mind in this regard. The works of these men might serve as ample warning against overemphasis of the distinction between language as *belles-lettres* and language as a practical art. In poetry an element of down-to-earth craftsmanship always exists, and craftsmanship at its best—literary or otherwise—contains authentic overtones of poetry.

7 Standards of Social and Group Life

Man is, in his very essence, *socius*, a "political animal," as Aristotle called him. Purely individual man, with no social relationships, is a myth; in such a state he would be without the use of language, and therefore less than human. Man's social nature finds expression in two ways: in his individual or personal relationships, and in his membership of a group. Not only has man always lived in personal relationships with his fellows, but these relationships have always occurred within the context of a group or groups. The group ranges all the way from the loosely knit kinship group or clan, found at the very primitive level, through the more developed form of the tribe, to the highly complex forms of group life at the civilized level.

In the course of his evolution, man developed values that brought order into his social life—made it more satisfying. Some of these values pertain to individual relationships, while others specifically concern his conduct as a member of a group. Both kinds of value find expression in certain forms of control which one encounters at all levels of human development. These controls are of four main kinds: law, custom, convention, and morality. Let us examine each of these in detail.

The law is an explicit sanction calling for a specific penalty for non-conforming conduct. This form of control is present at all levels, as the anthropologist Marett pointed out in answer to those who picture primitive society as entirely dominated by custom.

Custom is control of the present by the past, or imitation of our forebears, as one might phrase it. Custom is the dominant form of control in primitive society, a condition due, not only to force of habit, or rooted merely in mental laziness and the preference for the easy, ready-made way, but containing an element of reason. The outlook of primitive man, we noted previously, is animistic— the fear of offending one of those "spirits of the cornfield and the wild" is never far from his mind. The "easy way" is also the safe way. Fear can make a civilized man cling to the old ways either because he is constitutionally timid (as often in old age) or because he apprehends some bad impact on his vested interests.

By way of contrast with custom, convention may be described as imitation of our contemporaries, rather than of our forebears. Conventions are thus subject to constant change, and when they are very variable we call them "fashions," or in some cases, "fads." They are an expression of one part of man's social nature, the need to conform, and this need alone seems sufficient to account for conventional behavior. The tendency to conform will receive comment in a later connection, but here the important question is that of the relation of both custom and convention to another form of control—morality.

Morals are commonly regarded as a more important, more penetrating form of control than custom and convention, but the line of demarcation is often far from clear. This point has led some thinkers to the view that there is no absolute or final distinction between morality and custom, that morals are in the last analysis merely customs or conventions where social pressure to conform is much stronger. It is of prime importance to come to terms with this latter contention.

The evidence for the idea that there is no absolute distinction between morality and custom lies, according to its advocates, in the fact that morals, like custom and convention, seem to change with time and place. Consider what time has done to the four controls: law, custom, convention, and morality. Let us imagine, for example, a circle divided into segments, with each segment representing one of these controls. Thus, there exists a region where judgment is based on law, or custom, or convention, or morality, or perhaps some combination of these factors. To complete the picture, we should add a segment representing the region of indifference, the kind of behavior, taking a walk or a snooze after lunch, for example, that is not socially judged at all, but is rather left to the free choice of the individual.

It is necessary to go back only a few hundred years in history to realize how some forms of conduct have moved from one segment of this circle to another. Cock-fighting was once sanctioned by law, custom, convention, and morality. Today cock-fighting is both illegal and held to be immoral. Precisely the same alteration in attitude has occurred with regard to slavery.

One hundred years ago, a man who staggered along the street under the influence of an excessive amount of alcohol would be considered culpable for flouting convention—overindulging in drink was the kind of thing that simply "was not done"—but condemnation stopped short at that. Today, the same man is liable to arrest in some countries, and many persons would certainly consider his behavior downright immoral. Similarly, not very long ago, a woman who ventured to attend a concert unchaperoned, or to smoke a cigarette in public, would have been regarded as acting unconventionally and perhaps even immorally. Such conduct is today regarded as a matter for indifference.

Lest we tend to believe that changing from one segment of the circle to another is confined only to the past, consider the fact that homosexual behavior was once regarded as profoundly immoral and was subjected by law to serious penalty. A few years ago, however, the British House of Commons decreed that the law would have no concern with homosexual behavior, where only adults were involved in such conduct.

A similar variety of judgment is apparent with change of place. In certain parts of the world, bull-fighting is regarded as both illegal and immoral, while in others it has the full approval of custom and convention, with no suggestion whatsoever of immorality. Not to labor the point further, it may be stated that if we take a world-wide view, including societies at all levels of development, the social anthropologists have brought to light such a variety of judgment with respect to conduct that the logical conclusion appears to be that such judgment is really determined by time and place. Ethical or moral relativism, as this principle is called, seems to have all the evidence on its side.

Nevertheless, on closer scrutiny, a certain pattern underlying this bewildering variety of moral judgment is discernible. There appear to be ways of behaving that are always approved, and others that are invariably condemned. What are these universals or constants of moral judgment, as we may call them?

Truthfulness or veracity would appear to be one such universal. The man known to his fellows as one who would not deliberately mislead them by false statement—the man of the straight tongue— is judged a good man, and his conduct is considered right. He behaves as a man ought to behave. By the same token, the man of the crooked tongue, who is prepared to resort to false assertion when it suits his purpose, is judged to be bad, and his conduct is considered wrong. Where exceptions occur, and they occur often enough to mislead the unwary, there is good reason for them, the kind of reason that shows that they are not really exceptions to the general principle that truth-telling is good and right, and that lying is bad and wrong. The tribesman, for example, may take liberties with veracity when dealing with an outsider, liberties not permissible in his dealings with fellow tribesmen. The distinction between the "in-group" and the "out-group" is apt to be very clearly drawn at primitive levels, and to belong to the "out-group" is really to be outside the pale as far as ordinary standards of intercourse are concerned. Nor is this attitude confined to the primitive levels, as a little reflection reminds us.

Is this attitude towards veracity not also true of certain other standards or values held to be basic at civilized levels? Let us examine the value of respect for human life. Once again, the factor of "in-group" and "out-group" may function here. Custom, moreover, may decree that it is not only permissible but also laudable to take life, as in the case of the head-hunter, for instance. But custom always very clearly defines the situation in which killing is permissible, and the one in which killing is wrong. Nowhere, it may be stated, is the taking of human life considered on the same moral level as the taking of animal life.

Kindness or sympathy—which philosophers broadly call "benevolence"—is considered good, and cruelty is looked upon as bad. At all levels and in all times, the man who relieves the suffering of his fellowman when he can is sharply and favorably contrasted with the man who is indifferent to his neighbor's pain, or who derives satisfaction from inflicting pain.

Respect for the property of another is universally approved, and the taking of it from one's neighbor by guile or force condemned. Loyalty, be it loyalty to person, cause, or institution, is universally approved, and its opposite condemned. Indeed, one of the outstanding philosophers at the turn of the century, Josiah Royce. went so far as to consider loyalty the most basic of all moral values. Be that as it may, it seems clear that without the tissue of loyalty, social life, and particularly the group forms of it, would be held together only by the insecure bonds of self-interest and mere gregariousness. The object of this loyalty may of course be good or bad, but we are thinking here of its value *per se.* Honor among thieves is still honor.

The reader can doubtless cite further examples of such universal values, or he may indeed have doubts about one or more of the cases that have been cited here. The preceding analysis makes no claim to precision or completeness. The essential point, however, remains that moral values are not reducible without remainder to customary values. Good or bad, right or wrong, as applied to conduct, *means more* than just in accord with or contrary to custom.

Try to imagine a society in which the murderer, the liar, the thief, the robber, the cruel man, or the treacherous man is not only feared (as he must be) but approved and even admired, and where the man who can be trusted to respect the life and property of another, to tell the truth, and at sacrifice to himself to be loyal to friend or cause, incurs disapproval and contempt. It is a difficult picture to imagine, and it remains so in spite of the following curious report by Ruth Benedict, a social anthropologist:

> The Dobuans amply deserve the character they are given by their neighbours. They are lawless and treacherous. Every man's hand is against every other man . . . . Dobu has no chiefs. It certainly has no political organization. In a strict sense it has no legality. And this is

not because the Dobuan lives in a state of anarchy, Rousseau's "natural man" as yet unhampered by the social contract, but because the social forms which obtain in Dobu put a premium upon ill-will and treachery and make of them the recognized virtues of society.[1]

Miss Benedict then adds:

Nothing could be further from the truth, however, than to see in Dobu a state of anarchy. Dobuan social organization is arranged in concentric circles, within each of which specified traditional forms of hostility are allowed. No man takes the law into his own hands except to carry out these culturally allowed hostilities within the appropriate specified group.[2]

This latter qualification turns what at first glance appears to be a stark exception into a fact that is really not at all exceptional.

Let us note, in passing, a philosophic question: how did man come to acquire the basic standards or values that we have mentioned? Some attribute them to man's possession of a "natural light" that enables him to discriminate clearly at all times between good and bad, right and wrong—this is very much the traditional idea of "conscience." Philosophers have offered more sophisticated explanations. Those who have seen in evolution the master key have suggested that these values represent ways of behavior that possess high survival value. Societies that "evolved" these values survived, while others that did not develop them disintegrated and disappeared.

The pragmatist, while generally accepting the evolutionist's explanation, adds that these values are inductions that men have more or less consciously made on the basis of experience as to which forms of social behavior are most satisfying and rewarding. According to the moral realist (or intuitionist), such values are the expression of an innate moral sense that perceives the quality of goodness in the direct, immediate way in which the eye perceives color. Religion tends to include, in its explanation of the problem, the factor of divine revelation. It is not part of our purpose to examine the pros and cons of each of these explanations, but it is

[1] *Patterns of Culture* (The New American Library, 1946), Ch. 5, p. 121.
[2] *Ibid.*

important to draw attention to a factor implied in all moral development whatsoever, a factor that becomes evident in the following
illustration.

In the family group, the child can come to realize the point that
his mother wishes to convey when she tells him that his brother has
as much right to a piece of cake as he has, although he probably
perceives this idea by insisting that *he* has as much right to something as his brother. The family itself can appreciate what is meant
when it is told that other families in the community have rights
equal to its own, and the psychology of this process is clear enough.
By a feat of imagination—sympathetic imagination, it has been
called—one individual can put himself in another's place and come
to see the other not only as an *alter*, but as an *alter ego*, a person.
One ethical philosopher, Leslie Stephen, an adherent of the Evolutionary School of thought, expresses this idea in the following way:

> To realize the world as a material whole, I must have representa-
> tive perceptions of time and space. To realize the world of thought
> and feeling, that world upon which my life and happiness depend at
> every instant, I must have representative emotions. "Put yourself in
> his place" is not merely a moral precept; it is a logical rule implied
> in the earliest germs of reason or a description of reasoning itself, so
> far as it deals with other sentient beings. Sympathy and reason have
> so far an identical factor—each implies the other.[2]

Leslie Stephen calls this capacity "reason," reason in the sphere
of feeling; it is reason as applied to the values that regulate conduct. To appreciate the precise meaning of reason in this connection
is of first importance because it enables us to come to terms with a
dispute of long standing in moral philosophy, that between those
who argue that morality is fundamentally an expression of man's
rational nature, and those who hold that its basis is not reason but
feeling. For the one school of thought, moral behavior is a matter
of intellectual training, training in the right use of reason; for the
other, it is a matter of habit or "conditioning," conditioning of the
feelings brought about by more or less protracted social training.

Advocates of this latter view accuse their opponents of the error,

[3]*The Science of Ethics* (London, John Murray, 1907), pp. 220-221.

an error typical of philosophers in general, of attributing to cold reason an importance that it does not possess. Protagonists of reason see in the conditioning theory an approach that would ultimately place human development or education on the same plane as animal training, and they sense something radically wrong in such an attitude. Let us then ask precisely what we mean by "reason," and in so doing, let us choose an illustration of the reasoning process from a field other than conduct, scientific investigation.

Consider the example of Sir Isaac Newton reasoning his way to the theory of universal gravitation. Newton brings together two very different facts, planetary movements and a falling apple, and shows that from the physicist's point of view these are not different at all. He eventually synthesizes a large number of seemingly disparate phenomena into a comprehensive whole, and this procedure provides us with the very clue that we require for our argument.

Reason is a mental movement towards extending the *application* of a particular concept, principle, or idea. The essence of reason, or at any rate an essential feature of it, is comprehensiveness. When we speak of reason in the moral sphere, the sphere of values that regulates conduct, the movement is the same. The mother of the child, in our illustration of the family group, sees, from her special mother's point of view, no difference between one of her children and another as far as the cake is concerned. She tries to convince the demanding child to share her standpoint, and in so far as she succeeds, she has given that child a lesson in one of the basic social values, justice. Considering the basic values to which we have referred—respect for human life, truthfulness, and the rest—the movement is again towards an ever-widening range of application, from the family to the tribe, to the nation, and to humanity as a whole. Reason is the active principle in the process by which the restricted boundaries are steadily pushed back until, ideally, humanity as a whole becomes the field of application of these basic standards.

One very important example of the extension of the range of application of these standards is found in the values specifically concerned with the regulation of group or political relationships.

As group life developed, man discovered certain principles on which satisfactory relationships within the group seemed to depend. These principles received expression, and on the whole adequate expression, in the slogan of the French Revolutionaries: "Liberty, equality, fraternity."

"Liberty," in this connection, implies that it is wrong for one person or group to treat another person or group merely as an instrument or tool. Liberty also implies, more positively, that it is right to remove any obstacle to an individual's development, where such removal is possible and humanly desirable. "Equality" implies the ultimate acceptance of Jeremy Bentham's formula: "everybody to count for one and nobody for more than one." More specifically, equality implies equality before the law: the incidence of laws should not be affected by irrelevant considerations, such as class or wealth. Into "fraternity" we read two meanings. The more sentimental one, probably intended by the Revolutionaries, implies that our concern for our fellow man should proceed beyond merely according him bare justice—it should include benevolence, an interest in actively promoting his welfare. The more philosophical meaning of "fraternity" may be stated as co-operation in the pursuit of common purposes. It is clear that such principles are indeed the extension to group relationships of the basic values regulating individual or personal relationships.

Such, then, is the meaning of reason as applied to the ends or purposes to which conduct is directed, a meaning which the English philosopher, Henry Sidgwick, sums up in the following abstract statement that he calls the "maxim of equity," and that might also be termed the principle of reason:

> It cannot be right for A to treat B in a manner in which it would be wrong for B to treat A, merely on the ground that they are two different individuals and without there being any difference in the natures or circumstances of the two which can be stated as a reasonable ground for difference of treatment.[1]

We can now understand the error of the philosophers who argue that reason has no part in the determination of values. Modern

[1]*Methods of Ethics* (7th ed., London and New York, Macmillan Co.) Bk. III, p. 380.

psychologists on the whole have supported this view, insisting that ends or purposes are determined by the instincts, emotions, and generally the non-rational part of man's nature. Where reason appears to be a determining factor, it is revealed, on closer examination, to be not reason but rationalization—in others words, the use of reason to justify ends that are in fact non-rational in origin. Reason, many psychologists hold, is concerned always with means, not with ends; its function is to adopt and adapt means for the attainment of ends.

It is indeed true that an important part of reason's function is the discovery of means to attain ends. It is a mistake, however, to regard this function as the sole one of reason, and to think that there is any essential difference between reason operating in this way and in the way described above, where reason is concerned with the ends themselves. The same principle of comprehensiveness is applicable in both cases.

When a politician subscribes to a charity from no motive other than the desire to garner votes, his subscription is a means to an end, an end in which charity plays no part. The politician views popular voting in a wider context, one that connects it with the feelings that people have about charitable conduct. Whenever an individual seeks the means to achieve an end, he tries to see that end in a more comprehensive way in which it includes factors whose relationship to it is that of cause and effect. The *Gestalt* psychologist expresses this condition by asserting that the effect of reason is to produce a better configuration or totality, inclusive of both means and end. In this fundamental sense, Dewey is right in describing the distinction between means and end as a false dualism. But let us return to Sidgwick's statement of the "maxim of equity."

Sidgwick's qualification concerning "any difference in the nature or circumstances of the two which can be stated as a *reasonable* ground for difference of treatment" looks like a begging of the question, since the term "reason" is used in the definition of reason. What is meant, however, is that the same test of comprehensiveness should be applied to the difference in question. If we examine this qualification more closely, we obtain some idea of the complexities and perplexities entailed in the practical application of Sidgwick's principle.

Discovery in the field of moral values is the story of how man has extended the application of the maxim of equity by bringing into clearer focus differences in nature and circumstances that do *not* provide a reasonable ground for difference of treatment. In education, a difference of social class could make all the difference between opportunity and no opportunity. Men have discovered that social class is no longer a defensible ground for difference of treatment in this regard. Men are now in process of discovering (we say "in process" because discovery in this sense does not come about suddenly) that color of skin is also an irrelevant consideration.

A more fundamental example is that of the right to the pursuit of happiness, to use the phraseology of the American Declaration of Independence. It is difficult for us to realize how senseless it would have appeared in the Middle Ages to say that the serf in his hovel had a right to happiness equal to that of the baron in his castle. An essential part of the mental outlook or ideology of the serf class was the belief that a man's first duty is to be content with the state to which God has called him, whatever the disabilities of that state might be. In like manner, the caste system of India placed certain individuals beyond the pale in so far as any question of right was concerned. Today the movement is in the direction of denying legal recognition to the caste system.

The word "discovery" has, as we have implied, a special meaning in this connection. It does not mean simply that someone has thought of an idea—equality, for example—and given it expression. In that sense of the word, Plato could be said to have discovered the idea of educational opportunity for everybody and the idea of the political equality of women. It would be hard to point to any idea that is not an old discovery in this sense. "Discovery" in the present context means that the idea in question has found its way into the thinking of the public, and though it may give rise to debate, the debate concerns not the idea itself but some aspect of its application.

This realistic meaning of the word "discovery" serves to remind us that the process of moral discovery is still going on, and with ever-increasing ferment. Consider the principle of equality once again. The color line, let us agree, is irrelevant with respect to educational opportunity and political franchise, but what of inter-marriage and policies of immigration? Immigrants might bring with them fundamental differences of religion and general cultural background that could, conceivably, with uncontrolled immigration, submerge the culture of the North American continent. Is there anything unreasonable in holding that such differences are grounds for "difference of treatment"? The reader is doubtless aware of other principles of social and group life in which reason is working towards an extended application on the one hand, and, on the other, towards unravelling differences that have or have not an important bearing on the process of moral discovery.

While it is erroneous to think of reason as always concerned with means and never with ends, nonetheless those who fall into this error base their view on a sound principle, namely, that ends, aims, purposes, values—whatever we may choose to call them—are ulti-mately a matter of *feeling*. We have therefore to note the opposite error, which is the error of the rationalists, the supposition that there are ends of purely rational character, in which feeling is not at all involved. This outlook contradicts the very idea of an end or value. A value is never merely intelligible; it is, by definition, *attractive*, which means that feeling is of its essence.

What both sides in this dispute fail to realize is the fact that the human being can develop a *feeling for reason*. Reasonable conduct, purely as such, comes to possess a quality of attractiveness; in other words, it becomes a value in the strict sense. The beginnings of this feeling may be seen in the earlier years, when the child shows a marked sensitivity to inconsiderate and selfish conduct on the part of others, or perhaps to conduct that is so inconsistent and unpre-dictable that it does not make sense. With social training, the child begins to apply a like standard to his own behavior. The time arrives when selfish or inconsistent conduct on his own part leaves him more or less disturbed, if not with an actual feeling of guilt.

The feeling of value that the individual comes to attach to reason-able conduct as such need not be taken to mean that he develops a high-souled regard for reason in the abstract; that would be rather an austere motive to attribute to ordinary people. This feeling of value is probably bound up with the individual's sense of his own personal dignity and worth. He comes to think of himself as acting on a higher plane when he does not fall in with the usual way of following the dictates of self-interest, custom, or convention. The latter are the "easy ways," and "there is no merit in them," as Dickens' Mark Tapley would probably phrase it.

The philosopher Kant, it is interesting to note in this respect, although he took the stand that truly moral conduct is an expression of man's rational nature, with no admixture of feeling, found that in the last analysis he could not exclude feeling altogether. Kant admitted this fact in the form of a feeling of respect—respect for moral law. If, instead of using the phrase "respect for the moral law" (which is the law of reason), we employ the term "respect for oneself as a rational creature" (which is not quite the same thing), then we are in line with what we have stated previously.

There is substantial evidence of the emergence and the importance of this sentiment for reason in the individual's development. What appears to be an early manifestation of it occurs in the young child's reaction, or rather over-reaction, to manifestly unjust treatment at the hands of his elders. The boy who says of his teacher: "He's a brute, but a just brute," adds a qualification that possesses much significance for his personal development. A clearer manifestation of this sentiment is encountered in adolescence and the phase of lofty idealism—in the adult's view highly impracticable idealism—through which the adolescent typically passes. The adolescent would, for example, accept the maxim of equity at face value and have little patience with any "grounds for difference of treatment," such as those suggested earlier. One might discount this idealism on the part of the adolescent as pretentious gesturing, a desire to appear liberal and broadminded, coupled with an unwillingness to think out the implications of his principles. This view appears somewhat harsh and unfair, for the adolescent takes his idealism very seriously, with a quality of earnestness that is incompatible with mere posing or unwillingness to do the hard thinking necessary to follow reason all the way. The qualification of a moral principle, when a question of its practical application arises, appears to the adolescent an unworthy compromise with the demands of his rational nature.

It is one thing, however, to recognize the existence of such a sentiment for reason in *homo sapiens,* and quite another thing to exaggerate its importance as a motive. The evolutionist sees in this feeling a late product of the evolutionary process, and, as such, a sentiment that is very vulnerable to the impact of more elemental drives. Even the individual who possesses sufficient strength of character to resist his lower impulses, and who conscientiously tries to conform to the standard of reason, is liable to honest error of moral judgment in the face of complex situations in which he so often has to exercise that judgment.

Nor is this the only respect in which the standard of reason is vulnerable. It is precisely in these complex situations, where the right course is far from clear, that the individual tends to succumb to a lower level of motivation, compounding with his conscience by giving non-rational motives the appearance of good reason. Psycho-analytical psychologists have shown us the extent to which this process of rationalization, along with other mechanisms, such as substitution, projection, and compensation, can operate to distort the individual's judgment of his own motivations.

There is yet another possibility relating to this question of reasonable conduct, one that is unfortunately more than a bare possibility. *Homo sapiens* is always capable of frankly repudiating reason in so far as his personal ends are concerned. He may choose to use the faculty of reason in the service of selfishness, prejudice, hate, or lust for power, while rendering to the higher standard, if any recognition at all, merely the hypocrite's homage of expecting other people to conform to it.

For a large-scale illustration of the struggle between reason and the lower motives, one need only examine the world of modern politics on the cosmopolitan and the international level. Never before has there been such widespread sentiment in support of political justice for all peoples, backward and advanced, primitive and civilized. To be sure, the sincerity of this sentiment in some quarters is more than open to question. What stands out clearly, however, is the fact that such groups are at special pains to conceal their insincerity, and this is indeed something new. Heretofore these groups had a free hand, with no questions asked, or at any rate without serious pressure upon their activities.

Our century may thus be said to have discovered the maxim of reason, in the sense of the word "discovery" that we have stressed. It is in relation to the qualifying clause—"reasonable grounds for difference of treatment"—that complexities and perplexities are becoming increasingly apparent. In this regard, therefore, the old bad motivations (not to mention plain bad thinking) are likely to operate and muddy the political waters. No group is immune to these motivations, and it is dangerous self-delusion, for example, to consider them as a peculiar malaise of Communism. Those who think in this way darken still further the prospect of an eventual victory for reason.

The reader may question the need for this rather long philosophical preamble, and perhaps even the point of it. By way of explanation, let us add one further general observation concerning the more practical aspects of social and political education. Any question of clear practical importance, the answer to which calls for an examination of basic issues, usually divides the interested parties into three groups: those who accept one or other directly opposed answers and, between the extremists, the confused individuals who are clear only on one point, namely, that there is much to be said *against* both sides. Education involves a number of questions of this type; for example, the question of whether such a thing as formal mental training, in the sense of training that results in a general enhancing of intellectual capacity, actually exists.

The topic that we are about to discuss, the education of man in society, is another very important instance of this kind of problem. It is hoped that the present chapter may aid us in adopting a middle course in this discussion, one divorced from the confusion and uncertainty to which the *via media* is usually subject.

8 *The Education of* Homo Socius

The discussion in the preceding chapters of three of the forms of social control — morality, custom, and convention — indicates the nature and aim of education with respect to social values. This education is concerned with values that appear to be universal in human living, the constants underlying the variables of custom and convention. Veracity, respect for human life, justice, kindness (or sympathy, or benevolence, or love—as this quality has been variously called), and loyalty, seem to be clear cases in point. These values constitute the fundamental decencies of living without which our lives, to use Hobbes' phrase, would be "nasty and brutish," whether or not they would be "short."[1]

The distinction between morality and custom is important, but the dividing line between the two, as already pointed out, is not always clear. Every community presents examples of standards or controls that have the outward look of custom, but that, on reflection, may appear to have more basic significance. Offering one's seat to a lady or to an elderly person in a crowded bus may have more underlying it than merely the sanction of custom or convention. It is an easy matter for the rebel against custom or convention to find himself challenging more than he had initially intended. Indeed, the flouting of any standard of behavior prevalent in one's community is not something to be practised lightly. Consider the minor conventions, such as table manners, the amenities of polite conversation, the way to decline an invitation to dinner or a game of bridge, and

[1] *Leviathan,* Ch. 13 ("the life of man, solitary, poor, nasty, brutish, and short").

so forth. The individual who asserts his independence of the code in these matters, who puts his knife in his mouth, who expresses his difference of opinion in a way that implies the other person's downright stupidity, who refuses to use the formal technique for refusing an invitation and, instead, gives expression to his actual feeling that he would find the occasion only a disagreeable waste of time, finds his behavior deeply resented. That resentment would seem to be traceable to one or both of two facts. He is forcing his fellows to give their attention to matters which they have been taking for granted and which they feel ought to be taken for granted. And his motives are suspect. They may amount at bottom to a form of egoism which takes this method of drawing attention to the ego or, it may be, a mean satisfaction in creating embarrassment and unpleasantness.

True, our rebel may be expressing resentment at controls that interfere with his freedom and force him into insincerities of talk and action. The crux of the difficulty here as in so many of the choices in life is that values are liable to clash with one another. Individual liberty, even in small things, is a value but so, too, is social harmony. If choice has to be made, it should be made responsibly, and a good rule for ensuring this is for the individual to begin with a healthy suspicion of his own motives.

Again, there is always the danger of suppressing the kind of rebel that society needs, the rebel who will turn out to be a prophet. That kind of rebel is of rare occurrence, no doubt, but there might have been many more of the kind had it not been for the manner in which society tends to treat such people. And yet may we not ask whether the rebels who became prophets and left their beneficent mark on history were really persons who had any quarrel with the ordinary amenities governing social life? Were their attacks not directed against rather deeper feelings? John Stuart Mill said of one of these rebels: "Mankind can hardly be too often reminded, that there was once a man named Socrates."[2] Mill might have added that Socrates seems to have worked out for himself a *modus vivendi* with his notorious scold of a wife, Xantippe, and, furthermore, when his friends arranged for him a means of escape from the cell where he was awaiting death, he replied by treating them to a stern lecture

[2]*On Liberty,* ch. 2.

on the importance of obeying the laws, even admittedly bad laws. Jesus was a rebel who came "with a sword" but not to attack the minor amenities (with which he seems to have lived quite at harmony) but rather the fundamental concepts of religion as he found them in his day. But we may leave the reader to follow this line of thought for himself. Let us return to the more basic values and the question of what education can do about them.

These values represent points at which civilized man can make contact with primitive man and also with members of other civilizations. Contact of one civilization with another presents a special problem because of the vast accretion of values, rooted in custom and religion, that conceal similarities of attitude and outlook, such as might offer a starting point for mutual understanding. The Westerner, for example, who makes an honest effort to understand the Oriental, the Indian, or the Arabic outlook, is likely to go badly astray by projecting his own deep-rooted customary values into the minds of these alien people. He may assume, for example, that their attitudes to women, to competition, and to wealth accumulation are the same as his own. Or he may conclude that his own world simply has nothing in common with these alien worlds, and in this supposition he would, of course, be mistaken.

Why, it might be asked, should education concern itself with values that are by nature universal? Why not leave these values to develop in their own way and in their own time in the individual? As basic traits of human nature, may they not simply be taken for granted as so much moral capital that social training can use as a starting point? The answer is obviously that, althought these traits are indeed rooted in human nature, so are their opposites. Sympathy or kindness is a trait of human nature, but so is sadism. The young child sees a creature suffering, and being human, he may do something to help, or, also because he is human, he may find the spectacle pleasurable and act in such a way as to intensify the creature's suffering.

Some persons argue that this is not really sadism, but rather a regrettable expression of childish curiosity. The Marquis de Sade likewise had his curiosity very strongly aroused by the contortions of his victims, but his basic psychological motivation was nonetheless pleasurable excitement at the spectacle of suffering. One might also reflect on the case of a normal child, one not at all a patho-logical liar in the technical sense, who has, however, become so thoroughly conditioned by a bad social environment that he cannot understand any argument against lying and theft except the danger of being found out. The basic decencies are by no means self-perpetuating; education must re-create them in every generation.

No one today needs to be alerted to the danger of assuming that these universal values are now securely based, that civilized men are too deeply committed to the fundamental decencies of living to accept any code of conduct that is an open, wholesale rejection of them. The twentieth century has demonstrated the fallacy of this assumption with appalling clarity. If, in the middle of the nineteenth century, an author had regaled his readers with the picture of a political regime in which the government so controlled the sources of public information that its subjects were kept in ignorance of, or grossly misinformed about, what was being said and done out-side their own state, and outsiders found it hard to get reliable knowledge of what was happening within that state; of a govern-ment that silenced criticism and suppressed opposition by means of a secret police organization, trials involving torture, both physical and mental, entailing slow death in a concentration camp; of a government that systematically ferreted out and murdered the mem-bers of a racial minority group integrated for centuries into the national life and contributing very notably to its scientific and cul-tural achievement; of a government, finally, that had forced its universities to falsify science to support a preposterous theory of innate racial superiority—and if the author had presented this pic-ture as a preview of what might happen in Europe within less than a hundred years—then his readers, far from taking this picture seri-ously, would have dismissed it as the grisly figment of a morbid imagination. Yet today we consider George Orwell's book *1984* believable enough to be frightening. Not the least alarming develop-ment of the twentieth century is the human awareness that this horrible vision can become reality, and that the social and psycho-logical techniques for making it happen have been invented. This is surely a lesson of history that it would be perilous for education-ists in our century to ignore.

The problem, then, is how to transmit the universal values from one generation to the next. In the preceding chapter it was pointed out that this transmission is possible at all only because of another trait inherent in human nature—reason. The child is able to acquire language, which is one expression of the reasoning faculty. He can also enter imaginatively into the mental states of other persons, and this sympathetic imagination, or imaginative sympathy, is another expression of reason—it is reason concerned with the understanding of other people. Reason, in these two senses, enables the child to identify situations denoted by terms such as justice, honesty, truthfulness, kindness, and their opposites. Initially, reason does no more than this; it is fallacious to infer that reason by itself will be sufficient to influence conduct and to secure conformity to the standards implied in the given terms.

Consider the behavior of the child who takes pleasure in teasing and tormenting his little brother, sister, or playmate. To try to reason with him, that is, to talk him out of it, will help somewhat, in that it will impart to him the idea that his teachers and other adult mentors *have* reasons for what they are doing and that they are not merely capricious meddlers with his fun. But the child must also be given the idea that what he is doing is not only unreasonable but also bad. His feelings must be aroused, feelings of aversion to a way of behaving, and this is brought about at that early stage of development by direct and impressive experience of the emotional attitude of others to his conduct. Forthright, implacable prohibition, even without any support of reason, can be effective.

Conformity thus secured is of course based on compulsion, and it therefore has little or no ethical value. It is, however, the necessary basis for a conformity that is self-imposed and self-directed, for the truly ethical level of self-discipline. At the ethical level, as we explained in the preceding chapter, the individual develops a feeling for reasonable conduct as such, a feeling strong enough to become a main factor in the regulation of his conduct. This is the final fruition of the sense of moral values, an outcome difficult to attain, and one probably never completely realized. As growth proceeds, reason increasingly broadens and deepens the feelings of value. Society, however, requires all its educational resources to give our most basic moral values a more secure foundation than reason can provide by itself.

What are these educational resources available to society? There are five specific educational agencies in civilized society today. They are: (1) the family or home; (2) the church; (3) the peer group; (4) the mass media of communication; (5) the school. The mass media can be more usefully discussed in a later context. Let us consider the others here. While it is obvious that they do not operate independently of one another, each is fitted to contribute in a special way to education generally and to social education in particular.

With respect to the influence of the family, it is important to keep certain special features of that influence in mind. It is the earliest to operate. Psychologists have stressed the importance of early pre-school training. One can agree with them without endorsing the crucial importance attached to the infantile stage by Freud and his disciples. Like the Jesuit who reputedly said: "give me the child for the first seven years and anybody can have him after," they are probably exaggerating the importance of an unquestionably important period.

Again, family influence is more continuous than that of any other agency. On the whole, this remains true despite the weakening of family control, of which one hears so much and which in any case is true mainly of the later stages of childhood. Family influence, moreover, is directly personal and intimate, by contrast with that of the other agencies. Finally, the family being an association with a biological basis as well as legal and social sanction, it is permeated by a sense of responsibility for the young which is peculiar to it.

Because of its continuous and intimate relationships, the contribution of the family to the fostering of the amenities of acceptable human behavior—manners as distinct from morals—is an obvious one. In the family context more than in any other, these standards can be presented and inculcated, not as arbitrary controls of conduct, a mere meddling on the part of the grown-ups, but for what they really are, forms of consideration for the feelings of others.

As a group, the family possesses a distinctive structure, one involving personal relationships of a specific kind: parents to each other, father to son, father to daughter, mother to son, mother to daughter, children to one another, older children to younger children, and so on. These relationships have their impacts on the child's development, especially on his emotional development, and such impacts may be transient or lasting, for good or for ill. Modern psychologists have drawn attention to the nature of these relationships, and to the psychological mechanisms at work in them.

The church is officially and specifically the agent of religious education. Whatever purposes it serves, and it serves many, the primary purpose is to foster religious belief and feeling both in adults and in children. In Chapter 2, we pointed out the fundamental needs that religion aims at subserving. One of these needs, we saw, is the need to find an ultimate sanction for human values, especially the values regulating conduct, the moral values, in short. Religion supplies a supra-natural sanction for these values. They are not merely man-made standards; they are rooted in a supranatural order, belief in the reality of which is an essential feature of religion, certainly of religion as the term is meant when we talk of religious education.

This means that religion introduces a special concept into our moral judgments, the concept of the "sacred." To put it negatively: certain kinds of behavior are not only morally bad or evil; they are sacrilegious or sinful, an offence against the sacred. This is what is meant by saying that "sin" and "sinful" are theological concepts, not just concepts of ordinary moral philosophy. To supply that sort of sanction to conduct clearly gives a peculiarly compulsive quality to the demand for conformity. How does the church implant and foster this concept in the mind of the young?

Partly, of course, by direct instruction. Along with direct instruction operates another influence, at least equally potent. This is the indirect influence of the church as an association. A church is an association of individuals like-minded in matters that ultimately rest on faith rather than logic and the association as such tends to confirm the individuals in their common faith. The association, moreover, reaches into the past to include the believers who have gone before. The young, moreover, find themselves here in an association in which the grown-ups are themselves participants; they, too, are on the receiving end of the learning process. It is a psychological fact that interests, beliefs, and feelings which are thus seen to be widely shared are *ipso facto* strengthened. The individual who boasts that he can be as good a Christian outside of the church as anybody inside it is probably deluding himself. Beyond a doubt, religion in the last analysis is a matter of what the individual does with his "solitariness" (as Whitehead has it) but the churchmen have been right in their belief that as a practical, going concern, religion flourishes best in association.

Such, then, is the special contribution of the church to the education of *homo socius*—the implanting of belief in supra-natural sanctions. Religious education is of course more than the implanting of that belief. Human beings have felt the need to *know* something about the supra-natural order and out of that need has grown a body of *dogma*. They have also felt the need to *do* something about it, to act in ways that bring them nearer to it and enable them to affect or influence it, and by this way they have developed a body of *ritual*. Religious education means the instruction in certain dogmas and rituals, and the investment of these with the same compulsive, supra-natural sanction.

Dogma and ritual vary from one religion to another and in some measure from one religious sect or group to another. There is yet another complicating factor. Religions and religious sects have established special tabus or conduct controls, with religious sanction attaching to conformity to them. Divorce, birth control, euthanasia or mercy killing, and the use of alcoholic beverages are cases in point. With one religious group, for example, divorce may be a purely secular matter, with secular law the controlling factor. With another group the final control may be not secular but sacred; severing of the marriage bond may be sacrilegious as well as morally bad.

When we use above the phrase "complicating factor," we have in mind one aspect of religious education which has presented democratic society with a peculiarly awkward problem: the extent to which and the manner in which the school should participate in religious education. The democratic state stands committed to freedom of religion. The architects of the American Constitution had learned one of the few clear lessons of history, for them still quite recent history: it is futile to use the powers of the state, through the school or otherwise, to enforce conformity to a particular religion. The only exception is the right of the child to education in the sense of literacy, training in the three R's. The state is prepared to enforce that right, should a particular sect take the stand that such education runs counter to its religious beliefs. On the other hand, the recognition—albeit reluctant recognition—of "conscientious objection" on the part of an individual to perform the time-honored duty of fighting for his country shows how unwilling the democratic state is to interfere wherever *bona fide* religious convictions seem to be involved.

Freedom of religion is thus a factor working against any satisfactory participation by the school in religious education. There is another factor working even more powerfully in the same direction. This is the view that religion is not merely one interest in life co-ordinate with other interests such as art, science, morality. Its writ runs over the whole region of the humanities and sciences and the idea that any one of the humane disciplines is something that can stand on its own legs, something autonomous with its own ineluctable standards, is in the last resort indefensible. It is the view, in short, that the concept of a purely secular education is invalid.

It would take us too far afield to consider here the many and varied devices adopted or suggested for having the state schools participate in religious education. Let it suffice to say that anyone who would work out a practical solution of the problem should satisfy himself at the outset that the crux of the difficulty lies in the operation of the two factors pointed out above.

Let us now consider the influence of the peer group. In the young, this form of influence usually occurs most notably during two periods of growth: the period of childhood proper (from six or seven to twelve or thirteen years of age) and the period of adolescence. In the period of infancy (up to about six years of age), family influence dominates. In passing from infancy to childhood, the individual passes from an intimate but restricted into a much wider sphere of social relationships, peer group relationships. The stage is typically marked by a certain withdrawal from the world of the grown-ups. The withdrawal may be very noticeable. How many a mother has been heard to say that her boy, aged eight to eleven years, is now a stranger to her! The fact is that his interest has turned to boys about his own age. True, a mother—or father—

has often enough said the same thing about the teen-age son or daughter. But there is a very significant difference between the two cases. The withdrawal of the child is due to temporary indifference to the adult world, while the adolescent's withdrawal as we shall see, is very far from being due to that factor.

We are concerned here with the manner in which the consciousness of social values, especially what we called group or political values, is developed as a result of the larger social experience incidental to childhood. Two agencies are of outstanding importance. The first is organized or group play, the second is the school itself.

The importance of play for mental development in general has been very properly stressed by the psychologists. It is not, however, the innate play tendency as such that is relevant to our purpose here. Our concern is with the organized group activities into which the play instinct has been elaborated and which realize developmental purposes far in excess of those of the instinct itself. If the Groos theory be true (the theory that play is an instinctive preparation for activities at the adult level), the general form of play would be largely determined by instinct, but from our point of view the interest centres on those features of the game which are of directly social origin and are transmitted, often with an interesting conservatism, from one generation of childhood to another.

From the moment he begins to play the game or games proper to his age, the child finds himself heir to a fairly elaborate system of rules and standards. These "rules of the game," which are his social play inheritance, are of peculiar importance for several reasons. To begin with, they are generally definite and detailed, and in this respect they are to be contrasted with the seemingly vaguer and more variable prescriptions which have hitherto claimed to control his activities. These rules are peculiar in another way. They are enforced with a fine stringency which refuses even to contemplate exception. As a participant in the game, the child finds himself a member of a group, the watchword of which is justice and equality. In the incidence of rules, all distinctions vanish, everybody counts for one and nobody for more than one.

To ask the psychological explanation of children's extreme

punctilio in this regard is to propound an interesting question which we may leave to the psychologist. All we need say here is that this, too, is part of his social inheritance with respect to the game. He accepts it as unreflectively as he accepts the rules themselves and, moreover, he finds this rigid application of the rules congenial and satisfying. Why? The answer at bottom is probably that the situation meets a need he is beginning to feel rather acutely by this time, the need for order and predictability in his world.

Attitudes and habits are thus developed in strict accordance with the meaning of political justice and equality. The child is familiarized with the notion of laws and standards impartially enforced within a given group. But the training in group life goes deeper than this. In this same context he comes to realize in a practical way another fundamental fact of group life, the educational importance of which we shall have to refer to in another connection. This is the fact of the essential *inequality* always implied in the healthy functioning of the group. In the game, he is speedily made to realize his personal level, to apprehend his personal capacities and limitations and thus to discover his proper niche in the group. He realizes that, if he is not to forego the many satisfactions of the game, he must limit and control himself in certain ways. He must follow, obey, imitate here while he can dictate and initiate there. The discipline of the playground thus early engenders habits of social action and standards of judgment which are the starting point for the articulate political ideals and standards of later life.

In like manner, the appreciation of the value we called loyalty or fraternity has its origin here. Play offers the earliest opportunity for conscious, deliberate co-operation with others for the realization of a common purpose and gradually habituates the child to the willing denial of purely individual impulse which such co-operation demands. On the whole, the organized play group may be said, in one important respect at least, to represent an ideal form of association, for here the individual is at once means and end. The presence of individuals who are *mere* means is completely alien to the spirit of the group. To be in it is to be of it; such is the first principle of this form of association.

The educational limitations of play, however, must be recognized. These are apparent in its very nature. The nature of play is adequately described by saying that the satisfaction resides in the activity itself, while the end to which the activity is consciously directed has only a make-believe value. This is an obvious inversion of the order of things as the child will find them in real life, where he will be called upon to prosecute activities not in themselves satisfying for the sake of an end of value. The training afforded by the school thus approximates more closely the conditions of real life. The school may and does, of course, interest itself in the activities of the playground and thus gives the child the additional satisfaction of feeling that the grown-ups attach value to what he is doing for the sheer fun of the thing. But the school contributes in its own special way to the training we are concerned with here.

The period of adolescence has been receiving special attention in our own day. The general psychology of adolescence has received attention from the psychologists for at least half a century owing to the inspiration of Stanley Hall's monumental work.[3] What has attracted special attention in our day is one aspect of adolescence, the apparently organized revolt against adult values and controls, especially against the authority of the home.

Let it be said at once that adolescent rebelliousness is itself no new thing. Consider the following paragraph from J. B. Priestley, a good observer of the manners of his own time.

> The truth was of course, that Mr. Smith's children *were* foreigners, not simply because they belonged to a younger generation but because they belonged to a younger generation that existed in a different world. Mr. Smith was perplexed because he applied to them standards they did not recognize. They were the products of a changing civilization, creatures of the post-war world [post World War I]. They had grown up to the sound of the Ford car rattling down the street, and that Ford car had gone rattling away, to the communal rubbish heap, with a whole load of ideas that seemed still of importance to Mr. Smith. They were the children of the Woolworth Stores and the moving pictures. Their world was at once larger and shallower than that of their parents. They were less English, more cosmopolitan. Mr. Smith could not understand George and Edna, but a host of youths and girls in New York, Paris, and Berlin would have understood them at a glance.[4]

[3] *Youth; Its Education, Regimen and Hygiene, 1907.*
[4] *Angel Pavement,* second ed., 1930 (The Musson Book Co., Toronto) p. 57.

Even the more extreme forms of rebellion are apparently not new. Here is a passage from the correspondence columns of the *Sunday Times* of London, dated May 31, 1964:

> The Brighton Pavilion was the scene of unruly rioting on Saturday, when a group of young men in distinctive dress and calling themselves "Bucks" came into conflict with the police. Some damage was done to the Pavilion, and there seemed to be some dispute between the "Bucks" and another group of young men who arrived by coach. The exact extent of the damage has not yet reached us, and it is feared that several were wounded.

The correspondent points out that this quotation is from the column "A Hundred Years Ago" in "The Western Morning News." One is tempted to dismiss the whole matter with a facile "there is nothing new under the sun," but that will not do.

What is distinctive of our own day is that the adolescents have become conscious of themselves as a group. This lively group consciousness has largely outmoded the former picture of the adolescent as a restless soul, withdrawn, sensitive, introspective. If he is restless, it is under adult restraint, if withdrawn, it is from adult interests and values, if introspective, it is not in lonely isolation but in reassuring communion with his own crowd.

This group consciousness appears to have resulted from specific and fairly obvious causes.

Many more adolescents than heretofore proceed to the high school (not to mention the university) and develop group feeling along the way. When education terminated for the large majority at the onset of adolescence, the young person remained at home working under his parents or left home for some form of apprenticeship. In either case he remained subject to adult standards and control.

Again, the new media of communication have done much to foster adolescent group spirit. The advertiser in particular has seen in the adolescents a most promising special market for his wares. Here, of course, the situation is not so much one of plain cause and effect as one of interdependence: the advertiser sets out to exploit a group spirit that he knows exists and in doing so intensifies that spirit.

But underlying it all is a more serious causative factor. Heretofore the "storm and stress" of adolescence was quite properly regarded as due to the inevitable maladaptation incidental to the transition from childhood to adulthood. The adolescent felt himself no longer a child and was anxious to put away childish things. At the same time, he felt he was not quite accepted by the adults as one of them. There were often other factors to which the psychologists have drawn attention, such as excessive strictness during the period of childhood, indoctrination with definite ideas and beliefs which the adolescent is finding unsatisfactory and disturbing and from which he is trying to shake himself free, the occurrence of deep-seated physiological changes entailing disturbance at the conscious level. Psychologists have explored the whole field very thoroughly.

But today the serious causative factor to which we have referred is something apart from all of the factors mentioned. In the past, the adults could present the young person with a set of definite values to live by—often enough too definite for his liking. Today the adult value system has seemingly broken down and produced confusion not only, or primarily, with respect to the more minor forms of conduct but also with respect to the more basic values. Consider a few examples.

Take the matter of war between civilized nations. All that the adolescent is sure of here is that adults have very recently made a shambles of the world, with the young people having to bear more than their share of the brunt of it. The angry young man can make out a good case for being angry. What have the adults to offer as a way out for the future? Nothing but confused counsel. Resorting to war or not resorting to war used to be a matter for argument. Certainly in the pre-1914 world, the rightness or wrongness of war was a matter for legitimate debate. The topic made a good "bull session" for students of those days. Today, it is clear that war is out, so far as the great nations are concerned. But it would take a very great optimist to say that it cannot and will not happen. A great nation may feel that its way of life may be so radically menaced that it might have to resort to war. Hence the hideous dilemma facing the public today. In a dilemma where either horn offers nothing but unmitigated disaster, and there appears to be no middle course, the situation is exactly right for hysteria, mass hysteria alternating with mass apathy. Something of the kind is noticeable in the adult world today with respect to war, and the adolescent senses it to the full.

Other examples could be cited. The color line, ethnic differences entailing deep-seated cultural cleavages, differences of social and economic class, sex morality, have created issues with respect to which the adult attitude is apt to be ambivalent: purported devotion to high principles, but with private and, it may be, unconscious mental reservations. This, too, the adolescent senses and he does not like it. He can see a symptom of it in a political election, for example, where the political parties do not appear to have any real quarrel with one another but seem to be concerned only to outbid one another in alluring promises to the electorate!

The adolescent thus feels himself thrown on his own resources and his impulse is to get together with his fellows. The outcome is the adolescent group with its own mores to which the individual conforms with a loyalty and punctilio which, differently directed, would satisfy the most exacting of domineering parents. The new mores cover a wide range of values. In personal appearance, blue jeans and tousled, unkempt hair may be the mode. In speech, every year or two brings a new dictionary of standard slang and colloquialism. In sex relationships, the new codes can be disturbing to grown-ups and with good reason when, for example, high school marriages threaten to become fashionable. In ways of thinking, certain beliefs and attitudes concerning matters of politics, morals, art, religion, become the vogue, the winds of doctrine here being as unpredictable as the other fashions. The individual, in effect, becomes "other-directed" in a very thoroughgoing way. The quality most highly prized by the group is the individual's ability to get along with the other members of it.

But it would be a bad mistake to think of the adolescent peer group as a herd-like association with a set of mores on the one hand and conforming individuals on the other. On the contrary, the presence of the peer group offers an occasion for expansion and intensification of social experience, notably in two directions Sex relationships acquire a new significance and the psychologists have done full justice to this development But it is not only *l'amour* that becomes important now; *l'amitié* or friendship plays a new part. Adolescence is the period for intense personal attachments either in the form of friendships or of hero worship, attachments which engender a new interest in and concern for the basic values governing the relationship of individual to individual.

To return to the peer group: it is interesting to note that the same tendency to group formation, with the same value attached to conformity and congeniality to the group, and probably largely due to the same cause (lack of a clear system of stable values), has appeared in the adult world itself. W. H. Whyte Jr., in *The Organization Man*, presents the adult parallel to this other-direction. He tells us how those responsible for staffing the great industrial organizations put the top premiums on one quality in their prospective employees, the ability to get along with one's fellows. Tests are devised to measure this quality and whether these tests really measure the individual's ability to get along with others or not, they serve to make the alert recruit aware of what is expected of him; his experience as a member of the organization completes the task.

One implication that Whyte evidently intends us to read into this process is that it constitutes a threat to the very thing it aims to promote—efficiency. The innovation that results in progress comes from independently-thinking individuals who possess the touch of rugged individualism that can be quite disruptive of smooth social relationships. The answer of the organization itself to this objection would be to point out that it has a department specifically concerned with research, and that these individualists would find their niche in that quarter. But the fact is that research itself is infected with the organizational virus; research tends to be organized into co-operating groups calling themselves "teams" —a reassuring word, until one reflects that it may easily create the wrong atmosphere for scientific discovery. Scientific research, of course, is no longer the haphazard thing it used to be, but the intellectual organization and co-operation that it has developed are essentially impersonal in character and not aptly described by the word "team."

Whyte points out, moreover, that the criterion of personal adaptiveness with a minimum of friction is not confined in its application to the office and the workshop; it is extended to social and private life. In these spheres, it takes the form of further contacts of the same "good mixers," with their wives included. The leisure part of life is thus also dominated by the organization, and becomes in effect an extension of the working segment of life. One wonders what John Dewey would think of this exemplification of his idea that the distinction between work and leisure is a false dualism.

We are principally concerned in this study with the young. One might conclude that the peer group mentality is nothing more than the imitation of what young people observe in the adult world, but this would be a mistake. As we have pointed out, there are more basic or universal factors operating in this regard than simply the mentality of the "organization man." Priestley's observations about George and Edna are sound, although Mr. and Mrs. Smith, and other parents of that day, were not "organization people." At the same time, the situation that Priestley describes, wherever it happens to exist, serves to give implicit adult recognition to the separate world set up by the "younger set" for themselves. Education must therefore do what it can to offset undesirable consequences of a way of life in which social adaptiveness is the ruling value.

In this argument, however, one should not forget that, however complete the peer group influence or "other-direction" at the adult level, it is easy to exaggerate its importance at the adolescent stage. Adolescents as a crowd can be implacably indifferent to matters that their elders consider important, but as individuals they can be and are sensitive and tractable. There is ample evidence that the individual adolescent is basically often dissatisfied with the shifting, erratic mores that his own crowd would impose upon him. Particularly in questions of moral right and wrong he searches for something more solid and dependable. The adolescent begins to sense the crucial fact that what is right and what is wrong is something more than just a matter of that which is customary and that which is opposed to custom—the thing to do and the thing not to do in the eyes of his peer group. Here is something that the school can take hold of and build on.

The contribution of the school to this aspect of education should be governed by a definite principle: the community should not delegate to the school any task which would interfere with the efficient performance of the school's own proper function, or any task which, because of its special structure, the school is not in a position to undertake with any prospect of success. Certain social changes have resulted in a growing disregard of this essential principle. Heretofore the family and the church made moral and religious education their special domain. The influence of the family has weakened, as has the influence of the church. Moral and religious education are nevertheless as important as they ever were and therefore the school—so the argument runs—must assume responsibility for them. Leaving aside the question of religious education, it is important for society to reassess the responsibility of the family in relation both to morals and to manners.

The influence of the family, as we have seen, begins early—it is continuous, direct, and intimately personal. The family influence is thus best able to foster the feelings and attitudes which are the very tissue of desirable social behavior. The school has many opportunities to co-operate, but its co-operation should be incidental and occasional. On this basis there is ample opportunity to reinforce the efforts of home and church, and indeed of any other social agency, to foster truthfulness, honesty, loyalty, and kindness, and to suppress the opposites of these values.

It is always true that the extent to which the teacher needs to concern himself with such fundamental matters depends on the kind of community from which his pupils are drawn. At one extreme, he is in the happy position of being able to take it for granted that a solid foundation has been laid. At the other extreme, he finds himself under compulsion to do what he can to cope with the consequences of no early training or possibly even of bad training. The teacher's compulsion should be that of his own professional conscience; the community should not hold him responsible for correcting the effects of its own neglect and carelessness.

In the main, the special contribution of the school to the appreciation of the basoc social values does not take the form of explicit training. Instead, it takes the indirect form of providing these values with the variegated, liberalizing background that grows out of acquaintance with literature and history. This background is liberalizing because it frees values from limitations of time and place, revealing them as the common concern of all men, always, everywhere. The true literary classics are classics in virtue of this perennial and universal appeal. History presents human nature in the large, in its goodness and evil, its nobility and baseness. By clear implication or open verdict, history usually leaves no doubt as to which is the one and which the other.

But the indirect influence of the school in the making of *homo socius* is by no means limited to the impact of studies such as literature and history. In so far as the school performs its proper function of fostering appreciation of all the basic values that we have discussed, it is accomplishing the same indirect result. Educationists who have stressed the importance of social adjustment in the sense of harmonious, satisfactory relationships with one's associates are correct in so doing. Discovering that people are important, developing an interest in them, and finding out how to get along with them—these are aspects of learning in which failure means more or less serious personal loss. At the same time, to allow one's judgments, beliefs, and values to become a mere reflection of the shifting attitudes of one's crowd is to adopt a way of life that leads to intellectual and moral rootlessness.

The school should provide the counteractive against unthinking acceptance of the passing vogue in questions of what is good and bad in art, right and wrong in morals, true and false in knowledge. The school can accomplish this, not by furnishing the individual with clear-cut, incontrovertible standards in advance, but by implanting in him a firmly-rooted conviction that there *are* standards of truth, beauty, and moral goodness, and by giving him experience and training in the critical reflection necessary for the apprehension of these standards. To leaven moral integrity with intellectual integrity is the school's special purpose, and if it fails to perform this function, the educational product will not be of high standard.

Whether the school accomplishes this task depends in the last analysis on the calibre of its teachers. If teachers as well as pupils fall into line with, for example, the more transient and superficial values prevailing among the adults around them, the teachers will fail to make the contribution of which they alone are capable. In *The Organization Man,* Whyte relates how some parents expressed to the superintendent their concern over their children's apparent backwardness in the fundamentals of reading, writing, arithmetic, geography, and other subjects. The superintendent explained that his schools were giving priority to something more realistic, more pertinent to the demands of later life—to social adjustment. Social adjustment was the dominant value in this particular community.

The school fails in another and opposite respect when its outlook is restricted to the values of a vanished past, when it proceeds in disregard of the needs and challenges of the contemporary world, and operates with a curriculum, methods and procedures that have no justification other than mere tradition. Clearly the ideal in such a situation is an attitude that lays due stress both on what seems valuable and deserving of allegiance in tradition, and on the demands, the often harsh and frightening demands, of the contemporary world. To look for teachers to possess this attitude of interested, appraising detachment themselves, and to ask them to impart a real measure of it to their pupils is certainly a lofty goal. But, is it, however, expecting too much of teachers at least to possess this attitude, however well they are able to impart it?

In spite of all that has been said and written on the subject, the special role or function of the teaching profession in the community has not been sufficiently clarified. At the one extreme, the teacher's role is conceived of as the duty of directing the young along the same paths their elders have taken, so as to fit them into the existing social scene. Teachers with an idealistic outlook have rejected this servile conception of their function. At the other extreme, some teachers claim that it is the duty of the profession to work directly for a better social and political order—a frankly political conception of the role of the profession, and one that the community in its turn rejects as unrealistic and megalomaniac. Parallels with other professions can be misleading, but it is nevertheless pertinent to observe that the medical profession does not accept at face value either grandmother's remedies for physical ailments or the medical nostrums and fashions that appear from time to time. The medical profession simply appraises these agencies from its own point of view. The teaching profession must build up an image of its own place and part in the scheme of things and contrive to impart that image both to its own members and to the community it serves.

To complete the discussion of the education of *homo socius*, we must give more careful consideration to what we have referred to as group or political values. Twentieth-century democracy has presented these values in a new light, and it will be better to deal with them later in Part II.

9   General, Liberal, Cultural Education: The Development of Individuality

We have discussed at length the desirable basic traits of men, the development of which constitutes a movement towards human excellence. In virtue of these traits as a whole, rather than of any one of them, man claims for himself the title of *homo sapiens*. These are the qualities, moreover, as the preceding chapters emphasized, that are the concern of education in the more fundamental sense, the sense in which it is usually referred to as "general education." The terms "liberal" and "cultural" are customarily applied to education in this context, and it is clear that each one of these words is apposite in its own way.

"General" reminds us that such an education does not aim at the achievement of a limited or specific purpose, such as preparing the individual to take his place in a particular social class, or training him for a specific vocation. General education is a form of education that has relevance for every human being. The term "liberal" implies essentially that education liberates or frees the individual from the limitations of his merely animal nature and directs him towards the way in which he can realize his true humanity. This idea was implied in the historical usage that equated liberal education with the education appropriate to a free man or man of leisure. A "cultural" education implies the idea of growth, of cultivating and bringing to fruition those traits of human nature that are worthy of development, and that will not develop without the right kind of nurture.

These values are the materials that education makes use of in performing its function. They are, however, only the materials for education. Believing that nothing else is required to accomplish the educational process is much like providing the prospective owner of a house with bricks, mortar, wood, glass, and all the other necessary building materials, and then leaving him to manage as best he can with them. The architect and the builder, both of whom will most likely have ideas that clash with the owner's personal feelings about what he wants, are indispensable to creating the house. In this analogy, we may think of the architect as the educational system and the builder as the teacher. Both architect and builder must take into consideration the general character or style of building in the particular region in which they are constructing the house. In other words, general education is a matter of developing in the individual an appreciation of the basic cultural values as well as an integration of these values into a personal pattern that is an expression of his individuality.

A correct interpretation of the terms "appreciation" and "integration" in this context is essential. From the discussion of basic values in the preceding chapters, the reader has doubtless already arrived at the proper meaning of the term "appreciation." Appreciation of science, for example, implies an overall understanding of the methods and standards of science, together with a general grasp of the significance of this pursuit for human living. This meaning of "appreciation" likewise applies to art in its various forms. "Appreciation" involves the *humane* approach and outlook, as distinct from the specialist's preoccupation with his particular art or science. The specialist views his specialty as a coherent, logically-ordered whole. He works on the frontier, so to speak, and his concern is with discoveries that will push back the boundaries of knowledge.

The specialist may, it is true, combine his specific interest with the humane outlook, but more than likely he will not. The specialist may not only don "blinkers" when dealing with his specialty (as he normally does), but he may also keep his blinkers on all the time, in which case he personifies that not uncommon phenomenon, a specialist in one of the arts or sciences who, while he perhaps renders a highly valuable service to his fellows, is not himself an educated man.

The distinction between the humane and the specialist point of view, a distinction that is familiar enough today, is presented in an especially interesting way by the philosopher Jacques Maritain, in connection with his account of the educational philosophy of St. Thomas Aquinas. St. Thomas accepted from Aristotle the distinction between the intellectual virtues and the moral virtues. The former are represented (for Aristotle) by the philosopher in his quest for knowledge; the latter are expressed in the standards governing right conduct. Professor Maritain interprets the intellectual virtues in modern terms by identifying them with the pursuits of the specialists and research men, an interesting suggestion that Aristotle, were he alive today, would undoubtedly accept. The ordinary educated man is interested in what the specialists are doing, but interested in his own particular way. Maritain states his case in this way:

> Thus we have two quite different states for intelligence: *natural intelligence* and *intelligence as scientifically formed and equipped*, or, in Thomist language, *intelligence perfected by the intellectual virtues* . . . my contention is that education, especially liberal education, has essentially to cultivate and liberate, form and equip intelligence, and to prepare for the development of the intellectual virtues, but that this development itself, once the threshold of virtue has been crossed, is necessarily particularized to a given branch of knowledge . . . a kind of *universal knowledge* is possible at the level of *natural intelligence* or, at a level which is neither scientific nor philosophical . . . . At this level of natural intelligence, the youth can be offered, not scientific knowledge supposedly reduced and concentrated but some real, integrated, and articulate, though imperfect understanding . . . about the nature and meaning of that knowledge which is proper to men in possession of the intellectual virtues . . . The genuine task is neither encyclopedic inculcation nor what I should like to call nursery accommodation: it is basic liberal education, dealing with universal knowledge at the level of natural intelligence and using natural intelligence's own approach.[1]

Keeping in mind Professor Maritain's philosophic interpretation of the meaning of the term "appreciation" as applied to the arts and the sciences, let us move on to the question of "integration." The

[1] *Modern Philosophies and Education*: Fifty-fourth Year Book of the National Society for the Study of Education, pp. 61-62 (Italics by Professor Maritain).

arts, the sciences, and the philosophic disciplines obviously present a wide variety of cultural materials. It is easy, and quite fallacious, to think of education as, ideally, a matter of training in each of these disciplines, as much training in as many of them as the time available for education allows. This is a mechanical conception, one quite foreign to the idea of education as personal development. To restate this fact from the pupil's point of view: the problem is to extract, under the direction of his teacher, a personal pattern from this cultural variety. The variety must somehow be integrated, because personality is a unity, and this integration must, moreover, reflect the fact that every personality is, in the last analysis, unique and individual. Certain special factors exert an important influence in determining what the resulting personal pattern will be like.

The first and most important of these factors is that of individual aptitude and interest. The curriculum, as we have seen, must make provision for wide variety in this regard. Individual aptitude is "individual" in the further sense that the stage at which it begins to manifest itself varies with each person. In some instances, this stage occurs much earlier or later than in others. The school is in a key position to discover for the individual, or rather to put him in the way of discovering for himself, special aptitudes and capacities that have important bearing on the question of the true line of development for him. Whatever this line of development, it will approximate one of two types.

On the one hand, it may be similar to the more general type of development, development based on responsiveness to cultural interests as a whole. On the other hand, it may approximate the concentrated, specialized type of development, where response tends to be limited, and for this very reason presumably more adequate and penetrating. The former type of development concentrates on variety and breadth, and the latter on depth. Each kind has its peculiar defect or danger: in the first instance, this danger is superficiality, while in the second, it is narrowness. Whichever the development follows, it represents the reflection in the individual of the fundamental interests and pursuits that constitute civilized living. It is a simple matter to accept the fallacy (a form of what the logicians call "hypostatizing abstractions") of believing that these values of civilized living have an independent life, that they survive and grow by their own inner drive. In reality, however, they have no existence except in so far as education gives them vital, personal embodiment from one generation to the next.

The vocational interest is another important factor that influences the personal pattern of development. This is obvious at the higher levels of vocational training—preparation for the professions—where basic disciplines in science, art, or philosophy constitute part of vocational training. Training for medicine or engineering calls for the study of certain basic sciences; theological training involves contact with metaphysics; and legal training directly or indirectly raises fundamental issues of social and political philosophy. The teaching profession is in a special position, since a sound background of general education is an essential part of its vocational preparation.

The influence of the vocational interest is not, however, limited to the higher levels of education. This interest is more or less dimly present at earlier levels, and by the onset of the teens it may well assume major importance, although actual vocational choice may not occur until considerably later. Among the less tangible but very important changes brought about by democracy today is the elimination of the old notion of leisure as a profession, with a professional leisure class. Everyone regards the choice and pursuit of vocation as one of the inescapable obligations imposed by society, a fact that naturally exerts an impact on the individual's general sense of values.

Of much greater importance is the influence on the individual of the age or epoch into which he is born. Civilized development has not taken the form of continuous and uniform progress along the whole cultural front. In a particular age, notable advances may be occurring at certain points, while at others there is stagnation and perhaps retrogression. Every age presents a distinctive cultural pattern in which certain dominating values tend to color the cultural outlook as a whole. The contemporary cultural pattern is inclined to affect profoundly the personal pattern that commends itself as the right one—in short, it affects the conception of education.

The history of Western culture offers numerous illustrations of this principle. In the Middle Ages, cultural history was dominated by the religious interest. While it is true that this period brought about great artistic achievements, it is significant that the inspiration and incentives for these achievements were religious. The religious interest gave motive and regulation to the pursuit of knowledge, the most highly prized form of knowledge being theology. Concern for social and political issues was conspicuously lacking in an age that gave clear religious sanction to the *status quo*, and in which, moreover, the belief in the more or less imminent end of the world ruled out in advance the kinds of ideas implied in the concept of progress. Science was in its infancy, a troublesome and unwanted child.

The Renaissance witnessed a vigorous revival of interest in certain fields of the humanities, as we refer to them today: art, literature, and metaphysical philosophy. Science was growing, but its cultivation was still the preoccupation of a very small coterie of dedicated individuals. Social and political philosophy, on the other hand, became a dominant concern of the intellectuals in the period designated roughly as the eighteenth century. Philosophers had largely become impatient with theological speculation and sceptical of its value. This same spirit found candid expression in poetry, as in these famous lines of Alexander Pope:

> Know well thyself, presume not God to scan;
> The proper study of mankind is man.[1]

In the age that produced the French Revolution, religious scepticism became so fashionable that, as one writer remarked, even the clergy took it up. Nor was the spirit of frank and rank secularism confined to philosophers and men of letters. The amazing upsurge of religious feeling that John Wesley aroused among the masses in England is understandable if we remember that religious practice had in great measure settled down to an empty formalism that failed to provide sustenance and expression for genuine religious needs.

Throughout the nineteenth century, interest in social and political values continued to form an important part of the civilized picture. By the turn of the century, however, science attained a dominant position, and during the twentieth century science has been achieving an ascendancy over men's minds comparable to that of theology in the Middle Ages. A hundred years of practical applications, each increasingly spectacular in character, could not fail to exercise profound influence on the popular mind and its sense of values. As for the scientists themselves (no longer a small coterie, but an immense

[1]Pope: *An Essay on Man.*

army now) indications are that, by and large, they have been working on the more or less unconscious assumption that any knowledge which stops short of being scientific knowledge is not real knowledge. This assumption has no doubt had much to do with the development of another interest, the application of scientific method to the solution of social problems. To the optimists, *social science* holds out the hope of the same spectacular results already achieved in the field of the natural sciences.

The "spirit of the age" affects every individual and every institution, including educational institutions. Each generation employs hindsight to observe and appraise the spirit of former ages, but a given age must accept the particular force that is currently at work upon it. The spirit of the age appears to be one of those great impersonal forces considered by some historians to be the real factors determining the course of human history. This is especially true with regard to its operations in the earlier stages of civilized history, to which we referred previously.

In the course of time, however, a new factor, awareness or self-consciousness, began to make its presence felt. As men became increasingly conscious of the values dominating their lives, they tended to objectify them and thus to judge and appraise them with a growing degree of detachment. Many examples of the great difference that this factor has made in man's behavior could be cited. One topical illustration of this point occurs in the field of advertising. When the public realizes that it is being subjected to a steady barrage of advertisement, it becomes less readily manipulated by the advertiser. The advertiser finds that he is faced with overcoming resistance and criticism that awareness of his aims and methods produces in the public.

It is one thing for a particular age or epoch to be critical of the past, and another to be critical not only of the past but also of the present. Let us clarify what we mean by "being critical of the present." This phrase does not refer to a sympathy with those who express nostalgia for "the good old days," amid jeremiads over the "rising generation." The lament of such persons is probably as old as the human race itself, and is not to be taken seriously, except perhaps as one of the surer symptoms of the onset of mental senescence. What we are referring to here is a criticism on a much more philosophical and more sophisticated plane, and once again the history of civilization provides us with pertinent and instructive examples of what we mean.

The intellectual and moral standards of the Middle Ages possessed finality for the people of the times. History had not provided them with the sophistication that could enable them to be properly critical of themselves. In the same way, the eighteenth-century thinkers regarded their postulate that the study of man is the sole concern of mankind as a philosophical discovery that subsequent generations would accept without question. These thinkers lacked the perspective that is basic to effective criticism of the present as well as of the past.

In his well-known *Essay on Education,* Herbert Spencer made a telling plea for recognition of science in the curriculum of schools and colleges in an age that was notably scientific in temper and outlook. Spencer went still further, presenting science as the true gospel for "complete living." This is clear from the manner in which he adjudicated the issue between science and the fine arts, including literature. Of the fine arts, he declares that "as they occupy the leisure part of life, so should they occupy the leisure part of education," a judgment that he obviously considered binding not only on his own age but on all ages to come. The notion that some fifty years later the case for humanities would come up in a context which would make his own judgment appear hasty and unsound would simply not have made sense to Spencer.

In the past, criticism of education was directed mainly against its conservatism, its tendency to lag behind the spirit of the age. This criticism was usually a valid one, for education by its very nature creates a cultural lag. Adults, whether parents or teachers, tend to train the young in the way they have gone themselves. This conservatism posed no problem as long as formal education remained the privilege of the few. Parents had the means of bringing education up to date, such as the Grand Tour in the eighteenth century, and formal schooling could be left to Oxford or some equally conservative institution.

With the extension of educational opportunity to the general public, educational conservatism appeared in a new light: it now meant that education was failing to perform its proper task of preparing the individual for the life that he would have to live in society. Critics insisted that the needs and demands of contemporary society should be the prime consideration in determining educational policy. For the school to be behind the times, with its teachers living in the past, was felt to be the worst thing that could happen to education. With the people as a whole involved, the old remedy of supplementing the work of the school with training outside the school, training more relevant to the needs of the times and of a particular social class, was no longer applicable. The main responsibility for turning the individual into a worthy member of society, of society as it actually existed, was then left to the school.

This view led to a new order of tension in the field of education. Heretofore, the basic dispute had been between those who looked to the past and those who looked to the present for a guiding philosophy of education. The former presented their case as a stand for "fundamentals" and training in these they were convinced was the best preparation for the present. Their opponents discounted the so-called "fundamentals," as outmoded values and procedures with no justification other than mere tradition. These persons stood for realistic study of the present, with the adjustment of educational aims and curricula in the light of the results of this study.

The new demand was that the present, no less than the past, should produce its credentials in order to show positive proof why it should be accepted as the source and justification of educational standards. Being up to date no longer necessarily meant being in the line of progress. The spirit of the age, or the prevailing cultural pattern, as it is perhaps better called, no longer carried authority *per se*. Educational thinkers thus ultimately arrived at a two-fold realization: a philosophy of education must examine the past in order to correct the shortcomings of the present, and it must also examine the present so as to discover how much of what has survived from the past should be discounted as merely the result of the sheer momentum of custom.

10 *General, Liberal, Cultural Education: Parental Ascendancy*

A very important form of influence that can do much to determine the cultural pattern that the individual will develop is direct and deliberate personal influence. By this we do not mean the official or authorized influence of the teacher's personality exerted through the classroom and the school, but rather the influence brought to bear directly and systematically by some other individual who happens, for one reason or another, to have attained personal ascendancy over the young person. The most important instance in this connection is that of parental ascendancy. Other kinds of control do occur, but they are usually transient in character and sufficiently varied to cancel each other out.

Parental influence, early, continuous, and intimate, as we have seen it to be, can have profound effects if it is brought to bear systematically and with a clear end in view. A case in point is the father-child relationship when, as is always likely, the sentiment of *property* becomes involved. A man's property, as the psychologist William James pointed out, comes to be regarded by him as an extension of his own self, of his material self, as James called this segment of the human ego. The father tends to view his child in this very light: the kind of creature that his child turns out to be reflects on himself, favorably or unfavorably. The temptation is strong to mold his son into a form to which he can point with pride. The mother-child relationship, on the other hand, involves deep-seated instinctive elements that make the relationship more complex and not so likely to lend itself to this straightforward form of proprietary expression.

Some extraordinary examples of parental domination are on record, and as the data of these relationships are detailed and reliable, it is instructive to examine them. Perhaps the most famous instance is that of Lord Chesterfield and his son, as presented in the famous *Letters*.[1] Lord Chesterfield achieved distinction in politics and in the diplomatic service, but more particularly as a suave and cultivated man of fashion. His heart was set on seeing his son grow up to outshine himself both as politician and socialite. To this end, Chesterfield secured a tutor, whom he carefully briefed on the object in view—the production of an accomplished scholar, a man of affairs, and a luminary of fashion, all of course in the best eighteenth-century conception of these roles. From the outset, Lord Chesterfield exercised unremitting supervision over both tutor and pupil.

It is to the period of young Chesterfield's Grand Tour, the coping-stone in the education of every young aristocrat's life, that we owe the *Letters*. With every step of the journey (to exaggerate slightly, but only slightly) there arrived a fresh letter of advice, exhortation, and warning from the anxious father. The boy had to answer each letter with a meticulous account of what he was reading, which persons of note he had met from time to time, what they had said to him, and how he had comported himself. Young Chesterfield's letters have not been preserved (which is indeed a pity), but we can easily guess at their purport from the comments and criticisms contained in his father's letters.

For both pupil and tutor the letters did much to take the joy out of travelling. The tutor and his pupil tacitly conspired to conceal the truth, and the wily father, either because he distrusted the competence of the tutor to pass sound judgment on his pupil's progress in the higher social graces, or because he was not sure of the teacher's candor, had his own well-qualified spies in the places visited. As is often the way of spies, some of them reported only what they thought would please their noble employer, and others sent back more disturbing communications.

Perhaps the most remarkable feature of the *Letters* is not their

[1]*Letters of Lord Chesterfield to his Son* (J. M. Dent and Sons, 1929).

literary quality, which is of a high order, but the shrewd and sound observations on what and how to read, how to study and resist distractions, how to make "desirable" friends and influence the "right sort of people." The *Letters* require far too much editing, however, to give them lasting value as a contribution to education. They reflect all too clearly the cold and calculating cynicism of an elderly eighteenth-century aristocrat whose sole thought is how to get on in his own world. They harp, for example, on the importance of being a success with women, in which connection the lord recommends an occasional liaison, but always with married women, so as to benefit from their superior sophistication while avoiding the risk of any permanent entanglement. The educational highlight of the Grand Tour was, of course, Paris, for that city alone provided the last word in social and political *savoir faire*, including the political know-how of *cherchez la femme*.

What was the end result of this education? Not, it must be recorded, a famous educational victory. In the years of the Grand Tour the young man had developed into precisely the antithesis of his father, with no interest in politics, unprepossessing in appearance, uncouth in manners, and quite content to remain that way. Young Chesterfield also married a young woman who had never come within sighting distance of his father's world, but one who proved a sensible and level-headed wife. Tutor and pupil skilfully managed to keep the marriage secret from the benevolent tyrant in England.

Early in the correspondence, Chesterfield wrote:

> I hope, I wish, I doubt, and I fear alternately. This only I am sure of—that you will prove either the greatest pain or the greatest pleasure of yours, etc.

It was pain rather than pleasure that actually materialized, when Chesterfield finally met the young man on the return to England, but being Chesterfield, he did not permit the least ungentlemanly manifestation of his utter disappointment to show itself. Later, to be sure, he wrote to a friend who consulted him about the education of his children that one should consider "not so much what you would choose for them as what they are likely to succeed best in." In quoting this observation, one writer draws the moral of this example of parental domination when he comments: "It had taken the fiasco of a life to teach him that lesson."[2]

The education of John Stuart Mill, an outstanding philosopher of the nineteenth century, sometimes called the "father of modern logic," is our second example of parental ascendancy carried to an extreme. Mill, besides being a noted philosopher, was also, for a time, a member of parliament, and in that capacity he took an active part in furthering various projects of social and educational reform. His father, himself a philosopher, took charge of his education, and Mill left us a description of that education:

A considerable part of almost every day was employed in the instruction of his children: in the case of one of them, myself, he exerted an amount of labour, care and perseverance rarely, if ever, employed for a similar purpose, in endeavouring to give, according to his own conception, the highest order of intellectual education.[3]

"By the age of seven," J. S. Mill continues, "I had read, under my father's tuition, a number of Greek prose authors, among whom I remember the whole of Heroditus and of Xenophen's *Cyropaedia* and *Memorials of Socrates*; some of the lives of the philosophers by Diogenes Laertius; part of Lucian and Isocrates' *ad Demonicam* and *ad Nicolam* . . . the first six dialogues of Plato, from the *Euthyphron* to the *Thaetetus* inclusive; which last dialogue, I venture to think, would have been better omitted, as it was totally impossible I should understand it. But my father, in all his teaching, demanded of me not only the utmost I could do, but much that I could by no possibility have done.

But the lessons were only a part of the daily instruction I received. Much of it consisted in the books I had read by myself, and my father's discourses to me, chiefly during our walks . . . and with my earliest recollections of green fields and wild flowers, is mingled that of the account I gave him daily of what I had read the day before."

From eight to twelve years of age, in addition to coping with a program that resembles the prescription for an Honors Degree in Classics, Mill made a good beginning with mathematics:

[2]Shellabarger, *Lord Chesterfield and his World* (Little, Brown, and Co., Boston, 1951), p. 370.
[3]*Autobiography of John Stewart Mill* (Columbia University Press, 1924), p. 3.

I learnt elementary geometry and algebra thoroughly, the differential calculus and other portions of the higher mathematics far from thoroughly; for my father, not having kept up this part of his early acquired knowledge, could not spare time to qualify himself for removing my difficulties.

During this period, moreover, he carried on extensive private reading in the standard histories of his day, and about the age of twelve, he tells us, he began the study of logic.

Some of the forms of training that one usually associates with those early years in which Mill's education took place had apparently no place in his curriculum. About religious education, for example, Mill makes this curious observation:

> I am one of the very few examples, in this country, of one who has, not thrown off religious belief, but never had it . . . It did not seem to me more strange that English people should believe what I did not, than that men I read of in Heroditus should have done so.

He also tells us how his father carefully kept him

> from having any great amount of intercourse with other boys. He was earnestly bent on my escaping not only the ordinary corrupting influence which boys exercise over boys, but the contagion of vulgar modes of thought and feeling; and for this he was willing that I should pay the price of inferiority in the accomplishments which school boys in all countries chiefly cultivate.

There was a side of J. S. Mill's nature for which this early and intensive intellectual cultivation proved not only unhelpful but actually injurious. Mill speaks of his capacity for human sympathy when he states:

> My education, I thought, had failed to create those feelings in sufficient strength to resist the dissolving influence of analysis, while the whole course of my intellectual cultivation had made precocious and premature analysis the inveterate habit of my mind.

Unlike Chesterfield's son, Mill could look back on his educational ordeal and appraise it with critical detachment. As the previous quotation shows, he found his experience incomplete and ill-timed, but he cast no doubt on the intrinsic value of the training as far as it went. Chesterfield's son was clearly a stolid, unimaginative youth, for to him all "labour, care, and perseverance" was mere parental badgering, to be circumvented by one subterfuge after another.

The third example of parental domination that we have chosen differs from both of the others already examined. In this case, not only did all the effort and attention devoted to the son's education appear to him in retrospect disastrously mistaken in both conception and method, but it led to permanent estrangement from a parent whom he had always loved and respected.

Sir Edmund Gosse, a distinguished man of letters in the nineteenth century, devoted an entire book[4] to the topic of his education at the hands of his father. The father was himself a distinguished naturalist who had made important contributions to the study of marine life. His son accompanied him on his excursions, and the exploration of beach, rock, and cave in quest of minute forms of plant and animal life remained with young Gosse as happy memories, perhaps the only truly pleasant recollections of his childhood. In the father's view, however, happiness had nothing to do with the serious business of education.

Gosse's father and mother were both devoted adherents of a small and puritanical religious sect. Their hearts were set on making their son a preacher and leader of their small religious community. All might well have proceeded as planned, had a momentous event not taken place in the world of science. This was the publication in 1859 of Charles Darwin's *Origin of Species*, a work that aroused a furor of denunciation among religious groups that had accepted the account of creation in the book of Genesis as literal truth.

His father tried hard to keep Gosse away from the contaminating touch of the new ideas. The boy, however, was sufficiently mature to be drawn by curiosity to find out for himself what Darwin had said, and moreover, to reach the conclusion that the famous naturalist had presented an unanswerable case. The effect of this discovery upon the young man was to shatter the image of his father's infallibility. Such a change is normal enough, and it need not have led to an estrangement, which was deeply saddening for both parties. The father's intensified efforts to restore the relationship to its old footing and save his boy for the service of religion proved an unfor-

[4] *Father and Son* (Charles Scribner's Sons, 1908).

tunate consequence of the break. A few passages from the son's book suffice to indicate how he regarded the whole episode in retrospect:

> In consequence of the stern ordinance which I have described, not a single fiction was read to me during my infancy. The rapture of the child who delays the process of going to bed by cajoling "a story" out of his mother or his nurse, as he sits upon her knee, well tucked up at the corner of the nursery fire,—this was unknown to me. Never, in all my early childhood did anyone address to me the affecting preamble, "once upon a time." (p. 25).

After a short stay with a neighboring family, where an entirely different atmosphere prevailed, Gosse recalls:

> The Clifton family was God-fearing in a quiet, sensible way, but there was a total absence of all the intensity and compulsion of our religious life at Islington . . . For a short, enchanting period of respite, I lived the life of an ordinary little boy, relapsing, to a degree which would have filled my father with despair, into childish thoughts and childish language. . . . (p. 82).

> My father, ever reflecting on what could be done to confirm my spiritual vocation, to pin me down, as it were, beyond any possibility of escape, bethought him that it would accustom me to what he called "pastoral work in the Lord's service" if I accompanied Mary Grace on her visits from house to house. If it is remembered that I was only eight and a half when this scheme was carried into practice, it will surprise no one to hear that it was not crowned with success. I disliked extremely this visitation of the poor. . . . (p. 142).

> It was not in harshness nor in ill-nature that he worried so much; on the contrary it was all part of his too anxious love. He was in a hurry to see me become a shining light, everything that he had himself desired to be, yet with none of his shortcomings . . . (p. 216).

> He who was so tenderhearted that he could not bear to witness the pain or distress of any person, however disagreeable or undeserving, was quite acquiescent in believing that God would punish human beings, in millions for ever, for a purely intellectual error of comprehension. . . . (p. 321).

> He had recognized, with reluctance, that holiness was not hereditary, but he continued to hope that it might be compulsive. I was still "the child of many prayers", and it was not to be conceded that those prayers could remain unanswered. (p. 335).

The case histories of Lord Chesterfield's son, John Stuart Mill, and Sir Edmund Gosse are three human documents worthy of careful consideration. It might be objected that they present exceptional cases which, because they are exceptional, should be discounted. They are indeed extraordinary in the sense that they present a detailed record made in each instance by an unusual type of individual. They are exceptional in the further sense that all three examples present an extreme degree of domination, or at any rate a systematic attempt in that direction. But there is no reason to suppose that these illustrations are exceptional in the sense that the situation that they all depict—the unhealthy domination of a young person by a parent or other adult in a position to achieve domination—is of infrequent occurrence. On the contrary, it is safe to assume that similar unrecorded cases are only far too numerous and as unfortunate in their untoward consequences.

These three histories raise an interesting question of a general nature: Is it ever desirable to make education a matter of this one-to-one personal relationship, with the more mature personality in intimate and continuous contact with the less mature? Educationists have been inclined to regard this relationship as educationally the ideal situation, dismissing it as impracticable, but never questioning its validity. The relationship symbolized in the phrase "James Garfield and Mark Hopkins on a log" has served to fix the image of this educational situation. Teachers have thought wistfully in terms of smaller and smaller classes, with the idea of one teacher and one pupil as the ultimate in educational progress.

Perhaps the whole idea of the one-to-one relationship requires rethinking in the light of psychological realities. Is it not likely, for example, that teacher and pupil might become emotionally involved, with the disturbing concomitant tensions of personal like and dislike, attraction and repulsion, love and hate? If this were to happen, would it not make the relationship at bottom *unprofessional?* Is it not also true that the most beneficial professional attitude for the teacher is one of detachment or objectivity, with *understanding* as the real desideratum, and sympathy as a means to fuller understanding? With regard to the teacher, is not the truly professional feeling his feeling for the value of what he is teaching—love of his subject, in other words? Genuine concern for the *welfare* of the pupil is of course a professional *sine qua non,* but this is a different order of feeling from the one that we have been considering.

The optimal size of a class, in this view, will fall between two extremes: at one extreme, the class is so large that individuals become mere units and teaching a mechanical parade, and at the other extreme emotional factors of the sort referred to will tend to intrude themselves. In this connection, one cannot but wonder what kind of relationship would have developed between Rousseau's Emile and his tutor, had each of them been a real person and not a figment of the reformer's imagination. Lack of space prevents further examination of this intriguing question, and we turn now to the discussion of a topic arising out of the three case histories that we considered in this chapter—the distinction between content and process.

11 *Content and Process in Education*

We must consider two ways in which authority can successfully be exerted to result in good education. We can deal first with the actual *content* of education. When we say content we mean the subject matter, or the curriculum. But we mean more than this. When we say content we also mean not only the subject matter, but the special arrangement of the subject matter which is denoted usually by the word "method." The word method is the teacher's description of his way of organizing the subject matter to obtain what he believes will be the best possible results. In the sense that it is only the way of presenting the content, the method (a word you will commonly find used in educational circles) becomes a part of the content, even though the pupil may not see it in this way.

When you read the chapter heading you noticed the words "content" and "process." It is between these two that we must make a very sharp distinction. The most important activity caused by education is that which happens in the pupils' mind as a result of content. We call this activity *process*. On the evidence of the best in educational thinking today, we should define process as true education. We have already noted that content should be a reflection of the basic values that dominate education. Over the years educationists have accepted an established, traditional content, and have simply assumed that by implementing it they have effected an important change in the pupil. They have called this change education. This ritualistic outlook (as we have already called it) received its first clear challenge from those educationists who introduced the famous "plant metaphor" into educational thinking. But for many years few questions have been raised regarding process in our sense of the word.

It was in the writings of Pestalozzi, Froebel, and Montessori, among other educational reformers, that educational thinking began to move closer, by using the plant metaphor, to our definition of process. In the plant metaphor, the relationship of teacher and pupil is considered analogous to that of gardener and plant. While the plant metaphor has, in some quarters, led to sentimentalism and loose thinking, nonetheless its effect was, in the first instance, to place educational thinking on a higher plane. Educational thought was henceforth dominated by the fact that education is not, as with the potter and his earthenware product, a question of molding a more or less pliable piece of matter, but rather of directing the development of an organism. This was not, to be sure, thinking concerned with "process" in the fullest meaning of the term, but it was nevertheless an important step in the right direction. The relationship implied in the development of the child was at last seen to be of an organic, not a mechanical, nature. Let us look more closely at this difference that makes all the difference.

Where the relationship of one body to another is purely mechanical, effects can be explained in terms of the basic laws of motion. The influence of the one body on the other is of a purely external character. Where an organism is involved, however, a new factor appears. The organism, by virtue of its own internal structure, *adds* something to the effect. This "something" contributed by the organism as such makes the important difference; it is, for instance, the difference between the effects produced by the sun, rain, and soil on a dead plant, and the effects produced by these external factors on a live plant. In the first case, the change is one of mechanical disintegration; in the second, the organism initiates a series of developments from within itself. It is this contribution of the organism that is denoted by the term "growth."

At the level of animal life, the developments due to the nature of the organism are more complex than at the plant level. Reactions at the level of animal life are mediated by nerve structures, simple or complex. Whether simple or complex, these nerve structures have a distinctive quality; retentivity. The reaction of the organism to any particular stimulus tends to leave a permanent trace which affects all future responses. Here is a factor that produces still further complexity, and that means, moreover, that the analogy with the plant is no longer strictly valid.

At the human level, another factor appears that plays a significant role in "process," the factor that the existentialists call "imagination," as opposed to "perception"; it can be roughly equated with what the philosophers have traditionally designated "self-consciousness." At this highest level, mechanical factors do, of course, operate. So also does retentivity. But retentivity now takes the form of conscious recall. Conscious memory and imagination between them illuminate the present with an awareness of the past and an anticipation of the future, so that behavior occurs on a level —the level of *homo sapiens*—at which the analogy implied in the plant metaphor is inapposite and misleading. The importance of this in differentiating between content and process should never be underestimated.

Among the many points at which the plant analogy is invalid with reference to education, one is of special significance. This is the experience of association with one's fellows. Human association, even at the most rudimentary level, implies a capacity which we have no reason to believe is present at the animal level. This is the capacity of imaginative sympathy or sympathetic imagination, to which we drew attention in Chapter 7. A passage was quoted there from the works of Sir Leslie Stephen, in which he states that "put yourself in his place" is "a description of reasoning . . . in so far as it deals with other sentient beings." The exercise of imaginative sympathy is no doubt related to that other distinctive capacity of man, the ability to use language. In any case, to use the terminology of logic, imaginative sympathy is the *differentia* of human association. Such association includes, of course, processes also found at the lower levels of associated life, but by virtue of this added factor, human association is *sui generis*.

There is a special form of human association, namely, co-operation, to which the same factor of imaginative sympathy makes a crucial difference. Co-operation occurs among the animals, but on that level it is based on instinct, or, as with the wolf pack in the hunt, it is probably no more than a habit blindly acquired as the result of environmental pressure. At the human level, however, co-operation can take the form of a two-way process, a *consciously* two-way process: it is the expression of the deliberate acceptance of a common aim. Education is, or rather, ought to be, co-operative in this sense. In summary, one might state that education means (*a*) growth, as with the plant; (*b*) directed growth, as implied in the plant-gardener metaphor; and (*c*) directed growth based on conscious co-operation, with the plant-gardener metaphor inapplicable.

For an adequate understanding of the process that occurs within the child, it is necessary that we attach a precise meaning to the two key terms "growth" and "directed growth." Even as restricted to human beings, "growth" is too comprehensive a concept for our purpose. We must ask which particular aspect of growth the teacher should regard as his special province. Again, what are we to mean by "directed growth," in reference to the task of the teacher and the schools? Growth directed towards what end? It is by no means sufficient to dismiss the question by simply stating a general theory of the aim of education. Each of these questions must be considered in depth if a clear understanding of the meaning of process in education is to be reached.

With what kind of growth is the teacher specifically concerned? The teacher's specific concern is with the development of the higher intellectual faculties of the young persons committed to his care. To express the matter in this fashion is to invite vigorous protest from some quarters. Is this, it is objected, not once again merely the same arid intellectualism that was all too characteristic of education in the past, and the *bête noire* of educational reformers of whatever complexion? Does the whole idea of developing the higher intellectual faculties not rest on a fallacious separation of intellect from feeling and action?

The answer to these objections is that no such artificial separation need be implied. The life of feeling and action, in so far as the school is concerned with it, receives consideration in various other parts of the present essay. In stating that the teacher's concern is with the development of the higher intellectual faculties, we are not thinking of the intellect operating *in vacuo*, but rather of intellect that is actuated by feeling, that expresses itself in action, that makes both feeling and action very different from what these capacities would be without it.

To state this idea in another way, society entrusts the school with the task of training the young to use their human intelligence to arrive at a progressively more adequate understanding of the world in which they live. Whatever term we use to describe the capacity in question—"intellect," "reason," "human intelligence"— its basic function is clear: it is to convert what begins as a vague, chaotic conglomeration into an orderly, meaningful whole. As various philosophers have pointed out, reason is fundamentally a unifying agency, one which re-establishes relationships of a variety of kinds—relationships of cause and effect, space, time, and simi- larity—between elements that were initially experienced as separate and unrelated.

The precise analysis of the human intelligence at work, and the practical applications of this analysis to the tasks of the school, are the concern of the psychologist and particularly of the educational psychologist. The various schools of psychology have dealt with these problems, each from its own special point of view. The task of the educational philosopher differs from that of the educational psychologist; it is to indicate what should *result* from the effective application of the knowledge that the psychologist has to offer. The question for the educational philosopher is therefore: What is the value of the educational product, philosophically judged?

Every child possesses a general curiosity about the world around him, and he satisfies that curiosity in an *ad hoc,* unco-ordinated manner. It is the concern of the school to transform this innate impulse into something with momentous significance for his mental life—an interest in the progressive, systematic clarification of par- ticular features of his world. The physical world, the world of plants and animals and of human beings, provides a starting point for a training that will change the natural curiosity that the child has in common with many animals into a different level of curiosity, one which only the human being is capable of attaining.

"Curiosity," like so many of the terms that the social scientist and philosopher must employ, is a rather rough-hewn word, one which needs considerable chiselling before it will fit coherently into the present context. The curiosity that finds satisfaction in science is not curiosity in the ordinary sense. Scientific curiosity does not gain its satisfaction purely and simply in items of knowledge as such; essential to its satisfaction is the experience of an orderly, progressive acquisition of knowledge. A factor is involved here that is perhaps best described as "constructiveness." The same factor operates in the acquisition of any form of organized knowledge; it is *homo faber* at work, operating in the region of ideas or imagination, rather than in the realm of perception. This kind of curiosity, once it has been effectively aroused, tends to carry its own dynamic, to be, in other words, self-propelling. Here is a form of motivation easily overlooked, but one that is of first importance from the point of view of process in education.

Mental growth may be described as the development in the individual of curiosity about what is happening and has happened in the human, the animal, and the physical world around him. We are not forgetting, of course, that the mind is largely preoccupied with practical problems, where the work of the intellect is the devising of means to attain specific ends; education should do what it can to raise the level of efficiency in practical thinking. But here again, the intellect functions as a unifying agency. Devising the right means to attain a given end is at bottom nothing more than achieving a comprehensive view that sees means and end as, so to speak, parts of a single picture—the fact that Dewey has in mind when he insists that the distinction between means and end is a false dualism. The important point, however, is not that thinking with such practical motivation plays an important part in life (which is conceded), but that the mind which has become responsive only to this kind of motivation is a mind whose growth has been seriously stunted.

It remains to point out that all mental growth has practical significance, in the sense that the mind as a whole and not the intellect alone is affected. For example, consider the way in which the development of "curiosity," in the sense explained above, may result in the fostering of certain desirable practical attitudes. The child's interest in animals, for instance, is quite compatible with callousness and actual cruelty in the treatment of these creatures. The child, however, who has read and enjoyed *The Wind in the*

Willows, and who has followed the doings of Mr. Badger and his friends, may have his whole attitude subtly changed. Again, if the scientist succeeds in arousing the child's interest in animal life as science sees that life, the result may be still another alteration in outlook.

At the higher levels of mental life, one might point to more telling illustrations of the fact that the mind as a whole is affected in mental growth. In the general attitude to differences of color, race, religion, and levels of culture, there exists a kind of toleration that really amounts to indifference, to lack of interest. There also exists toleration that is accepted as a matter of abstract principle or vague sentiment, and that is rather likely to break down under the strain of the concrete, practical test. A third form of toleration is rooted in a positive, active curiosity about the ways of acting and thinking of human beings markedly different from oneself. This last attitude is of prime importance for mental growth.

We have examined the function of growth, the mental growth that is the teacher's primary professional concern in his consideration of content and process in education. It remains to discuss the problem of *directed* growth. With regard to the human being, direction takes two forms, both of which are dependent on the conscious two-way co-operation between teacher and pupil referred to previously.

The first form of direction with regard to mental growth is controlled by the curriculum, itself a reflection of basic values dealt with in preceding chapters. The curriculum represents an organization of subject matter, the study of which constitutes the content of education. Some organization of subject matter—in other words, some method—is indispensable, if direction is to occur at all. The curriculum, moreover, represents authority, adult authority. It must not, however, mean purely imposed authority. The task of the teacher is to secure a measure of co-operation from the pupil in meeting curricular requirements, which means, in effect, that the teacher must lead the pupil to attach value to the fulfilment of these requirements. In so far as this happens, we have authority without negation of liberty. From what has already been said in this study about the pupil as a rational creature, the basis of co-operation is always present in the pupil, provided that the teacher knows how to build on it.

To illustrate: it is easy to give the pupil direct experience of the importance of being able to "figure." School and life outside the school can, between them, accomplish this end very effectively. When this end has been accomplished, is there anything wrong then in having the pupil memorize the multiplication table? Certainly, the pupil is rational enough to be able to see that such memory work is all part of the important task of learning to figure correctly. Dewey deplores the practice of making learning a direct and conscious end in itself. He points out that "the cheapening of devices, like printing, for recording and distributing information—genuine and alleged—has created an immense bulk of communicated subject matter. It is much easier to swamp a pupil with this than to work it into his direct experiences."[1] By this, Dewey means that it is much easier apparently to impart content to a pupil than it is to impart the content in such a manner that the process, as we have already described it, occurs.

Dewey's observation is obviously true, but "direct experience" is an ambiguous concept. According to Dewey's interpretation, the term means knowledge discovered by the pupil himself in his efforts to solve problems arising out of his own experience. This is the meaning that Dewey's more enthusiastic disciples have been encouraged by his writings to adopt. The result of depending on the pupil's direct experience in this sense would be to leave his education "mostly holes." "Direct experience" should be taken to mean, broadly speaking, that the knowledge in question has significance or value for the child at the particular stage of growth that he has attained. Thus, in the first meaning of directed growth, direction takes the form of leading the pupil to an appreciative experience (process) of the cultural materials set forth in the curriculum, of the content, in other words.

The second meaning of "direction" was indicated in Chapter 9. General education, we saw there, implies leading the pupil to fabricate a personal pattern out of the cultural materials of the curriculum. Citing the plant metaphor once again, we find that

[1] John Dewey, *Democracy and Education* (New York: The Macmillan Co., 1916), p. 256.

with relation to the formulation of a personal pattern, it implies a very apposite analogy. When *homo faber* constructs a mechanical object, the test of whether or not the object is satisfactory is the degree to which the product serves the purpose that he happens to have in mind. When an organism, such as a plant or a human being, is involved in this development, however, the final value of the product is a matter of the degree to which it expresses its own true nature. There is the further difference, which is of particular importance where a human being is being educated, that no stage in the development may be rightly regarded as *merely* a preparation for a later stage; every stage of growth has value in and for itself.

In the preceding chapters, we mentioned certain factors that affect the development of the personal pattern, factors over which the teacher has no direct control. The basic factor, however, we saw to be the child's native aptitude and interest, and it is in this realm that the teacher has an opportunity and duty to exercise wise direction. Directing the development of a personal pattern in the pupil depends on a two-way exchange of communication and co-operation. In attempting to lead the pupil to attach value to curriculum content, the teacher is, in effect, trying to persuade the pupil to see and feel things in the teacher's way. It is true that the teacher must use whatever understanding of the pupil he possesses in order to accomplish this result, but the teacher's task is, in the main, to commend adult values to the pupil.

On the other hand, in order to lead the pupil to discover and develop the value pattern or integration expressive of the capacities and needs of his (the pupil's) personality, the teacher must, so to speak, come to the pupil, instead of having the pupil come to him. This requirement demands an attitude on the part of the teacher which is *par excellence* the professional attitude, and one that is, moreover, very hard to come by—respect for the pupil.

In the preceding chapter, we mentioned two possible forms of the teacher-pupil relationship: (1) The teacher may be emotionally involved with the pupil, a form of relationship that was characterized as unprofessional. (2) The teacher may have concern for the general welfare of the pupil, an attitude to be taken for granted, but one falling distinctly short of what we have in mind by the term "respect." Respect for the pupil means, to put it simply, that the pupil's inner life—his ideas, feelings, aspirations, his fumbling efforts to understand and come to terms with his world—be taken seriously.

Why is this attitude of respect so hard to come by? The main reason is that the adult's view of childhood, and of those elements related to childhood, is frequently one of condescension tinged with mild contempt. The child is looked upon as a grown-up in the making, with a long way to go in life before he should be taken seriously. The fact that the adult can recall how he himself thought and felt as a child need make no difference to him. Every adult, indeed, reaches a stage in which, if he looks back on his childhood days, memory shows him an individual whom he finds it very hard to identify with himself. To put away the elements of childhood means, for most people, more than just outgrowing such things; it means the rejection of them as insignificant and trivial. This attitude, let it be noted, need not imply lack of understanding, for the adult may still possess a perceptive understanding of children, derived from one source or another. If this is the case, however, the adult is then motivated not by imaginative sympathy (the real desideratum) but by imagination without sympathy.

The teacher must be on his guard against this very natural tendency to look upon the child in a condescending manner. The teacher's attitude should be one that differs not only from that of the adult towards children generally, but also from that of the parent towards his own children. In this latter relationship, emotional involvement is likely to exert an influence, and it may do much to prevent that detachment or objectivity which is a necessary element in the attitude of respect. The teacher, moreover, operates or ought to operate, under the guidance of a well-thought-out philosophy of education, an aid not usually present in the mind of the parent or other adult. All in all, as we have remarked, the attitude of respect, the truly professional attitude, is difficult to attain, and there are several specific influences which act in opposition to its achievement. Some of these influences are in the nature of pitfalls that are always in the path of the unwary teacher, while others are obstacles set up by society itself. Both types of pitfall require illustration.

In the passage that was quoted from *Democracy and Education,* Dewey draws attention to one factor which may operate to sabotage instruction. Printing has provided "an immense bulk of subject matter" that entices the teacher to take a shortcut which will, in fact, probably lead him astray from his desired goal. Typical instances of this occur when the wrong kind of textbook is used, or possibly, when the right kind of textbook is used wrongly.

Another and rather more insidious pitfall in this regard may result from the teacher's preoccupation with a particular method of instruction. The method in which he is interested may be quite sound. It may, in the first instance, have represented a valuable contribution to the art of teaching. But when the method comes to be used mechanically, without any feeling for the values that originally vitalized it, instruction is no longer effective. Unfortunately, no method is immune to the possibility of being turned into a lifeless, mechanical routine. Even the activity programs of the progressivists, despite the implied and essentially sound insistence on always keeping the acquisition of knowledge in a context that gives it significance, may become stereotyped procedures passed on to the teacher as "the thing to do," like a register for maintaining a record of school attendance.

Finally, it is important to mention another factor that may operate to sabotage instruction, one for which the teacher is not responsible, or certainly not solely responsible, namely, the examination system. We need not enter at length into a discussion of this issue which has long been a matter of concern, especially at the higher levels of education. On the one hand, there exists the need to find some way of evaluating educational achievement, and, on the other, the difficulty of avoiding a method of doing so which not only fails to accomplish this purpose, but also puts a premium on the kind of learning which is a travesty of true education. The examiner is confronted with the problem of devising questions which lend themselves to objective marking; indeed, he is often under pressure to do so. Yet, with some subjects in particular, and probably to some extent with all subjects, good marking should be determined not only by what the examinee states, but by what the right kind of examiner can read between the lines.

The suspicion of such subjective evaluation of examinations may be sufficient grounds to persuade some teachers to accept "cramming" as a necessary evil. At the higher levels of education, the intelligent student, with a sense of the intrinsic interest of the subject in question, may feel only impatience and contempt for the manner in which examination requirements force him to study that subject. He may console himself with the thought that, when the examination is over and done with, he will sort out the information with which he has crammed his mind, and make orderly sense of it. But this sorting out is not likely to happen. As with immigrants entering a country that has a strict immigration policy, so with ideas and the mind: nothing can make up for a wrong entry in the first place.

The effect of negative influences such as those mentioned is to stock the mind with what A. N. Whitehead inveighs against at some length as "inert ideas." These he defines as "ideas that are merely received into the mind without being utilized, or tested, or thrown into fresh combinations." In short, they do not qualify as "educative instruction" (to use Herbart's phrase), the progressive satisfaction of mental needs and interests. The intelligent pupil, in particular, is apt to feel himself imposed upon and thwarted, and, like the spirited pony in the riding school under the novice who does not know how to use the reins properly, he balks and ends up by throwing his rider.

It is hoped that the argument of the present chapter will help to clarify for the practical teacher a matter about which he may be confused because of what he has heard and read about education. This is the question of the teacher's rôle in the matter of instruction, the imparting of knowledge. Educational reformers appear to have built up a conclusive case against the conception of the teacher's function as that of filling the more or less empty receptacle which is the pupil's mind. The realization has been reached, in other words, that education does not mean mere content, that the process of mental growth that takes place in the pupil's mind is, in fact, the essential factor in education.

Some educationists would go so far as to say that instruction is not the function of the school at all. They claim that instruction is a task that the home and other agencies are quite well fitted to perform. The school's concern, they feel, is with matters that strike deeper, and that more properly merit being called education than does instruction. The effect of this opinion on some teachers, who are conscientiously resolved to be in the van of progress, is to create in them a kind of phobia about the imparting of any knowledge whatsoever.

Despite the convincing case presented by the reformers, however, the teacher is apt to find himself with a stubborn, residual conviction that, in some way or other, his main concern as a teacher is with instruction. He feels this way not merely because his own interest lies in knowledge, although this fact is an important consideration; the conditions of his work, imposing as they do very definite limits to his direct contact with his pupils, point to instruction as somehow his special province. Furthermore, as a good teacher, he exhorts his charges to make full use of library and other facilities outside the school in order to extend their knowledge, and this, too, he regards as an important part of their education.

Both points of view on this question are essentially right. In so far as instruction results in Whitehead's "inert ideas," the reformers are correct in discounting it as at best only better than ignorance. If instruction means the imparting of useful and interesting items of information as the occasion arises, then the reformers have John Locke on their side in regarding it as the least important part of education. On the other hand, if instruction is identified with what we have called "direction," in the twofold sense of leading the pupil to an appreciative understanding of the cultural materials reflected in the curriculum, and of guiding him to discover and actualize the right cultural pattern for his personal development, then instruction becomes *educative* instruction. The teacher is correct in regarding this kind of instruction as his special professional responsibility; he clearly appreciates the respective rôles of content and process in education.

It was pointed out earlier that the content of a curriculum should present a large variety of special subjects or disciplines. The important problem arises as to whether or not some of these subjects are of peculiar value from the point of view of mental training. In other words, are there some subjects, the study of which yields a general mental training, strengthening the faculties so that they can cope more effectively with any problem or situation that may present itself? Are there kinds of learning that raise the general level of mental efficiency? This is the question—the old question— of formal discipline.

12 *Formal Intellectual Discipline*

The education of an individual means, it is generally supposed, giving his mind a training that raises the level of its performance on the whole. Education is the whetstone that sharpens the mind and makes it, like the keen-edged knife, a better tool for all of the many purposes for which it may be employed. Are some subjects of study more effective for training the mind than others? The supporters of formal discipline have held that the answer to this question is in the affirmative.

The idea that some subjects are more effective than others for training the mind fitted well into the picture of the mind presented by those who adhered to the prevailing psychology at the time that the issue was first clearly raised. This picture was that of "faculty psychology," as it came to be called, by which was meant that the mind consists of a number of different faculties, such as perception, memory, imagination, and reason. According to faculty psychology, the exercise of one of these faculties on any particular material gave that faculty a general training. For example, if the individual received training in observing the parts, structure, and coloration of plan uld become a keener observer of his surroundings esult of exercising his memory on historical dates, deal more efficiently with geographical facts. If reasoning powers operated on geometry, that rove them for any other purpose for which they eeded.

The theory of formal discipline included more than simple intellectual training; it also took in training of character. One of the important faculties of the mind, according to the theorists of faculty psychology, is will power. Through formal exercise, they believed that the power of the will can be trained. In other words, the hard, uninteresting grind of learning Latin grammar would strengthen the will, so that the individual would find it easier to resist distractions and to concentrate on the task at hand. The main task of education was seen as the provision of this formal discipline, intellectual and moral, and among the many subjects of study available in the arts and sciences, the adherent of the school of faculty psychology believed that some are better adapted for the purpose than others.

This conception of formal discipline appeared early in modern thinking about education. Indeed, among the various theories of education, this one might be said to have been first in the field. Its appearance is usually said to have stemmed from the need to defend the key position of Latin on the curriculum when the practical importance of knowledge of that language was no longer clear. A knowledge of Latin, as we have seen, was for a long time an indispensable part of the equipment of the "clerk," whose vocation was one of the learned professions. In all scholarly writings, moreover, Latin was the language used, and without a knowledge of it no one could be a well-read person, for he was debarred from everything worth reading—or so it seemed, at least. Latin became a vested interest in education, and, as always with vested interest, any threat to it arising out of changed conditions rallied the interested parties to its support. The theory of formal discipline was the response of these persons to the challenge.

It would be more accurate to say, not that the challenge to Latin produced the theory of formal discipline, but rather that it gave the theory the vogue that it enjoyed for about two centuries. The idea of formal training, of subjecting the mind to a process of sharpening, is not a new one, however. Francis Bacon, for example, gave expression to it in one of the more famous of his *Essays*, at a time when Latin needed no special pleading in its defence. Numerous other examples could be cited to illustrate this idea from the works of writers who reflected on the meaning of education. Historians of education are right, however, when they state that thinkers who were searching for a rational defence of traditional practice saw in the theory of formal discipline a welcome answer to a question that had become rather pressing.

The historians of education were wrong, however, in assuming that to point out this fact was in itself enough to discredit the theory of formal discipline. In economics, one does not prove that a certain tariff is undesirable simply by showing that the industrialists who had it established in the first instance were actuated by ulterior motives. Nor is the theory disproved (as most of its critics have assumed) by showing that the psychology which made it plausible—faculty psychology—has itself been discredited and abandoned.

We stated the theory of formal discipline in a simplified and rather crude way, but we did so for the good reason that it was precisely in that form in which it became widely accepted among educationists. It was that same form of the theory of formal discipline which the experimentalists investigated. Their experiments covered a wide field, including rote memory, perception (e.g. ability to discriminate shades of color, lengths of line, and the like), imagining, and reasoning. No detailed résumé of the investigations need be offered here, but attention should be drawn to what was definitely established by these investigations.[1]

The formal or mechanical exercise of a mental function or capacity does not bring any absolute or general improvement of it. To "go through the motions" of exercising a capacity leaves its general level of efficiency unaffected. Exercise of rote or mechanical memory does not develop memory as exercise develops muscle. Learning the logarithms of numbers up to one hundred does not affect the power of memorizing other materials, or affects it so little that any improvement is probably due to factors other than a strengthening of the memory, and is, in any case, not worth the time and effort involved. To exercise the imagination and the reason on geometrical forms does not of itself make the individual

---

[1]*Note:* The experiments took no account of the possibility of a "delayed-action" effect. That still remains as at least a theoretical possibility.

imagine more vividly and reason more clearly when dealing with historical material or practical problems of ordinary living.

One practical outcome of the investigations is sufficiently clear: teachers were no longer able to turn the study of subjects such as history and geography into a chore of memorizing facts, justifying themselves with the plea that they were developing the memory. They could no longer drive the unwilling pupil from one proposition of Euclid to another with the claim that "geometry with tears" developed the pupil's reasoning powers. The elimination of this conception of what teaching means was all to the good. It seemed to follow, moreover, that there are only two sound reasons for studying any subject: its usefulness (memorizing the multiplication table, for example) and its intrinsic interest. One subject of study being as effective as another for purposes of mental training, selection should therefore be made on the basis of utility and direct interest.

At the academic level, this proposition led to the adoption in some quarters of the principle of free electives in the field of general education, with utility the governing factor in professional training. The principle was short-lived. Under its easy yoke, too many students were presenting university authorities with completed programs for the Bachelor's degree which were curiosities of random sampling of the very diversified wares that the modern university offers. On the theoretical side, moreover, the rejection *in toto* of the notion of formal mental training (a common formula among "up-to-date" teachers was, "Research has disproved all that") entailed another inference which certainly looked doubtful, namely, that there is at bottom no difference between the education of a human being and animal training. Was there something of significance in formal discipline after all, something that the experiments were not getting at?

It was pointed out earlier that the use of language is peculiar to human beings, and based on the ability to generalize, to detect the common element in different objects and situations. Generalization is an intellectual process. The everyday, unreflective use of language is a case of the rough-and-ready use of a tool which explicit training enables the individual to use with much greater precision and effect. Here, then, is intellectual discipline as general or formal as language itself. It consists essentially in making the individual conscious of language as a tool and in training him to avoid the easy and slovenly way of handling it.

Another kind of mental training exists, which is more specific in character, but nonetheless general enough to be classed as formal discipline. The reader may recall the distinction that was drawn between scientific knowledge and logical non-scientific knowledge. These two types of knowledge are the expression of two types of thinking, in other words, of two ways of using language. The scientist employs terms that are defined with a high degree of exactness or precision. This is possible, as we saw, because science is abstract, limiting itself to those features of reality that lend themselves to exact definition. Any science—physics, chemistry, geology, zoology, and the rest — offers an opportunity for training the individual in this way of using language, and the training thus acquired transfers, or ought to transfer, to any mental activity involving the scientific point of view and method.

What we called "logical thinking" (to distinguish it from thinking that is scientific as well as logical) operates in the main with the language of ordinary, everyday usage. The exception, of course, is the purely deductive thinking of mathematics, and, more generally, of formal logic. The language used in philosophy, history, and to a large extent in the social sciences, carries a wealth of fringe meanings that tend to give the thinking a subjective quality for which there is no place in science. Clarity and precision are achieved by way of judicious choice of words, skilful use of context, felicitous illustration, and, on a humbler level, repetition.

The social scientist finds himself in an awkward middle position. To some extent, he is concerned with matters to which the exact terminology of science lends itself. The economist or sociologist, for example, can deal with vital statistics in the exact manner of the scientist. "Births," "deaths," "marriages", "divorces", and "incomes" are terms admitting of no serious ambiguity. But when the economist uses words such as "values" and "needs," and the sociologist words like "happiness" or "welfare," these thinkers are employing language of a much less precise character than that of science, and they are confronted with a dilemma. On the one hand, they can admit that the terms that they employ are imprecise, in which case the natural scientists are reluctant to accept them on an equal scientific footing. On the other hand, the social scientist can give such terms an exact but esoteric meaning, in which case the ordinary man discounts their claim to be true scientists, for the reason that their findings do not, like those of the natural scientists, result in a body of clear and significant practical applications— their technical thinking fails to yield a technology.

Another form of mental training, which is more or less general in character, is training in the appreciation of the non-logical values of language. The appeal of literary art depends largely on such appreciation. In the purest form of this training, poetry, the emotional aura of language is the very essence of appreciation. The same poetic language appears merely irrelevant and distracting for scientific and logical thinking.

Poetry, moreover, contributes to our understanding of the world, but it does so in its own particular way. The insights provided in poetry are neither arrived at nor justified by logical reasoning, but rather come as illuminating flashes which are their own justification—it is sufficient that the flashes *are* illuminating. The test of the validity and worth of these insights is in this sense *subjective.* The insights deal with a region of experience that is not susceptible to the systematic procedure of logical thinking. The light that these poetic flashes of insight cast on this twilight region of experience may indeed be more penetrating than any illumination springing from logical thinking. The poet himself will claim that it is so, and there is no good reason for repudiating his claim, although there is also no objective way of substantiating it. Poetry has its intellectual side, which, however, does not lead our thinking towards a growing clarification of the obscure, but rather intrigues us with suggestive flashes of insight, ending, perhaps, as Keats has put it, by "teasing us out of thought."

It is the function of poetry to sensitize the mind to these non-logical impacts of language. The effects of this process will not be confined to poetry in the ordinary sense of the word, but will spread to other forms of literary art—to drama, fiction, and *belles-lettres* in general. This form of mental training thus has transfer value of a high order. Moreover, with the right sort of teaching, the effects will spread further, extending to those arts that rely primarily upon a medium other than language—to painting, music, sculpture, and architecture.

It might be objected that, as a matter of common observation, the transfer that we have just outlined does not occur. What is more common, the objector asks, than the musician who has little interest in and still less good judgment about literature, or the novelist who is indifferent to the world of painting? The objection is, of course, a valid one, but we must add that high native endowment in a particular direction is often, perhaps even typically, accompanied by narrowly specialized interest. Native interest and aptitude (the underlying psychology of which is still obscure) may leave the gifted mathematician very unresponsive to any interest other than mathematics. Such absolute cases are, however, exceptional; with ordinary individuals, interest is not specialized to such an extreme degree that the individual is rendered unamenable to the broadening influence of competent teaching.

Let us return now to the important point which, it was conceded, the experimentalists established, namely, that transfer is not automatic, that it does not happen as a matter of course. For transfer to occur successfully, the teacher must be aware of the educational values inherent in the subject that he is teaching, and, by suggestion and explicit statement, he must convey that awareness to his pupils. To the extent that this process takes place, formal training becomes formal *education*. True, this is not the result that the advocates of formal discipline had in mind, but it is a very important result indeed.

It should be clear from our discussion that those who dismiss the issue of formal mental discipline as one that is old-fashioned and discredited are rejecting more than they perhaps realize. One might even ask whether the discredit attached to faculty psychology is itself not due to a hasty and unfair interpretation of what its adherents actually meant. If these psychologists were offering terms such as "memory," "imagination," "reasoning," and "perception" as *explanations* of the processes denoted, they were guilty of gross fallacy—to state that we remember because we have a faculty of memory, or imagine because we have a faculty of imagination, seems no better than saying that we have a toothache because we have a faculty of toothache. The real error of the psychologist was not in resorting to verbiage of this sort, but in the idea that the faculties are simple entities, separate and distinct from one another. There are different kinds or levels of memory, and some of these involve imagination and even, to a certain extent, reasoning. Reason consists of memory and imagination operating in a particular way; and so with the other faculties.

At the same time, is the underlying *principle* of faculty psychology not basically sound? Through the imagination, the human being can experience an object which is not present to the senses. He can recognize that same object as one which he has encountered before, and here the faculty of memory is involved—memory on the conscious, as opposed to the unconscious or merely organic, level. He can manipulate the object so as to attain a desired end more effectively, and here he employs reasoning. Furthermore, is this same principle of special faculties not implicit in certain concepts which figure prominently in psychology at the present time, concepts such as capacities, aptitudes, and abilities? The older psychologist (and the layman still) would find such terms interchangeable with the term "faculty." What is needed is a clear definition of all such terms in order to avoid fallacious inferences from them.

Our discussion has shown that formal mental training is possible. It is not true that one kind of learning is as good as another for educational, as distinct from purely instructional, purposes. The extent to which mental training takes place depends on two factors. The first of these factors is the significance of the capacity at which the training is directed. This means the extent to which civilized living calls for the exercise of that capacity—how general is it? The second factor is the extent to which teaching has imbued the individual with a sense of the value of the capacity or mental quality, and thus led him to set it up as a standard to regulate his thinking.

Psychologists were accustomed in the past to draw a distinction between intellectual and physical habits. In the case of intellectual habits, the end is fixed, while the means is flexible and varied. With physical habits, the end and means are both fixed. For example, consider the practice (or habit) of scrutinizing the exact meaning of words in the particular context in which they occur. Obviously, the opportunities for doing this will be many and varied. Contrast the physical habit (or series of habits) represented by dressing one-self or by typewriting. Here the action is specific with respect to both end and means. Does this argument not amount to asserting simply that the formal training value of learning depends on the extent to which thinking is involved, always assuming that think-ing is not reducible to the kind of "conditioning" represented by animal training.

This assumption, it is true, might be and has been challenged. The extreme behaviorism advocated by some psychologists in the second and third decades of this century argued that thinking meant the operation of language mechanisms, the training of which was fundamentally a matter of mechanical conditioning. Bertrand Russell was no doubt right when he remarked that "it is humiliating to discover how terribly adequate this hypothesis turns out to be."[2] It was adequate, in the sense that there was no form of thinking that could not be described in terms of linguistic responses. Think-ing through the medium of visual imagery appeared to be an awkward exception, but the behaviorists denied the reality of the visual image. In any case, however adequate, the hypothesis was not fruitful; it did not serve to open up and direct fresh investiga-tion of the thinking process. It was, after all, only another ex-pression of the rampant, contrived "scientism" which was making itself felt in the social sciences in those decades.

Events have occurred in our own day which seem to lend support to the idea that all education is at bottom mere conditioning, the fixing-in of specific responses to specific situations. "Brainwashing" would seem to point to this conclusion; an individual can be sub-jected to a kind of treatment, physical or mental, which undermines and finally eliminates beliefs and values hitherto implicitly ac-cepted. In the absence of more careful investigation of this sinister phenomenon, it seems sufficient to answer that it adds nothing to

[2]*Analyses of Mind* (Allen & Unwin Ltd., London, 1921), p. 27.

what psychologists have long known. Under certain conditions—hypnosis, for example—the operation of the higher mental faculties can be temporarily suspended. Pain can have a similar effect. The old way of getting at the truth through torture had something to say for itself, if we ignore the moral aspect of the matter. It is also well known that extreme fatigue or physical debility can make the individual the helpless victim of suggestion. All of these facts serve to remind us that the higher mental faculties, as the latest products of evolution, are the most vulnerable part of man's endowment. This is very different from saying that these faculties are merely a disguised form of the more elemental characteristics of the nervous system on which conditioning is based.

13 *Formal Moral Discipline*

Faculty psychology did much to perpetuate a mistaken outlook, not only in formal intellectual training, but also in formal moral training, in the training of character. Will, according to the tenets of this psychology, is a special faculty, and, like the memory, imagination, reasoning, and the other faculties, it can be developed by exercise. Any exercise that demands sustained effort is therefore right for the training of the will. Learning mathematics, for example, is considered by the faculty psychologist to be such an exercise, and it thus serves the double purpose of providing training for the intellect and training for the will. According to the tenets of faculty psychology, it follows, moreover, that the less the study in itself attracts the individual, the more effort is necessary to cope with it, and hence the more effective it is in training the will. Such was the reasoning underlying the theory of formal training in its cruder form. Criticism of it was to be a matter of providing a more adequate and detailed psychology of the will.

Historically, however, the idea of formal moral discipline is associated with a concept other than a mistaken psychology, although the latter was always a factor in the case. Formal moral discipline is associated with a certain view of man's nature, the idea of the innate depravity or sinfulness of man. The theological doctrine of original sin put a premium on the repression of the natural impulses. Even the natural play impulse of children was suspect. It was not merely that the devil found some mischief still for idle hands to do; if young hands were not idle, but left free to choose their own congenial occupations, these occupations were likely to be inspired by the ever-watchful adversary. This idea was very much present in the thinking of the seventeenth-century Puritans. To thwart the designs of "that old deluder Satan," as the devil was called in 1647, in the first system of public education in Massachusetts, two elements were necessary: concentration on sacred as opposed to secular literature, and the curbing of the natural propensity to play.

This gloomy thesis found its antithesis in another idea which became current in the seventeenth and eighteenth centuries. Nature, in the sense of external nature, was extolled as the great model of goodness. The ways of nature were felt to be the ways of the benevolent Creator; the right manner of conduct for the creature was thus to observe and follow nature. John Milton, writing in the seventeenth century, tells us how

> . . . . most innocent nature,
> With her abundance, she good cateress,
> Means her provision only to the good
> That live according to her sober laws
> And holy dictate of spare Temperance."[1]

In the eighteenth century, the same idea is set forth with great elaboration by Alexander Pope: "One truth is clear, Whatever is, is right,"[2] a statement which Pope means as having reference to the works of nature, and not, except by gross misquotation (on the part of political conservatives, for example) to those of man. And again:

> Thus, then, to man the voice of Nature spoke—
> 'Go, from the creatures thy instruction take:
> Learn from the birds what food the thickets yield;
> Learn from the beasts the physic of the field;
> Thy arts of building from the bee receive;
> Learn of the mole to plow, the worm to weave;
>
> . . . .
>
> Mark what unvary'd laws preserve each state,
> Laws wise as nature and as fixed as fate . . .[2]

[1]John Milton, *Comus*, II. 761-766.
[2]Alexander Pope, *An Essay on Man*.

In due course, this sentimental idea of external nature was extended to include human nature. Just as the sentimental idea of external nature had not yet been disturbed by the theory of evolution, with its harsh note of nature red in tooth and claw, so the idea of human nature had not yet been affected by a psychologist such as Freud. There was thus the tendency to idealize original human nature by thinkers who were really concerned with protesting the view long imposed by the theologians.

The new doctrine of human nature as something innately fine and noble, but stifled, distorted, and corrupted by the artificialities of civilized society, found its most eloquent exponent in Jean-Jacques Rousseau, the prophet of the movement in literature known as "Romanticism." The true mission of the poet, according to Rousseau, is not to describe and interpret the natural and social world around him, it is to illuminate the world *within*. The poet's concern is with the unconscious, rather than the conscious, to use language more typical of our own century. To find free and adequate expression for the natural feelings, impulses, and insights which are the core of individuality—that is his special task.

Rousseau brought this conception to bear on education in his *Emile*. The result was a thoroughgoing radicalism. For the theological idea of education as a process of eradicating the old Adam from child nature, he substituted the idea of education as a process of providing stimulus and expression for a nature born free and good, but enchained and corrupted by society itself. In the *Emile*, the child encounters society only in the person of the tutor, whose sole concern is to adjust instruction to the needs of his pupil as they manifest themselves. It was Rousseau who introduced into education the idea of the so-called child-centred school.

It would be aside from our purpose to consider the practical prescriptions of the *Emile*—the "do's" and "don'ts" addressed to the teacher. It is sufficient to note that many of them are sound, some of them paradoxical (e.g. the dictum that the only habit the child should learn is that of learning no habits), but that they are always arresting and suggestive. The resulting picture in Rousseau's *Emile* is one of intense individualism in education; and later reformers, whose thinking has been governed by the ideal of individual self-expression and fulfilment—Montessori in the first decade of the present century, for example—are in direct line with the author of the *Emile*.

Such was the origin of the issue of formal moral discipline, the puritanical versus the romantic view of human nature. By the beginning of the twentieth century, this issue was no longer dominated by any such *a priori* view of man. It was conceded to the puritanical view that there are no doubt traits in original human nature which, if left to express themselves unchecked in a social context, will take forms recognized as morally bad. Some traits, on the other hand, are intrinsically valuable, and should be given free expression. Childish curiosity and the impulse to self-expression in song, dance, drawing, and poetry are in line with the romantic view. Even here, however, education fails in its task if, in its preoccupation with self-expression, it does not in due course imbue the individual with the feeling that there *are* standards with which he must come to terms. And so with all other desirable forms of self-expression: education must lead to awareness of standards, acceptance of which will make possible *truer and more adequate forms of self-expression.*

With regard to Rousseau's theory of education, one proviso for the safeguarding of the free, healthy development of the young met with very emphatic rejection in our own century. This was the idea of withdrawing the pupil from contact with the everyday world. As John Dewey saw it, there is no question of a repressive society operating on natural impulses, good or bad. Society is not something to be avoided if education is to achieve its true purposes; society is that which sets education its real purpose.

This does not mean that the values and modes of conduct actually prevalent in society set the goal for education. The philosophy of education must scrutinize these values, distinguishing the good from the bad, the basic from the superficial, the valuable heritage of the past from the worthless. Adjustment to this society (the aim of education) comes from living participation in it. Hence Dewey's picture of the school as a miniature society, a society "simplified" and "purified," to use his own words.

Dewey's view might appear to grant Rousseau's thesis that society is evil and therefore an influence from which the young must be protected. But this is not so, and Dewey sees social life as a *sine qua non* of man's humanity. Dewey reverts at this point to Aristotle's idea that man is by nature "politicus"; society is *natural* to him. Dewey develops this idea in the context of two governing concepts of our own century, the theories of evolution and of modern democracy.

It should be added that the romantic insistence on the importance of free expression for the natural impulses received support from another quarter in the twentieth century. The source of this support was Freudian psychology. Repression became associated with the idea of unhealthy mental development, with mental conflict, complexes, and other more or less abnormal traits to which Freud had drawn attention. In point of fact, this association was due to a careless reading of what Freud really meant by repression, namely, *harmful* repression. Nonetheless, Freud's authority was apt to be invoked to justify libertarian extravagances rightly felt by most people to be an outrage on common sense.

The second form of the issue of formal moral discipline did not turn on the question of any general view of human nature, but on the question of a more adequate psychology of the will, more adequate, that is, than the view presented by faculty psychology. The question of what is meant by the will led to the problem of motivation. Dewey himself gave a clear lead in passages such as the following, typical of many throughout his works:

> We need to discriminate between physical results and moral results . . . . A harsh and commanding tone may be effectual in keeping a child away from the fire, and the same desirable physical effect will follow as if he had been snatched away. But there may be no more obedience of a moral sort in one case than in the other.[3]

This outlook represents one extreme, the authoritarian extreme. Where the individual acts purely to avoid undesirable consequences artificially imposed from without (which is what "punishment" strictly means, as distinct from the undesirable *natural consequences* of an act), he is not a free agent; he is not motivated by his own sense of the value of what he is doing. At best he will devote to the task in hand the minimum of effort needed to evade the consequences of disobedience, and if any training at all is accomplished, it

[3]Dewey, *Democracy and Education, op. cit.,* p. 32.

consists, as Dewey has himself pointed out, in training in the habit of divided attention.

At the other extreme, the libertarian extreme, the individual is actuated by an immediate, direct sense of the value of what he is doing. By "immediate" and "direct," we mean that he is doing what he wants to do; the task entices him on its own account. Clearly, in this case, too, there is no *moral* discipline. So long as interest is thus spontaneous or direct, there can be no question of such discipline. It is between these two extremes that we must seek the kind of action that is motivated by the individual's own sense of value, but in such a manner that the performance of it entails moral discipline.

We must distinguish between different forms of value which may serve to direct conduct. There are three forms to be kept in mind: (1) direct or immediate value; (2) indirect or remote value, and (3) imitative or associative value. Let us examine the bearing of these different forms on the problem before us. The first form of value, as we have pointed out, does not concern us here. It is in relation to the second and third forms that the meaning of formal moral training becomes clear.

In considering the indirect or remote value, we are dealing with a situation in which a thing is sensed not as valuable in itself, but as a means to something else which is felt to be valuable. It was said of Michelangelo that when he looked at the block of marble, what he really saw in it was a finished statue. The analogy may be applied to matters of conduct. Certain ways of behaving are felt to be desirable, not in themselves, but because of the ends to which they are a means. Mathematics may not attract the pupil sufficiently to evoke the effort that study of it demands. Seen as a necessary means to admission to the engineering profession (the end which the pupil really desires), the subject of mathematics takes on a new perspective; it appears important and valuable.

Clearly, what happens is that the individual achieves a more comprehensive view of a certain way of behaving (studying mathematics) and of a certain result (engineering), and sees them simply as aspects or continuations of one another. Terms such as "means" and "end" imply a separation which is artificial. This is the point that Dewey has in mind when he deprecates the distinction between means and end in matters of conduct as a false dualism. At the same time, the distinction serves a useful purpose. It reminds us of the fact that the connection between end and means may not be obvious—on the contrary, a more or less strenuous intellectual effort may be needed to grasp it. Moreover, after the connection has been apprehended, another sort of effort is demanded, namely, the effort to act in the light of it and to persevere in such action until the desired end is attained.

Here, then, is an experience, an experience with three distinguishable facets, which it is the task of education to provide: (*a*) use of the intelligence to attain a more comprehensive view of an act; (*b*) exercise of effort to resist distractions which would prevent the individual from acting in the light of the more comprehensive view; and (*c*) experience of the satisfying feeling of achievement or creation which emanates from the successful prosecution of an end in this manner. By formal training, we mean nothing less than the attainment of these three goals. It should be noted, moreover, that each of the three facets that we have mentioned represents action on a distinctively human level. Formal discipline is here again something on a higher plane than that represented by animal training.

It should be noted that failure to give due recognition to the part played by the third form of value that may serve to direct conduct, the imitative or associative value, has done much to befog the issue of formal moral discipline, and indeed the whole question of authority versus liberty in education. While some values are a direct expression of the child's own spontaneous interests, and others are due to the means-end relationship, there are yet others which are due to association—association with the adult world. It is a mistake to suppose that standards imposed by the adult world are necessarily sensed by the child as external, alien, compulsive. On the contrary, the child is always in some measure, and usually indeed in large measure, sensitive in his own way to the obvious values of the adult world. Though they are not *his* values—the two sets of values may indeed clash—they are nonetheless sensed as valuable; they acquire value by association. Illustrations of this fact are found on every hand.

The teacher who adopts a new way of parting his hair or buttoning his jacket may find that his style of dress has spread like an epidemic among his students. The teacher for whom mathematics is very obviously a matter of great importance infects his pupils with something of his own feeling about the subject. This feeling is often a powerful motivation for students, and even justifies a demand for effort on their part, effort which is something more than a matter of compulsion. In the example quoted from Dewey's *Democracy and Education* (page 138) is there not an important difference between the child's staying away from the fire because it has actually burned him, and his staying away because he has been either snatched from it or harshly commanded by an adult? Does not the fact that the prohibition is social in origin tend to stimulate, however vaguely, some feeling or idea of value in connection with it?

It is thus not true that when we call upon the child to act in a manner at variance with his immediate, spontaneous interests, we are necessarily subjecting him to compulsion. His liberty is denied and adult authority abused only if he is made to continue acting in that way when we have failed to imbue him with any feeling of value, as was the case with Chesterfield's son; or if the influence of the adult creates in him a wrong or distorted sense of value, as we noted in the example of John Stuart Mill's relationship to his parents; or if the adult fails to pay due heed to the growth in the child of significant values different from his own, in the manner of Edmund Gosse's father. None of these abuses is likely to occur when the child benefits from a skilful teacher guided by a sound, well-thought-out philosophy of education.

Finally, it is clear that the question of formal moral discipline, like that of formal intellectual discipline, leads us back to the fact of man's rationality. Psychologists in the first two decades of our century developed a marked propensity for discounting reason as an important factor in the explanation of human action. At best, reason was suspect. The psychologists were certainly mistaken, however, if they left reason out of the reckoning in connection with formal moral training. Reason is implied, as we have seen, in the apprehension of the means and end relationship. In this same connection, moreover, reason appears in another form, intelligence. Once the individual has seen the means in relation to the end, as an intelligent being he will note the relationship for future use; he does not need to rethink the situation every time it occurs.

Again, the tendency of the child to react sympathetically to obvious adult values is a manifestation of reason already noted in the passage quoted from Sir Leslie Stephen. Stephen characterized reason as sympathetic imagination, the ability to put oneself in another's place, and referred to it as "reason in the sphere of feeling." To deny the reality of formal discipline, either intellectual or moral, would thus amount to the discounting of the very important factor of intelligence—intelligence of the human order.

14 *The Basic Skills: Language and Tool-using*

We have considered the basic civilized values and the problems that they raise for education. It is important now to examine more closely the two basic skills or tools which we referred to as distinctive parts of the human being's equipment in this situation. The first of these skills is language. The nature of the language sign has already been explained, in particular, the way in which it differs from non-linguistic signs and symbols. Attention was also drawn to the fundamental intellectual capacity implied in the ability to learn language, the capacity for abstract thinking.

The primary function of language is communication—the communication of ideas, wishes, and feelings. Language is not the only means of communication that man has devised. Music, dance, and ritual serve the same purpose, each in its own way, but for flexibility and range, none of these latter means can compare with language. The reason for this fact lies in certain changes which have come over language in the course of man's ascent from the primitive to the civilized level, changes which will be discussed in this chapter.

One of the essential changes that has taken place with regard to language is that it has been reduced to writing. This has meant something much more important than the appearance of a recognized or conventional manner of spelling words, although it has, of course, meant that also. With the reduction of language to writing, words have had, so to speak, to stand on their own feet in the realm of communication. At the pre-civilized level (as so often in conversation at all levels) gestures of face and hand, voice intonations, and the like are freely used to help to convey meaning. Such aids are not available in written language. Clear communication depends on more precise definition of the meaning of words, with greater care in the use of them, and the arrangement of them in a way calculated to convey the meaning without ambiguity. This latter means that language acquires a recognized or conventional structure—it develops a grammar and syntax. The curriculum must make provision for training the young to use language in this way.

Another essential change gradually comes over language, or, it is more correct to say, over man's attitude to language. The linguistic sign—the word—comes to be increasingly regarded as conventional or arbitrary, until, at the civilized level, it is realized that not only would a rose smell as sweet by any other name, but also that there is no reason why the rose should not be called by some other name. At the primitive level, on the contrary, the connection between the sign and the thing signified is felt to be something quite other than an accident of convention. It is vaguely felt to be real, so that the two cannot be separated.

Much of primitive man's magical beliefs derive from his identification of the name with the thing. For example, if an object is *tabu*, this means, among other things, that it must not be touched. This in turn comes to mean that the object must not be mentioned by name. The name *is* the thing, and to name it is to touch it. Again, the name given to a particular person will *do* something to that person; it will tend to give him the quality indicated by the name (e.g. brave fighter).

The tendency to feel a real connection between the name and the thing is not so noticeable in adults, but it is obvious enough among children. Tommy Smith would find it hard to believe it a mere accident that he was not called Billy Smith. Though not as evident in adults, the tendency is still there, and it takes a characteristic form, namely, the belief or feeling that if there is a word (or phrase), there must be something definite that it denotes. It is this feeling that Lewis Carroll is playing on, when he intrigues us with:

> 'Twas brillig, and the slithy toves
> Did gyre and gimble in the wabe;
> All mimsy were the borogoves,
> And the mome raths outgrabe.[1]

Words like "energy," "force," the "unconscious," especially when spelled with a capital letter, are apt to suggest to the untrained mind something more definite and concrete than is actually denoted by such terms. Again, as with words that denote really concrete objects —"house," "river," "cloud," and the like—meaning is thought of as fixed or permanent; allowance is not made for the fact that in the course of time the meaning of a word may change so greatly that the word can be seriously misleading.

The word "religion" provides an example of this phenomenon. To people in the Middle Ages, this word specifically denoted the beliefs and ritual of the Roman Catholic Church. Any other belief was classed as paganism or heathen superstition. Today the word "religion" encompasses a vastly more comprehensive meaning. "Democracy" is another such term. Ancient Athens, we are told, was a democracy. So, too, are Great Britain and the United States today. It is easy for the untrained mind, misled by the common generic label, to harbor very naïve ideas about resemblances between these political regimes. In all such cases, the trained mind tries to detect the features that really are common to all three and justify the use of the same word to designate them. That calls for abstract thinking, and therein lies the rub. The original or primary reference of words was to definite concrete objects, actions, and situations. The untrained mind does not find it easy to move on the plane of abstract thinking. It tends to lapse to the more primordial level of the concrete, and in this way to simplify—and falsify—its thinking.

Yet another change comes over language in the course of time— words acquire emotional coloring. Some words, such as "religion," "patriotism," and "communism," become so charged with emotion

---

[1]Lewis Carroll, *Alice in Wonderland and Through the Looking Glass* (New York: Grosset and Dunlap, 1946), p. 240.

that one tends to lose sight altogether of what they denote, that is, of their intellectual or logical content. There are, again, the familiar words bound up with elemental, universal experiences, words such as "father," "mother," "home," "death," "sky," "sun," and "sea." In the English language these "elemental" terms are mainly words of Anglo-Saxon origin. That is no doubt the reason why so much of the great poetry in English (it would be going too far, but not very much too far, to say *all* of it) relies mainly on the short Anglo-Saxon words. The poets have exploited the feelings latent in these words, feelings as elemental and universal as the things that the words denote.

Students of semantics have drawn attention to other changes in the use of language. For instance, language is sometimes used for ceremonial purposes rather than for purposes of communication. Certain linguistic expressions are right for certain occasions—they are "the thing to say." "How do you do?" is neither a true question, nor a rhetorical one; it is ceremonial formula. When the chairman has assured the meeting that the speaker "has done us a very great honor in consenting to address us today," one does not ask oneself whether or not the chairman is speaking the truth.

Again, it has been suggested that the words used to express moral standards—"good," "bad," "right," "wrong," and the rest—are not used with any specific logical reference at all; they do not denote any actual object or situation. What they do communicate are wishes or commands. "It is right to tell the truth" is a covert or disguised way of saying "I wish you to tell the truth," or "Tell the truth!" But for our purposes, we need not investigate these further subtleties of linguistic usage. Our discussion of basic moral values in the preceding chapter seems to make it clear that these words are not *merely* the expression of covert wishes or commands.

Communication by language is therefore not the simple, straightforward process that it is usually taken to be. It has become a major problem in civilized society for two main reasons. First, at the level of civilized society, language has a far broader function than it has at the primitive level. The more complex the society, the more exacting the demands on the medium which is the principal means of communication. Second, two factors already noted operate to make the process of communication by language a major problem, namely, the tendency to think that if there is a word or phrase, there must be something definite that it denotes, and the tendency of words to acquire emotional coloring.

As an example of this second factor, one might consider the phrase "collective security." This phrase had its origin in a complex and menacing international situation, and it expressed the need for a policy to deal with that situation. "Collective security" did not denote any definite object or situation—no one was clear as to what alignment of nations was implied, or indeed as to whether any such alignment was possible. The phrase was the expression of an aspiration, a hope, an ideal. But how many people came to think of it as denoting something concrete and definite? To be for or against "collective security" was for these persons the same as being for or against Tom Smith.

It should also be observed that both words of this phrase were emotionally charged. "Security" to an anxious world was a warmly comforting word, and "collective" suggested the reassuring idea of strength in numbers. Imagine (as happened often enough) the politician on the electioneering platform asked by the public whether or not he was in favor of collective security. The question was an awkward one for an honest and realistic individual. The candidate would at least hesitate, and a display of hesitation on such an obviously "good" and "right" idea was certainly enough to make his audience think that he was not a person to be trusted.

On the whole, then, we can see good reason why educationists provide language instruction with a prominent place on the curriculum. It is indeed true that what is actually done about language on the curriculum, the kind of instruction that is actually given under this heading, may be open to grave criticism. This situation may in large measure be the outcome of unthinking acceptance of traditional practices. The case for systematic language instruction in some form is, however, unanswerable. What the form or method of such instruction should be may be very much a matter of debate, but the controlling aim or purpose is always clear. This purpose is to train the individual so that he will use language like a civilized person, that is, make an effective tool of it, and never allow it to make a tool of him.

Let us turn next to the second basic skill of man: tool-using. What about the education of *homo faber*? Here we have a trait which is not only an essential facet of man's humanity, but which has been of profound significance for the realization of his human potentialities. Among the instincts which psychologists used to list (when they employed that concept more freely than they do now) was an instinct of constructiveness, an innate tendency towards the manipulation of the physical environment. All that we need say here is that aeons of tool-using must have generated in *homo faber* a deep-seated need for this form of self-expression.

Advocates of educational handiwork—shop in its various forms— would seem to be right when they insist that such training has significance over and above its utilitarian or vocational value. Activities providing expression for this need would seem to make their own contribution to the healthy growth or "culture" of the individual. In the pre-machine eras, the demands of living provided abundant scope for constructive activities, but all that has changed, so that this side of human nature is now left uncultivated. Most contemporary education concentrates on the intellect, ignoring an authentic expression of the intellect, the one that comes by way of hand and eye.

It might be pointed out in reply to this contention that the machine has not only created the problem of an uneducated side of man's nature, but that it has also provided a solution for it. Automation has very substantially increased the part of life allotted to leisure, and if it is true that there is a need of the kind mentioned, that need can be left to find ways of satisfying itself in leisure-time activities. Many of the so-called hobbies subserve this very purpose. Hobbies are peculiarly personal or individual, and the school should not use any of its already limited time to concern itself with that private side of life.

A point that was made in connection with our discussion of self-expression in art should be recalled here. Artistic creation, we noted, is itself an expression of *homo faber*. The peculiarity of it is that it is directed, not to an ulterior, practical purpose, but to the creation of an object that is satisfying in and for itself. The child may be encouraged to express himself in this way when left to his own devices in the matter. It was also suggested, however, that there is a place for definite instruction in techniques, instruction which will create sustained interest by opening up ways to more adequate self-expression. So, too, with many of the hobbies to which men turn for satisfaction. Instruction in certain elementary skills will make the "do it yourself" way more satisfying in the end.

Another important aspect of the general education of *homo faber* is the development of insight into the manner in which the tool, whether actuated by human and animal energy or by natural energy (and called a machine), has been a main factor in determining man's entire mode of living from one generation to another. From very primitive man with his digging stick, to man as a hunter and fisher, as a nomad with domesticated animals and an agriculturist with domesticated, food-producing plants, to man possessed of the resources of steam, oil, and electricity, the story is one of how the tool has not only changed the material conditions of human living, but how it has affected social and moral life generally. In Part II, we shall consider some problems which technological developments in the present century have posed for the educationist.

One important difference between the educated and the uneducated man is the difference of insight into the conditions that determine the man's way of life. The nomad wandering from place to place with wagon, dray animal, and herd no doubt regarded his way of life as the only conceivable one. Living, he reasoned, had always been, and would always be of this nature. When the sailing ship radically changed human habits, the new way of life that it brought with it was in time accepted as the one worth considering. When the airways reach the point where they are the normal avenues of intercourse, those reared to the new conditions will, if left to themselves, accept them in the same simple, unsophisticated manner as did their predecessors the other innovations. Education aims at imparting sophistication, the kind of sophistication that best results from viewing the new technology against the background of the past. The effect of this process is precisely the same as, for example, the effect of being able to see the democratic way of life in the light of its history. In both cases, this effect is to make the difference between the educated and the uneducated outlook.

The twentieth century has created new educational problems with respect to both of these basic skills, language and the use of tools. The development of the new media of communication, especially of the visual media, must be evaluated in relation to the basic medium, language. Tool-using, as represented by contemporary technology, places the whole issue of vocational selection and training in a new light.

Part II:

The Twentieth-Century Context

15 *The Mass Media of Communication*

Significant changes have taken place in the twentieth century, not only in the methodology, organization, administration, and costs of education, but also in the kind of problem that confronts the philosopher of education. The demand that the educational philosopher examine the basic educational values in a context that is in many respects without precedent, and one that has very important bearings on his attempts to translate these values into practical educational procedures, has greatly complicated his task.

The educational philosopher is inclined to one of two extremes. On the one hand, he can ignore this new context and confine himself to the timeless principles that constitute the energizing force of education at all times in the direction of human excellence. In so doing, he commits himself to the view that the twentieth century presents no new problem except that of extending to the people as a whole the culture that in the past was a class monopoly. On the other hand, the philosopher of education can become so deeply engaged in trying to understand and cope with the challenges of the new situation that he totally neglects the basic standards and values. He then loses a clear sense of direction. The former path is characterized by conservatism, and the latter by progressivism, both of them extremist outlooks.

It is important to examine carefully certain features of the twentieth century context that have particularly significant implications for educational philosophy. In the present chapter, the topic of discussion is the problem of communication. The inventions of this century have inaugurated a new era in mass communication. The radio has brought the living voice and the whole world of music into the home. The moving picture theatre and television have conjoined the living voice and the living picture; television has brought that combination into the home. Our approach in this study is to consider first the impact of these new media of communication on specifically moral values, and second, their effects on mental development as a whole.

From these various media, the young person derives all too many intimations of the false idols of the adult world. The most disquieting example of these idols originates with the modern advertiser and his thoroughgoing exploitation of the new media for his own purposes. His strident "excelsior"—his call to a higher standard of living, meaning always a higher standard of material welfare and enjoyment—constantly resounds in the ears of young and old. As the author of *The Status Seekers* and the *Wastemakers*[1] has so vividly pointed out, the main motive to which the appeal of the advertiser is directed is the interest in social status, which in itself is not a materialistic motive. When the aim of keeping up with and surpassing the Joneses is presented as exclusively a matter of the possession and display of material goods, however, it assumes and effectively creates a materialistic philosophy of living. Blatantly frank, without finesse or sublety, the new hedonism is relentlessly directed at young people as well as at adults, and it becomes a potent instrument for sabotaging the work of moral education.

The hedonism may not only persuade the young person to regard success in terms of Cadillacs and mink coats, it may also provide him with a premature and highly distorted view of the adult world, a picture of exciting struggle, tortuous intrigue, and ruthless violence. Whether this image of the adult world exerts a permanent effect upon the young person, or whether he outgrows it, discarding it with other impressions acquired in childhood, is no doubt a debatable matter. It is significant, however, that studies of delinquency report that young delinquents often insist that they do not believe that there is anything unusual in their wayward

[1]Packard, V.O. (1959-1960: N.Y., D. Mackay Co.).

mode of conduct, feeling that everyone acts more or less in the same manner.

In examining the general intellectual effects of the new media, their impact on mental development as a whole, we are concerned with a more subtle issue, one in which it is difficult to establish specific judgments. Communication in this realm is essentially a one-way process. When the newspapers were the main source of communication concerning events happening outside the individual's own community, news tended to foster discussion, whether in the face-to-face relationships by the village pump and in the general store, or in the columns of the press itself. A body of public opinion tended to grow up, and whether well-informed or not, it was at least the outcome of real reflection and discussion. Public opinion produced a fairly stable body of beliefs and attitudes that politicians and other public leaders took seriously. Respect for that opinion and deference to it, constitutes in large measure the meaning of democracy.

For sociologists, too, public opinion was an important phenomenon, and some of them—C. H. Cooley, for example, in his *Social Organization*[2]—recorded a penetrating analysis of it. Today, an analysis such as Cooley's (definitive for the time in which he wrote it) is in certain important respects either irrelevant or invalid. Public opinion, in this more stable sense, has largely disappeared. What we now have is rather a *climate* of opinion, one resembling the physical climate in several respects, including the feeling of the individual that he is powerless to alter it. Such is the result of the massiveness, the variety, and the tempo with which the new media make their impact.

Influencing the masses directly through the medium of the living voice is of course no new phenomenon. The pulpit is one of the oldest agencies for this purpose, and it, too, is a one-way medium. The information and ideas relayed from this source are, however, usually carefully sifted and controlled. Consequently, in spite of the hypnotic potencies always implicit in the living voice, and occasionally exploited by preachers as by other speakers, the pulpit normally contributes to the creation of a stable public opinion.

[2]Chapters XI and XII (New York: Charles Scribner's Sons, 1913).

Returning to the new media, in particular to the media of television and the moving picture theatre, it should be noted that teachers have sensed their far-reaching possibilities, and have rightly taken a stand for their more direct and systematic use for educational purposes. In science, for example, certain facts and processes can be presented with a clarity and vividness that allow the mind to retain them far more easily than through the usual media of oral communication and the static diagram. In the teaching of history, these media can present the life and general atmosphere of a period with an effect that can be matched by only the most imaginative of readers.

Television and the cinema can also contribute to art appreciation in a new and most effective manner. To illustrate, the great musical creations, to which the ordinary individual must repeatedly listen and closely attend before any real appreciation develops within him, are now readily available to him; he need not wait for the star performers themselves to appear in his community, as in the past. There is evidence that as a result of this the general level of music appreciation among the masses has already risen significantly.

In the view of the young person, there is inevitable prestige attached to whatever the various media of communication present, and this is particularly true of television. Young people feel that here they are face to face with real "celebrities" of one sort or another—and they are not very likely to be critical of the type of celebrity that they see. In this same regard, the association of these media with amusement is an important factor. Teachers who insist that learning can be "fun" are nevertheless thinking of learning as the ultimate aim, the amusement being incidental. But with regard to the media of communication, the situation is likely to be reversed —the "fun" becomes the important thing, and learning is incidental. Impressions acquired in this unconscious, indirect manner can be all the more lasting on that account, as we have already remarked in our discussion of moral values.

The fact that these media of communication operate on the level of direct sensory perception cannot be overstressed. They possess all the immediacy, concreteness, and vividness inherent in this most influential level of experience. True, they do not represent first-hand experience of reality, but the experience that they yield is only once removed; whereas language taken by itself, written or spoken, is experience twice removed, and demands the exercise of the imagination in order to give clarity and vividness to the object described. On the basis of the living picture, the individual is able to build more realistic knowledge of the world he lives in and of the many and diverse peoples who share it with him. Reading about other peoples and other cultures, one may easily fall far short of removing the feeling of their strangeness and remoteness. Unless the reader possesses unusual imaginative ability, or the writer exceptional powers of verbal description, understanding is likely to remain on a coldly intellectual, impersonal level. To actually see these people, however, as they live their daily lives and meet the needs and demands of life by the practice of their own skills and customs, is the one sure way of sensing their common humanity.

One might object that this process merely accentuates the feeling of difference between cultures, but on closer examination, any accentuation of differences is revealed to be only a superficial one. People of other cultures are no longer seen to be foreigners and outsiders. Emotional and moral barriers are in some measure broken down, just as science has broken down the stubborn obstacle of physical distance. The living picture *can* operate in this way— but, again, it may fail to do so.

To appreciate how the living picture can function in the one way or the other, one need only contrast its immediacy, concreteness, and vividness with the characteristics of language. Language, we have seen, is inseparable from some degree of abstraction and generalization. We noted the more general bearing of this fact on formal intellectual training. Its specific bearing on the present issue will become clear if we invoke a philosophical concept, the statement of which we owe to the philosophical school of idealism. This is the concept of the *concrete universal*.

Consider any ordinary object of perception, say, an orange. Seen directly and naïvely, an orange is simple, uncomplicated, unique, and individual. When the mind operates on the orange, it divides its perception of that orange into a number of different qualities or attributes—the orange has color, taste, smell, weight, and shape. These qualities are general; they do not pertain uniquely to the orange, for other objects have color, taste, and the rest. After the mind has thus analyzed the object, in this case the orange, the perception of the object is different from what it was initially. The object is still sensed as individual or unique, but as a unique combination of these general qualities. The object is still seen as a whole, but as a differentiated whole—it represents a better *Gestalt,* or "configuration," to use the language of one school of psychology.

Qualities or attributes are not the only aspects discerned and discriminated by the thinking mind. The relationships of the object to other objects are additional such aspects—causal relationships, for instance, such as that of the object to the conditions of climate and soil that produce it, and relationships of effect, such as that of the object's bearing on the economy of a country. Should the reader carry this analysis to its logical conclusion, he will probably ask himself whether the object is anything more than a fusion or bundle of qualities and relations. And if the object is nothing more than that, is it not then in its essence mental in character, since qualities and relationships are mental constructs? The proponents of idealism answer in the affirmative, while the advocates of realism escape from the quandary by insisting that qualities and relationships are not *entirely* mental in nature.

The arguments of the idealist and the realist are not of immediate concern for us here. The point that is very relevant to the topic under discussion is that the use of concepts, such as qualities and relationships, to enable us to obtain a fuller understanding of the object, is dependent on language. Such concepts and relationships represent thinking on a level for which language is essential. To be sure, thinking can occur on a lower plane that does not depend in the same way on language. It can even proceed on an animal level, and one can distinguish different degrees of *intelligence* in such thinking. Any sustained, controlled thinking not only rests on language, but also demands certain competence and precision in the use of that medium. Before we consider the practical bearing of these observations on the problem with which we are concerned in the present chapter, let us expand the concept of the concrete universal to include a more complex type of situation than that represented by simple sensory perception.

To this end, consider the following quotation from R. H. Lotze, a distinguished German philosopher of the nineteenth century. Discussing "two general modes of fallacious thought," Lotze says:

> The first is doctrinairism, the second narrow-mindedness. The doctrinaire is an idealist, who refuses to see that though ideas may be right in the abstract, yet the nature of the circumstances under which and of the objects to which they are to be applied must limit not only their practicability but even their binding force. The narrow-minded, on the other hand, can recognize and esteem no truth and no ideal, even the most universally valid, except in that special form to which they have become accustomed within a limited circle of thought and personal observation.[3]

Examine these two forms of bad thinking, doctrinairism and narrow-mindedness, in connection with the bearing of the new media, especially the movies and television, on the individual's understanding of cultures other than his own. If the individual depends on reading, he must draw on the resources (if he has them) of a vivid, concrete imagination, or his thinking will be abstract, sketchy, and relatively empty. If he applies such empty thinking, he will become doctrinaire, for he is too much occupied with universals, and not enough with their concrete setting. If, on the other hand, he depends on the picture presented by television and the cinema, then he must carry out the analytic synthetic process described above. If he does not accomplish this, he then becomes narrow-minded, for he remains so preoccupied with the concrete that he tends to lose sight of universals altogether.

Clearly, then, the visual media may serve only to leave the mind well stocked with a variety of pictures that stay with it as passive memories. The case is similar to that of the globetrotter whose contacts have supplied him with a great variety of direct experiences which, however, have done little or nothing to enhance his interest in other peoples and cultures or to deepen his understanding of them, a state of things probably more common than one

[3]*System of Logic:* Vol. I (Oxford: Clarendon Press, 1884), p. 285.

might imagine. Reflection is needed to make such direct experiences meaningful in the best sense, and language, used with deliberation and precision, is indispensable to such reflection.

It is with these considerations in mind that one should approach the specific and very important questions concerning the extensive use of the media of communication for educational purposes. A very crucial question is their influence on reading: Do they tend to replace reading, to leave it, on the whole, unaffected, or to act as a positive stimulus to it? Social scientists on both sides of the Atlantic have investigated this important matter, and it turns out to be less simple than it first appears. On the whole, the question is still an open one—and a very crucial one as well.

Again, learning through the visual media is a one-way process, for the long-approved principle of pupil participation is seemingly abandoned, although it should not be beyond the ingenuity of the teacher to devise ways of avoiding this unfortunate result. Are these so-called visual aids functioning, however, as aids or as substitutes? If they function as the latter, is there not then real danger of educational sabotage? This would be the result if, to take only one example, the vivid and interesting pictures associated with the teaching of science were enjoyed merely on their own account, instead of functioning as a stimulus for the effortful, systematic thinking implied in scientific instruction at any level where it is seriously undertaken.

It would be a mistake to commit oneself to any definite stand on such questions, for the media of communication are being developed at such a rapid pace that it is all but impossible to accurately anticipate future innovations or achievements. Whatever the future holds, the main question for the teacher will nevertheless remain: Are these developments stimuli and aids to thinking, or are they thinking-saving devices? One can, however, venture to say that there appears no good reason why these scientific developments could *not* be used to function in the right way—the right way being not only to stimulate thinking, but also to link it securely to the realities of living by providing a foundation of vicarious experience, vivid, extensive, and authentic.

16   *Science and Technology*

Among the more spectacular changes brought about by twentieth-century science and technology is the practical elimination of the space barrier. At the primitive level, the life of the tribe was self-contained; other tribes figured only as potential enemies or objects of an occasional marauding raid. When tribal society developed into the modern state and nation, the outlook of the average individual, though no doubt greatly broadened, was still definitely circumscribed by state and national boundaries. One is tempted to say that modern science, through its elimination of the old space barriers, has created something in the nature of a world community, but this would be far from a true picture.

Physically, India is now on our doorstep. Spiritually, however, it is still very far away. The combination of physical proximity and spiritual remoteness has created a field of possible tensions hitherto unknown. In the past, our civilization could largely ignore other contemporary civilizations—the contacts could be and were limited to matters of trade and commerce. No thought was given to the fact that beyond the periphery of these contacts lay a vast hinterland of religion, morality, and deep-rooted custom, of ways of thinking, feeling, and behaving alien through and through to our own.

Missionaries, it is true, occasionally glimpsed into this region, but they were not primarily concerned with understanding and giving an account of it. Adventurous travellers had their strange tales to tell, but these stories were taken with more than a grain of salt.

More recently, professional students of ethnology and social anthropology cast some light on the picture. Their interest, however, was mainly confined to the more primitive levels. But the common man still tended to lump together life in the jungle with life in an ancient civilization, and to dismiss both as merely "the heathen in his blindness."

At one point only has there been a beginning of real interpenetration of our own and other civilizations, namely, in the world of science. Science will not remain the exclusive possession of the West much longer. Scientific procedure readily lends itself to being taught and learned. Science, moreover, can coexist with those fundamental differences of spiritual outlook to which we have referred, and which are, after all, the ultimate dynamics of any civilization. Even within our own civilization, science is apt to make this quality of moral neutrality a matter of pride. One cannot therefore assume that the assimilation of Western science by other civilizations will work towards a lessening of fundamental tensions—it could serve only to make them more dangerous.

The situation, then, is without precedent in three respects: direct and continuous communication with alien cultures is inescapable; the new media could raise the level of such communication, making it informed and intelligent as never before; and the consequences of failure in this regard are already so starkly clear that one need not dwell on them.

How is this better understanding of other cultures and civilizations to be achieved? Journalists and novelists have in their different ways contributed towards it. These writers, as is the way of artists, are not concerned so much with systematic analysis as with the object of making the alien way of life come alive, and this is all to the good. In neither case, however, is the writer primarily concerned with producing an objectively accurate picture. For this purpose, systematic research is needed, and the graduate schools of our universities should undertake it. This means that a new kind of research would have to come into being, since the graduate schools have in the main limited their efforts to strictly scientific research. They have tended to avoid investigations in which the scientific method is not fully applicable and in which findings cannot be reported in scientific terms. The new type of research would be a combination of scientific and non-scientific study.

In the study of an alien culture, there is always much that lends itself to scientific investigation. Geography, climate, soil conditions, food, disease, and other such material factors present no problem, save that of finding the men and money for the job. This, however, is only a part—probably the less important and certainly the easier part—of the investigator's task. To "explain" an alien civilization, the investigator must study not only the externals of custom, law, morality, and religion, but also achieve an insight into the underlying value-patterns, the ideas, feelings, and general world-outlook with which these externals are bound up, both as cause and effect. Here he must take leave of science, in the narrowest limits of the term; what is needed now is disciplined, percipient, and objective thinking, with an unusual endowment of sympathetic imagination, the faculty of "putting oneself in the other person's place."

The main pitfall in the path of such research is clear. The investigation is directed towards values, and the investigator is himself the product of a civilized value-pattern. Objectivity is thus hard to come by, especially where moral and political values are concerned. For example, by the time he has reached the level of graduate research, the investigator may have already committed his mind to a political ideology. Whether this has come about by way of sincere and independent thinking or by some accident of personal influence matters not; the important thing is that it impairs his capacity for objective observation and report. Yet it is in this group of young people, who have long been concerned about politics, that the graduate schools would be likely to find their most eager volunteers for the new type of research.

Another and a rather less obvious difficulty stands in the way of the desired kind of research into alien civilizations. In all such studies, the frame of reference is inevitably one's own civilization, Western civilization. To make comparisons with another civilization meaningful and valid, there must be a clear and true picture of the real, as distinct from the ostensible or professed, values of one's own civilized milieu, and this is hard to come by.

Can our universities produce such a core of creative scholars, dedicated to the task of appraising alien contemporary cultures—as de Tocqueville did with America in the early nineteenth century—and perform the task more systematically, but with the percipience, not to say remarkable prescience, displayed by the Frenchman? It should be noted here that some of the graduate schools in the United States have already made a beginning in this direction. The drive no doubt came in the first instance from the need to obtain a realistic picture of the Soviet Union, and to counteract the effects of a generation of propaganda and distortion. In this case, ignorance was felt to be a positive menace. It is already becoming clear, however, that the Soviet Union does not provide the only instance where ignorance is dangerous. As already remarked, regions once remote, such as India, the Middle East, and China, whose civilizations have roots deeper in the past than our own, are now on our own doorstep. Insight of the kind that we have described may not be a sufficient condition of coexistence, but it certainly seems a necessary one.

A most impressive appreciation of the long-range significance of technology appears in a recent publication.[1] Professor McLuhan's thesis is twofold. First, the invention of printing effected a cultural revolution, in the sense that, prior to that invention, the spread of knowledge—as far as the vast majority of the people was concerned—was a matter of direct, personal communication by way of platform, pulpit, or other personal agency. The wide dissemination of the printed word pushed all such agencies into the background, leaving them only a secondary, incidental role. Knowledge became available to the individual, as an individual, not as a member of a listening group, nor as one at the receiving end of a directly personal relationship. This part of the author's thesis is certainly convincing: the change meant a revolution, a silent and long-drawn-out one, but a revolution nonetheless.

The second part of Dr. McLuhan's thesis holds that electronics is putting an end to the era of the dominance of the printed word and reinstituting, now on a world-wide scale, the era of direct face-to-face communication and influence. The ultimate effect, the author maintains, will be to turn the whole world into a community, like the small community strictly so-called, where direct, face-to-face

[1]H. M. McLuhan, *The Gutenberg Galaxy: The Making of Typographic Man* (Toronto: University of Toronto Press, 1962).

relationships were continuous and, in respect to influence, decisive. Are we now headed for the small town writ large, as large as the world itself?

Two observations should be made about this interesting prediction of the shape of things to come. One cannot assume (although Professor McLuhan's thesis seems to imply it) that electronics will do to the printed word what the printed word did to older forms of communication, namely, push it into the background and make it a relatively unimportant part of the process of communication. One had best leave that an open question.

Again, there is a long and hard way to go before such a cosmopolitan community comes into being. If we accept the sociologist's three criteria of community—a common territory, direct, face-to-face relationships, and a sense of identity, of "belonging together," we can see that electronics can, in its own way, produce the first two of these criteria, but that these two need not produce the third—they may work against it. *Homo sapiens* finds himself facing the stark alternative: One Great World, accommodating somehow its myriad of differences—or no world at all. And already St. Paul's stern injunction is literally applicable, every word of it, to man's case: "Work out your own salvation in fear and trembling."

Returning to the topic of specific changes due to technology, it is important to note that this century has brought another alteration that poses a problem for education. The basic sciences of mathematics and physics have acquired for the general public a new practical importance. Heretofore, the practical importance of basic scientific research was taken on trust—on the word of the scientists, and usually with a certain amount of scepticism. Developments such as nuclear weapons and space travel have changed all that. The practical urgency of research on the frontiers of basic science is now clear to everyone, and it is also evident that this means not only a long and arduous scientific training, but a training that presupposes special talent of a high order. Our educational institutions have the task of drawing on the population as a whole for the supply of such talent, of detecting it as early as possible, and of making governments aware of the facilities required to bring it to fruition.

Twentieth-century technology has placed the whole issue of

vocational training in a new light. Unskilled and semi-skilled occupations are being steadily eliminated. Trade union officials and others are already pointing with dismay to what appears to them a new and terrifying form of the spectre of unemployment. Advanced technology has resulted in the need for a new type of technician, one who is better called a "technologist" than a technician, to signify the higher level of technical expertise he will represent.

The number of individuals in the forefront of basic scientific research today is quite small, and indeed it may never be large. But the number needed for the practical applications of basic research will steadily increase. These technologists will range all the way from individuals with a competent knowledge of basic theoretical science to those on a much lower level of scientific understanding, the technicians properly so-called, the individuals well versed in "the tricks of the trade." We are apt to picture the final outcome of automation as an industrial order with two levels of worker: at the top, the scientist engaged in the advancement and application of scientific knowledge; at the bottom, the automated worker, the limit of whose expertise is pushing the right button at the right time.

This picture of the final outcome of automation is grossly oversimplified. Among other things, it obscures the important fact that society will depend for the inventions of the future not so much on the scientists as on the high-level technologists. The quality of mind needed for scientific discovery and that needed for practical application of discovery are not necessarily the same. A high order of endowment for the pursuit of theoretical science may well co-exist with indifference to practical applications—indifference amounting to something like stupidity. The story of how Sir Isaac Newton, when he wanted to give his cat and her kitten access to his study, cut a large hole in the door for the cat and a smaller one for the kitten, is doubtless apocryphal, but it is believable. Or it may be that Sir Isaac had a keener insight into the ways of cats than most of us! In any case, the new technology will offer scope at all its levels for satisfying participation in significant practical activities, and at its higher levels for the exercise of the inventive faculties.

This means that twentieth-century technology will make available to *homo faber* new forms of self-expression to replace the old, natural forms so largely eliminated by a century and a half of industrialization. The tool, so long dependent on human and animal energy, evolved into the machine, which was actuated by natural energy and which relegated the human being to a relatively passive role. Now the machine is evolving once more into a new form, one dependent again on human energy, energy of mind, not of body. Seen in this light, vocational training, or rather, vocational education is not only worthy of an important place in the curriculum of our higher educational institutions, but charges them with a responsibility that they cannot afford to ignore. The innovations and modifications that will be needed to cope with this task are matters of organization and administration that do not concern us here.

Among other things, our educational institutions will have to come to terms with questions of a novel order. One such question has been implied in our discussion of the new media of communication. If these media should begin to undermine the rôle of the printed word, what are the schools going to do about it? Apart from the effect on reading generally (we suggested that that is still in doubt), there is evidence that, so far as "news" is concerned, television is replacing the newspaper for many people. How far that movement has spread among the masses would be an interesting question for the sociologist to investigate.

If the technology of communication is indeed moving in that direction, the school will have to incline towards one of two policies. Either it will fall in line with the movement and set itself to make the most of the new media for its own purposes, or, if satisfied that communication by the printed word has the special educational value we claimed for it in the discussion referred to, the school will set itself to conserve that medium and develop competence in the use of it.

Another question concerns the teaching of science. Scientists have been protesting that the whole approach of the schools is quite out of line with the needs of an era of increasing automation. The teachers in their turn might well protest that the scientists have left them with no clear lead as to what precisely is wrong with science teaching and how, precisely, it could be put right. For example, there is no clear answer to questions such as these: (1)

Should there be a difference between science teaching for purposes of general education and science teaching for purposes of technological preparation? (2) What specific changes should be made in the teaching of arithmetic, mathematics, and the natural sciences? (3) At what level of education should these changes be introduced and, in particular, how far, if at all, should the work of the primary school be affected? With respect to this last question, some scientists seem to be demanding something the primary school is already doing and has long been doing. Others are silent, while others talk as if they thought that every primary grade has quite a large quota of budding Bertrand Russells and A. N. Whiteheads!

Over and above these more specific issues, there is a more general issue which, though by no means new, has acquired peculiar urgency in the twentieth century. It calls for a chapter to itself.

17 *Science and the Humanities*

In comparatively recent times, it has become common to think
in terms of the opposition of science to the humanities. In the
Middle Ages, the opposition was not of science to the humanities,
but of the humanities to theology. The term "humanities" in that
era designated studies of a purely secular kind. "Theology" meant
the cosmology or world view and the ethical doctrines developed by
the Church on the basis of biblical teaching. The cultural cleavage
was between the religious and the secular, the Christian and the
pagan. The humanities at this stage consisted essentially of the
philosophy, literature, and art of Greece and Rome, or rather, that
part of them that the Church tried to integrate with its own thinking.

With the Renaissance, there came a great extension and enrichment of the field of humane studies. Theology, still prominent, was
distinguished from the humanities, but with the boundary line less
sharply drawn than in the Middle Ages. It was not until the
seventeenth century, however, the century of Sir Isaac Newton
and the founding of the Royal Society, that the activities of the
scientists began to arouse general interest. The post-Renaissance
period, the seventeenth century and the first few decades of the
eighteenth, brought with it another shifting of the cultural scene:
theology came to figure as one of the humanities, maintaining an
uneasy liaison, broken by occasional outbursts of strife, with secular
philosophy. The rise of science, with its disturbing and often openly

disruptive implications, finally drove theology and the humanities into the same camp. So much for a very bare outline of an intellectual drama in which the scenes, as history portrays them, were charged with intense human interest. In our own day, the curtain has gone up on another exciting scene in this drama.

By the beginning of the twentieth century, science had secured a firm foothold in the curricula of the schools and colleges. The cleavage between science and the humanities became increasingly marked, and for this there were several reasons. Proponents of the humanities showed little disposition to re-examine the meaning and relevance of the humanities in the light of modern needs and values; they fought staunchly for the old curriculum, pure and undefiled. The humanities thus presented a sharp contrast with the vitality and the progressiveness of the sciences. Again, scientific research needed facilities and financial resources on a scale which only well-supported institutions of higher learning could provide. Competition developed within these institutions, competition for financial support as well as for the interest and allegiance of the students. Finally, science found itself in a wholly unprecedented rôle. In the past, political power turned on considerations such as manpower and industrial potential. In the quest for the means of naked power, the universities had no part. The struggle for power in the old form has become outmoded because of science—science at a level with which only the universities can cope.

How should one distinguish between science and the humanities? What is the precise nature of the cultural rift implied in the distinction? If one were to ask the ordinary man of average intelligence how science differs from the humanities, he would probably answer that the humanities are concerned with persons, and science with things—and in so saying he would be a better philosopher than he knows.

It is clear that literature and history are directly concerned with human beings. Drama, fiction, and history present human beings as "going concerns," actuated by certain feelings, motives, purposes, and aspirations. The humanities present man, and they present him because he is intrinsically interesting as an object of contemplation. In this they are living up to their name: they "humanize" us in the sense that they broaden and deepen our knowledge of our fellow humans. Let anyone who doubts this fact try to imagine what his knowledge of men and women would be like without benefit of the contribution of history, drama, fiction, poetry, folklore, and mythology. Left to his own direct experience and reflection, he would find his knowledge of human beings limited to a degree that it is not easy to imagine.

But this principle of division does not take into consideration a cultural area ordinarily regarded as part of the humanities. Philosophy is a case in point; it does not concern itself directly with human beings. Like science, philosophy seeks to expand and deepen our understanding of the world we live in. Indeed, it had attained a ripe maturity in this inquiry before science was born. We must look for a broader principle of division than the *content* of the disciplines in question. This difference turns out to be that of *method.*

In Chapter 3, we described at some length the method of modern science and the point of view implied by it. By way of this method, science arrives at knowledge that is "public," in the sense explained in that chapter. We contrasted scientific forms of knowledge with other forms, particularly with that kind of organized knowledge that is not based on scientific method but on logical consideration of available data. Philosophy is one of these non-scientific disciplines. It accepts what science has to offer, but proceeds with its own constructive work without benefit of scientific method.

History has been mentioned in connection with literary art. History is art in the hands of the historian, who is at once conscientious about his facts and concerned to invest them with flesh and blood, to make the characters and situations of history come to life. History, however, may be presented in another way, the way of Henry Thomas Buckle, Oswald Spengler, and Arnold Toynbee. Here the historian assembles and evaluates the facts with the object of bringing to light important principles of social and political philosophy. It is history in this sense that is intended by those historians who mistakenly claim that history is a science. Political philosophy, law, and the like belong to the same category of humane, non-scientific studies.

From the preceding analysis, it is evident why the discussion of the issue of science and the humanities often becomes confused: the disputants are talking at cross purposes. The men of letters are apt to think in terms of the narrower criterion, content, and to restrict humane studies to the field of *belles-lettres.* As for the other great area of non-scientific studies, they leave it to the scientist to deal with as he likes, and the thing that he will *not* do is accept it as part of his domain. Our analysis, moreover, enables us to dispose of certain specific arguments intended to deny the validity of the distinction between science and the humanities, or at any rate to minimize its importance.

With regard to the first of these arguments, there are those who insist that there is really no cleavage between science and the humanities in the cultural life. Without necessarily being disciples of John Dewey, the advocates of this argument align themselves with his teaching in regarding the distinction between science and the humanities as a false dualism. Science, they claim, is itself one of the humanities, and a very important one at that. This line of reasoning, to which the scientist himself usually subscribes, will not stand up under examination.

Science is, of course, a human creation, one expression of the human mind, but this fact does not mean that it is one of the humanities. All forms of culture are by definition human products. Again, science is used in the service of human needs. Indeed, one of the principles underlying the growth of scientific knowledge is this practical motive. Men have realized that the kind of knowledge that is power—power in the sense of power over nature—is above all scientific knowledge.

It has become mere platitude to state that the impacts of science on the conditions of living have always been far-reaching, and that in our own day they are of spectacular importance. Thinking has perhaps become confused in this connection. The fact that science is so directly and deeply significant for human living has led to its being classed with the humanities. This method of reasoning would, however, also lead one to believe that the study of climate belongs to the humanities. In fact, all knowledge with any bearings, actual or possible, on human living would fall into the same category. The result would only be to deprive the term "humanities" of all serviceable precision of meaning.

There are those who take their stand on the theoretical principle of the ultimate unity of knowledge. Does this principle amount to anything more than the assertion that all knowledge is of a piece, in the sense that it all consists of true or false propositions about reality? It is clear also that the different kinds of knowledge have bearings and impacts on one another. The historian, for example, may use the resources of the chemist to help him to date a document. The logical thinking of a philosopher like Locke or Berkeley can prove very suggestive for the physicist, and help him to clarify the presuppositions of his science. The social sciences, as we shall see presently, are very intimately bound up with non-scientific forms of thinking. But none of these considerations affects the fact that science employs a procedure not available to the other disciplines, and that it confines itself to those aspects of reality that lend themselves to that particular procedure. Finally, it may be remarked that it is usually scientists, or those whose minds have been dazzled by the glamor of science, who make much of the fundamental unity of all knowledge. Is it not permissible to suspect that what they really mean is that, when all the chips are down, it is only science that has the genuine stamp of knowledge, an idea that we have already seen good reason for rejecting?

How then does one classify the social sciences—sociology, social anthropology, and political science? They claim to be sciences, yet their subject matter is human beings. Up to a certain point, each is a science, strictly so-called; the process of learning presents phenomena that lend themselves to scientific observation and verification. This is also true with regard to the processes of production and distribution of economic goods, and to vital statistics, population movements, and the like. In cases like these, human beings take on, in effect, the status of things. But scientifically accredited knowledge is only a part of what these disciplines have to offer. It is supplemented by logical examination of data neither obtained by scientific procedure nor yielding conclusions tested in that manner.

The matter is further complicated by the fact that judgments of *value* are present, although they may, and usually do, operate quite unconsciously. In economics and in sociology, the inquiry is governed by the interest in determining the modes of production and distribution, the kinds of social organization, population distribution, and so forth that contribute best to human welfare. "Welfare" is unconsciously interpreted in terms of the civilized standards that the economist or sociologist has come to accept implicitly; and although the standards may be broad, as broad as Western civilization itself, they may even so be too parochial for the universality of science. In short, the social sciences are an amalgam of (1) real science, (2) organized knowledge, and (3) philosophical assumptions. It is easy to understand why the social scientist is peculiarly subject to the temptation of being uncritical in his application of scientific standards.

If these latter paragraphs appear to labor the obvious, they are directed at those who would tell us that the distinction between science and the humanities should be classed with those seemingly self-evident ideas that turn out to be illusory, such as the idea that the sun travels around the earth. The effect of denying or obscuring the distinction between the humanities and the sciences, of minimizing its importance, is to sidetrack an educational issue which in our day is assuming paramount importance. With the increasing demands of science and technology, what is to happen to general education? Is the whole idea of general education becoming outdated, impossible of realization?

Specifically, what about provision for some real, vitalizing contact with the humanities for (1) those who will become the pioneers in scientific advance; (2) the much larger number of persons needed to cope with the exacting demands of the new technology; and (3) those headed for the scientific professions, such as medicine and engineering, students whose time and effort are being increasingly absorbed by the demands of their rapidly developing vocations? We should first clarify our minds on this crucial question: precisely what will be lacking in the education of these specialists if their training admits of no significant attention to the humanities?

In deciding upon our answer to this question, let us consider the distinction between knowledge and wisdom. Clearly, there is a difference. To have a mind well equipped with knowledge does not of itself guarantee wisdom. Learning and foolishness are not mutually exclusive; this much the ordinary man would concede at once. At the same time, the ordinary man feels that knowledge has some bearing on wisdom. In this, too, he is right: there are forms of foolishness for which the remedy is more knowledge. The difficulty arises out of the fact that historically the word "wise" has often been used to mean simply "learned."

In the true sense of the word, "wisdom" is the ability to judge and choose rightly among different and often conflicting values. The values, moreover, are those which have to do with the regulation of *conduct*, the manner in which the individual deals with the various practical choices arising in the course of day-to-day living. This will determine the kind of person that he will become. In so far as he chooses in a manner tending to create a pattern of living which the moralist calls "the good life," he is wise. He possesses the kind of knowledge that Socrates had in mind when he argued that virtue is knowledge, that right conduct is a matter of right knowledge. Whatever that knowledge, it is not just a reserve of factual information, scientific or non-scientific. Socrates would comprehend at once the point of the observation made about James I of England, that he was "the wisest fool in Christendom."

How does the individual acquire this wisdom? It comes in the first instance from two main sources. One source is the direct influence of society, from early childhood onwards, exerted in a manner that we have already examined. The other source is the individual's reflection on his own experiences of actual living. The humanities add another dimension to this level of moral training and experience by providing a vicarious experience that serves to broaden and deepen the sense of values.

Literature introduces the individual to a world that reveals his most private, personal feelings as something he shares with his fellows; and the individual views this common human nature through the discerning eye of the artist. This is a vastly larger world than that of his actual experience, making available a range of feeling which would otherwise remain closed to him.

History reveals the greatness and the baseness of human nature, and thus makes possible those insights which are essential to human wisdom. Ideas and practices of government which the individual once casually took for granted as obviously right and necessary are seen as only the latest chapter in the long story of the struggle of man for liberty. No one with this kind of perspective is going to assume naïvely that the way of democracy need only be shown to backward peoples in order to be appreciated and put into effective practice.

To the effect of literature and history on the individual must be added those of the fine arts. Of these, music and painting especially reveal to the individual that the aesthetic feelings aroused by his own experiences are but very small intimations of a great region which his fellow men have been exploring in the past.

The overall result of contact with these influences is a sense of "cultural heritage," to use that overworked phrase. Science is, of course, a part of this heritage, but it is coming to be less and less a distinctive part of it. As already remarked, science, with its practical applications, is an exportable commodity. It is the other part of the heritage that will constitute the distinctive character of the Western civilization which it is the task of education to conserve and further. It would seem, moreover, that the most humanizing part of that heritage (in the sense of "humanizing" already pointed out) is that in which the medium is language: poetry, *belles-lettres*, history, and philosophy in its various forms—social, political, ethical, and metaphysical. Music and painting make their contribution, in their own ways, to humane education, but appreciation of them is always compatible with narrowness of human interest and outlook. More importantly, they do not provide training in a kind of thinking or an order of knowledge which, without presumption, one can assure the scientist is at least not less important than his own. One could indeed go farther and argue that this non-scientific thinking plays a far more important part in the life of the ordinary man than does the thinking exemplified in science.

Universities have so far been experimenting with one or both of two ways of protecting humane education from the pressures that would force it into the background. The first of these is to require the student to take a limited number—of necessity a very limited number—of specially selected courses in the humanities as part of his regular program. The average student (to say nothing of the exceptional student who combines a real flair for science with a mental and temperamental intolerance of anything that is not science) is apt to look on such courses as gratuitous obstacles put in the way of his getting on with the real task—an attitude which in itself can go far to defeat the whole purpose of such courses. The more versatile student no doubt derives something from a few such courses, and he may even derive enough to enable him to carry on later by himself in this realm, with confidence and competence, should he desire to do so. But that would indeed be the exceptional case: "later" is likely to be too late.

The second way that the universities have attempted to protect humane education has been to offer courses in the history of science with a view to showing the impacts of science on human living. In this manner, they hope that the cleavage between scientific and humanistic studies will be overcome. John Dewey contributed much to giving currency to this "socialized approach," as he himself would call it.

Two observations are pertinent regarding such a course. First, the historical part will consist largely of a review of the crudities and deficiencies of early science, and of how they were in due course overcome. Does this approach not merely amount to more science? Is it not, moreover, typical of the scientist (as contrasted, say, with the philosopher) that he is not interested in the errors of the past? Since these aspects of early science have been proven to be in error, they are over and done with.

Second, if the impacts of science on human living are brought out with any degree of thoroughness, one certainly penetrates into the field of the humanities. But is the field of the humanities not too large a one to be taken as an incidental or side issue of a program of scientific studies? How far, if at all, can a student, with no real knowledge of the religious outlook and assumptions of the seventeenth century, appreciate the impact of Sir Isaac Newton? Would it not be better to deal with the matter directly, by a study of history on its own account, leaving the student to make the connections for himself? For the most part, such connections will be obvious enough.

Some universities provide for a more systematic training in the humanities by making the B.A. degree a prerequisite to professional training, particularly to training for the profession of medicine. This type of program might well provide a sound basis for a permanent and more extended interest in the humanities later. The main difficulty with it (apart again from the fact that it will appear to many students a serious and unnecessary obstacle) is the economic difficulty in that it adds substantially to the cost of a training which is already costly and time-consuming, and steadily becoming more so.

The situation, then, may be summarized as follows. The provision made for humanistic training for students of the sciences is already far from adequate for what is now required and what will be urgently needed in the future. With the sciences growing as they are, and the need for scientists as pressing as it is, one can expect that the provision will become progressively less. This will mean that in due course those in the forefront of scientific progress and research, the individuals with the means of naked power in their hands, will mostly be individuals for whom the humanities are a *terra ignota,* individuals with no knowledge of history or philosophy, with artistic judgment untrained, and with linguistic competence limited to the language of their specialty. Add to this (if rather spectacular recent evidence is not to be discounted) the fact that their training will leave them capable of an outlook on political matters so naïve as to be nothing short of frightening, and one has, on the whole, a very disturbing picture.

Our universities will have to come to terms with one fact underlying the whole situation: they are expecting something unreasonable from the young people with whom they are concerned. The universities expect students of about seventeen or eighteen years of age to be interested in the humanities, or, rather, in the approach to the humanities which the university must adopt. This approach sees the humanities not as mere entertainment and relaxation, but as an opportunity for the highly rewarding exercise of higher mental faculties. Reared in the atmosphere of the twentieth century, the young person, especially the young person with some flair for science, very naturally finds his interest centred on some aspect of science, and has little or no interest left for the humanities. One cannot but wonder how many young people of an earlier generation who chose the humanities would have headed in the direction of science, were they students today. The fact is that there is very little in the adult world around these young people that is likely to make them take the humanities seriously, as seriously as they take science.

This observation suggests a final question: Are these young people, merely because they failed, and very naturally failed, to respond to the humanities at this early stage in their studies, to be permanently denied the chance of a real education in the humanities? Can the university devise a way of giving them a second chance at a later time when they might be better prepared to respond?

It is not uncommon to meet individuals who in later life express a sense of regret about their lack of competence in one or another field of the humanities, and who want to do something about it. If the realm of study that they have in mind is, for example, philosophy, then one can tell them of certain books with which they may make a beginning. These they can read with interest, but there is one thing, perhaps the most important thing, that they will not acquire through reading: they will not derive the feeling that they are on the right track and really making progress. Sooner or later, and more likely sooner than later, they will give up their reading. What is needed here, as at the earlier student level, is systematic training under competent teaching.

Were the universities to undertake this project they would have to cope with a number of specific problems. They would have to devise a special type of matriculation examination for the purpose of testing the competence of these individuals. There would be no point in asking the candidate to rummage out his yellowing high school parchment. The test would be devised not only to detect the right sort of person, but also to reject the wrong sort: the "crackpot" whose idea in taking a course is to enlighten the benighted teacher, and the person who "has no time for reading," but who thinks that his mind stands in need of re-charging, and others of that ilk.

To overcome these problems, the universities would need to devise a special teaching system based on a combination of correspondence, evening classes, radio, and television. They would also have to insist on dropping those who were not making reasonable progress, as ruthlessly as many of them now drop an idle or incompetent freshman. Some form of degree or diploma would be needed to give the student a target to aim at, and to leave him with a sense of definite achievement.

As for inducements of a more concrete kind, it is not easy to see what could be done. A real inducement might present itself under a system of "weighted" voting. With the present principle of "one man, one vote" as a basis, society might devise a system in which factors such as level of education, marital status, and record of public service on boards, philanthropic bodies, and commission would make the individual eligible for additional voting power. To those who would see in any such plan an attack on the very citadel of democracy, it may be suggested that, with the increasing urbanization of the population and the new media of communication and influence, it is dangerous to assume that "one man, one vote" is the last word in democratic machinery. Reluctance to take such a project of adult education seriously may well be related to another factor—unwillingness, despite all the evidence to the contrary, to take education seriously.

In this connection, encouragement, as well as much significance, is contained in the new slant on adult education implied in a recent pamphlet: *Are Liberal Arts Colleges Becoming Professional Schools?*[1] In this pamphlet a good case is made for adult education of the calibre that we have indicated, but a more comprehensive provision is outlined than one for the humanities alone. We would suggest that, if such an innovation is to be fitted into the permanent structure of the education system, there is good reason for giving priority to the humanities.

What about the converse problem, the provision of scientific education for students of the humanities? C. P. Snow, after deploring the fact that the scientists of his acquaintance do not get beyond

[1]Earl J. McGrath and Charles H. Russell, Teachers' College, Columbia University, N.Y., 1958, pp. 21-26.

"touching their caps to the traditional culture," has this to say about the humanistic scholars:

> Once or twice I have been provoked and have asked the company how many of them could describe the Second Law of Thermodynamics. The response was cold; it was also negative. Yet I was asking something which is about the scientific equivalent of: *Have you read a work of Shakespeare?*[2]

It will help us to clarify the whole issue of education in science and the humanities if we examine this analogy more closely.

Compare the two tasks: training the scientist to read a play of Shakespeare so as to achieve enjoyment and appreciation of its great qualities, and training the humanist so that he can understand the precise meaning (not to say follow the proof) of Einstein's Theory of Relativity. The latter task clearly implies more than merely a good teacher and an interested student. It implies a student endowed with a very specialized form of intellectual talent, the ability to cope with the highly abstract concepts of mathematical physics.

Appreciation of Shakepeare's works implies no such specialized intellectual capacity. It can be achieved on the basis of an ordinary endowment of intelligence. The reason for this is that one is not dealing here with purely intellectual concepts of a highly abstract nature. Shakespeare portrays the thoughts, feelings, motives, and aspirations that are the substance of ordinary living. He enables ordinary men to see their common humanity through *his* eyes; "appreciation" means that the great mind has raised the average mind to a level where there is genuine sharing of insight.

The case is similar in other areas of the humanities that are concerned with human beings and the values that govern their lives: philosophy in its various forms, history, and religion. Understanding usually implies no specialized intellectual capacity in these subjects. Given that interest is aroused, the individual can possess himself of the knowledge—and the wisdom—that these disciplines make available. Furthermore, there is nothing to prevent him from drinking deeply from these wells of wisdom—an

[2]*The Two Cultures*, p. 13.

important consideration—because shallow draughts will exert no appreciable influence upon him.

The difference between these two problems, that of providing a scientific education for the humanist, and that of furnishing a humanistic education for the scientist, should now be clear. For the general answer to the first of these dilemmas, the reader is referred to Chapter 4. The needs of the case are met if education has given the humanist (1) an appreciation of the scientific point of view and of scientific method; (2) the ability to recognize scientific thinking and procedure when he sees it; and (3) an appreciation of the impacts of science on human living. These qualities should be sufficient to provide him with an understanding of the language of science, an understanding that is correct as far as it goes. They need not, and in most cases probably cannot, go far, but it is enough, in short, to make him scientifically literate. One may add that they will be enough to make him an intelligent supporter of science and to inoculate him against the periodic outbursts of intellectual mobism, occasioned by the impacts of science on intellectual vested interests and fanatically closed minds.

Providing the humanist with an education in science is thus not a matter of bringing him *au courant* with the most advanced work (to date) in the field of science. Few, as we have suggested, will be capable of appreciation in that sense. With the scientists, on the other hand, it is a matter of bringing him *au courant* with the *best* that the humanities have to offer. The best in this case is not necessarily the most advanced (in the sense of the latest), as it always is in science. Again, while we suggested that a few courses in science well taught could be sufficient for the scientific training of the humanist, his scientific confrère would require much more thoroughgoing contact with the humane studies, guided and inspired by good teaching. It is thus surely far off the mark to state that the inability to explain the Second Law of Thermodynamics is the scientific equivalent of never having read a work of Shakespeare. The former is compatible with a good general education (including a high degree of scientific "literacy"), while the latter (for one whose native tongue is English) is at least strong presumptive evidence of the lack of it.

Let us consider the rift between the two cultures at a level other than that of academic study, namely, at that of the work of creative artists. While the scientists proceed with their discoveries, doing no more than "touching their caps" to the traditional culture, are the novelists, dramatists, and poets proceeding as if man had never launched a sputnik and began his venturing into outer space? Have these artists come to terms with the new *Weltanschauung* that science has created? If not, and if literature is a "criticism of life," as Matthew Arnold called it,[3] then literary authors are not performing their mission as men of letters. Examining the matter more closely, however, we find that the question is not *whether* science should play a part in the thinking of literary artists, but *how* science should affect their thinking.

It is valuable to consider here an example from the realm of psychological science, one in which scientific knowledge would seem to be obviously relevant to the work of the novelist. During the first two decades of the present century, Freudian psychology, together with its special terminology, attained wide currency. Many writers of fiction turned to it for material with which to illuminate their work. They created characters who obviously exemplified the processes of rationalization, projection, substitution, mother-fixation, and so forth. They wrote to a scientific formula, always a wrong approach for the artist. Their productions may have had some interest as case studies in Freudian psychology, but they were not true contributions to literature.

Yet Freudianism can have immense significance for literature. It profoundly affected, for example, D. H. Lawrence's view of life. The philosophy of Henri Bergson (which attained quite a vogue in the first two decades of our century), with its emphasis on intuition and instinct as against intellect, was probably also an important influence in shaping Lawrence's outlook. But whether it was Freudian science or Bergsonian philosophy, Lawrence made use of it to create live human beings, interesting purely as human beings, and not merely as samples of scientific or philosophic principles.

[3]*Essays in Criticism—Second Series* (London, Macmillan & Co., 1911), p. 5.

By the same reasoning, the right kind of entente between literature and science today will not come about by any premeditated and deliberate effort on the part of the men of letters to come to terms with the cosmos that science is revealing. Literary artists have no call to turn themselves into writers of science fiction. The point is not that fact has become so fantastic as to put science fiction out of business as serious art, though this may be true; it is simply that great literature does not come into being in such a way.

This situation is not without precedent in our cultural history, and the period designated as the Renaissance would seem to present a parallel. The confining world of the Middle Ages was being disrupted and destroyed in the Renaissance: Columbus, Vasco da Gama, Magellan, and other explorers were doing for men's ideas of geography what Copernicus had done for their ideas of astronomy. The new interest in the literature of ancient Greece and Rome accomplished the same broadening of men's perspective on the perennial problems of morals and politics. The more active intellect of the day simply absorbed the new outlook, which meant not so much that they found new things to write about, but that they wrote about the old things in a new way. They were not themselves aware of what was happening to their perspective; the hindsight of the historian would have been required for them to appreciate that. A nineteenth-century historian phrased it thus:

> Vast spiritual and material continents lay for the first time displayed, opening fields of thought and fields of enterprise of which none could conjecture the limit. Old routine was broken up. Men were thrown back on their own strength and their own power, unshackled to accomplish whatever they might dare.[4]

Today the astronomers and atomic scientists are creating a world outlook that exerts an impact on the imagination not unlike the one that affected the men in the Elizabethan age about whom Froude was writing. The creative writers of our century may be left to adjust themselves, in their own special way, to this expanding universe. In so far as this process of adjustment occurs, the rift between "the two cultures" will disappear. And adjustment will

[4] J. A. Froude, *Short Studies of Great Subjects*, Vol. I (Longmans, Green and Co., London, 1901), p. 443.

become a reality if these artists address themselves, with determination and integrity, to their proper task of making literature "a criticism of life," in the sense of something deeply significant for human living. This means more than the absorption of the world outlook created by the physical and biological sciences. It means the artist's "engagement" in the whole contemporary scene, in the French existentialists' sense of the word, a sense not quite adequately rendered by the English equivalent.

But the rift will broaden and deepen if the *avant-garde* of the humanities, literary or other, comes to consist of professionals with nothing to offer of any clear significance either to the professional scientist or to the common man—if it becomes, in other words, an esoteric cult with its own language, intelligible only to its own members. The *avant-garde* of science, we have seen, also has its own language, beyond the reach of the ordinary man. But that is due precisely to the fact that it is the *avant-garde*; it is producing every day spectacular evidence of the fact that it is in the true line of scientific advance. Some of the artistic innovators may indeed be in the main stream of artistic progress, but some of them are certainly in eddies and backwaters—it may be, frothy eddies and muddy backwaters—of the main stream. Neither the scientist nor the ordinary man is in a position to decide what is ephemeral and what is lasting. The professional critics who ought to help them are too often unhelpful, for the reason that they, too, are preoccupied with their own arcana.

Such is the issue of science versus the humanities in the broader aspect. In education it appears in the old, familiar form, the question of an "all round" education. The twentieth century has brought with it a development that has given a new practical urgency to that question, namely, the practical acceptance of the democratic ideal of "education for all."

18 *Democracy and Education: The Basic Issues*

The present chapter is concerned with some of the more obvious issues implied in the acceptance of the democratic principle of the right of every individual, irrespective of social class or economic status, to the opportunity of receiving an education. It might be objected that the twentieth century cannot take sole credit for this principle. Beyond a doubt one finds the idea expressed, and expressed with vigor, in the preceding century by social reformers of the time, such as John Stuart Mill, the historian Thomas Babington Macaulay, and others. But these reformers were thinking of literacy, the ability to read, write, and count, rather than of education as we mean it today. These men expected very much in the way of human betterment from a people made literate, especially from a people that had learned to read, and it is curious to look back some hundred years later on these great expectations. As for education beyond the level of mere literacy, that was still quite generally accepted as a privilege of class and wealth.

It was not until the present century that the idea of full educational opportunity for everyone was accepted as a *sine qua non* of the democratic way of life, accepted at any rate in the two great English-speaking democracies, the United States and Great Britain. In both countries the change has created new and serious problems, a fact hinted at in the phrase commonly used to denote this change —"mass education."

Let us note first that this change is not simply a matter of making available to the people as a whole the kind of education that in the past was limited to the few. The humanities and the sciences (allowing for historical limitations) were the core of the traditional curriculum. Were we to think of this same curriculum as the right educational pabulum for today, we would expose ourselves to challenge and pertinent criticism on two counts, namely, believing that education in the past was along the right lines (within its class limits), and that the same lines are indicated for our own day.

What was the actual educational picture in the past? The favored classes (educationally speaking) consisted of two main groups. There were those, a relatively small number, who made good use of what the arts and sciences had to offer, and who, by any sound standard, became truly educated men. Some of these, indeed—men such as Erasmus, Leonardo da Vinci, and Benjamin Franklin—stand out as personal landmarks in the pursuit of human excellence. But there was also the much larger group of men for whom contact with the arts and sciences, and the institutions that stood for them, was primarily a mark of class status, an attitude quite compatible with little or no seriousness of educational purpose. Even with those who took their educational privilege seriously, no question arose as to the rightness of an education sanctioned by long-established custom. Education represented the right ritual, and, as we remarked earlier about ritual in this or in any other connection, it is implicitly accepted as "the thing to do."

The existence of the democratic state, with its commitment to the principle of educational opportunity for all, has led to a new demand. This demand is that the subject matter hitherto offered and implicitly accepted as the core of education—in a word, the curriculum—must show its credentials and make good the claim advanced for it. So long as education was the private preserve of a relatively small group which not only financed education but also made the taking or leaving of it a matter of free choice, society as a whole had no vital stake in raising questions about its quality. When the democratic state made education up to the level of the primary school mandatory for all, however, it needed good reason to justify such exercise of its power of compulsion. But there was no difficulty on that score; the case for literacy at any rate was clear enough.

It was a different matter with higher education. Here the question was not that of compulsion, but of the provision of opportunity. The question went even beyond that to include the devising of an educational system aimed directly at making sure that those fitted to benefit from the opportunity of higher education would take full advantage of that opportunity. The democratic state as such had to accept this policy not only as a matter of duty but of interest —long-range interest, perhaps, but nonetheless vital, for the democratic state needs all the highly-trained scientists and professional men that it can produce. It also requires as high a level as possible of general education, and high schools, colleges, and universities have to justify their offerings in face of this new demand.

Are these institutions truly geared to the pursuit of "human excellence," to the production of "trained minds," "developed personalities," "socially adjusted individuals," or whatever formula we may adopt to describe the aim of education? There was a time when, for example, study of classical language and literature could be offered as the necessary and sufficient condition for general education. Such an education today would fail to provide social adjustment, using that phrase in a broader sense than it usually bears. The basic values, in other words, must be brought into the context of twentieth-century society.

There is a further question to consider. Even if the cultural opportunities offered by the educational institutions are above suspicion, are these opportunities being used in a manner that will insure the full realization of the intellectual and spiritual values that the institutions represent? The ability of the student is not the sole consideration; the question of his inclination is no less pertinent. On this point, Edward Ferrars, in Jane Austen's novel *Sense and Sensibility*, states:

> There was no necessity for my having any profession at all . . . and a young man of eighteen is not in general so earnestly bent on being busy as to resist the solicitations of his friends to do nothing. I was therefore entered at Oxford, and have been properly idle ever since.[1]

[1] *Sense and Sensibility*, Chapter 19.

The twentieth century, with its "harsher" approach to life, has rendered this attitude to an institution of higher education outmoded.

Our examination of the educational values inherent in the sciences and the humanities stressed the point that serious and strenuous intellectual effort is a condition of the appreciation which alone makes them truly educative. Without such serious interest, higher education becomes again the superficial thing that it was apt to be when it was regarded as a mark of class status. Today, it is true, the interest in class status may not be in evidence, but equally irrelevant motives may be operating. For example, it was no doubt a great gain when industrial corporations began to attach importance to the possession of a degree in general education by their prospective employees. Is there not a danger, however, that such a requirement may clutter the educational institutions with a large number of persons whose attitude is from the outset incompatible with the purposes of general education? A reasonably exacting standard of attainment, ruthlessly enforced with the co-operation of an enlightened public opinion, is the only protection against such dilution of the academic population.

One issue that democracy raises concerning education has received a great deal of attention, and the tendency is to dispose of it more perfunctorily than is warranted. This is the question: Does education for all mean the same education for all? One is tempted to answer "No," and to leave it at that. The educationists who attach crucial importance to individual differences will certainly follow this line of reasoning. The simon-pure traditionalists will answer with an equally emphatic "Yes." They will add that good education is at bottom always the same kind of education, and that past examples of it will serve, with only minor adjustments, as models for the present.

If the traditionalist overstates his case, as he is prone to do, this should not blind us to the fact that he has a case. "Individual differences" is a blanket term covering a wide variety of personal qualities, from idiosyncrasies with no educational significance to highly specialized aptitudes with very great significance. Moreover, the individuals who are the bearers of these differences are always human beings, and as such they are the embodiment of resemblances or similarities, as well as of differences. They are all sharers in a common humanity. The phrase "common humanity" is, after all, more than a sentimental expression of one's kinship with all one's fellow men. It points to capacities and traits in the development of which educationists have always seen the primary reason for their own vocation. Aristotle himself gave a clear lead in this respect with his concept of human excellence. Let us look more closely, then, at our question: Does education for all mean the same education for all?

In part it does, for everyone needs training in the basic skills underlying all education. These skills are roughly described as "the three R's." This description will suffice if we take "reading" to mean not only the ability to read one's mother tongue, but also to express oneself in it with clarity and grammatical correctness. Again, both intellectual and moral discipline, in the sense explained in Chapters 13 and 14, are an essential part of any education that fits the individual for civilized living. Finally, appreciation of the basic values which we have seen to constitute the meaning and dynamic of our Western civilization, and therefore the core of general education, is an aim with validity for everyone.

Democracy is committed to the task of distributing the benefits of this general education as widely as possible. As we have seen, democracy is committed to this task on two grounds: first, that of duty, in that it concedes the right of every individual to this opportunity, and second, that of interest, for its own workability or survival is at stake in a world which has evolved ideas and regimes implacably hostile to it. No such duty towards the individual is implied in totalitarianism. With regard to interest, raising the level of general education in a totalitarian state is apt to be sensed—with good reason—as a menace to the regime itself.

In that sense, or rather in these senses, education should be the same for all. But our analysis of the meaning of general education also takes account of the aspect stressed by those who would answer our question with a firm negative. Their thinking turns on a different definition of education. They are considering education not so much in terms of human excellence or mental discipline as of personal development or growth, and the concept of personality essentially implies individuality, uniqueness.

The reader will recall that the outcome of education should be to create a personal pattern out of the basic values, a pattern that will be a reflection of significant differences of native aptitude and interests. Our complex society, moreover, needs the development of important specialized talents, and provides abundant scope for their exercise. Our humane and scientific heritage, in other words, is a "house of many mansions," with ample accommodation for individual differences which have clear significance for personal development and for the needs of a complex and highly dynamic society.

Let us turn to the next main question: What can the schools do, in a specific way, to train the individual for democracy? Today's teachers have been devoting much attention to the question of education for democracy. Indeed, they have been the targets of much criticism on this score, and the gist of the criticism has been the claim that one *cannot* teach democracy. This line of criticism has enough truth in it to lead one into serious error; much depends on what is meant by "teaching democracy." The enemies of democracy have put forth spectacular evidence of what can be done to teach their own political philosophies, and these philosophies, it is true, usually represent clear-cut, definite ideologies that for that very reason lend themselves more easily to being taught. But are there not certain features of democracy, features essential to it, that also lend themselves to teaching, both direct and indirect? The outcome of the struggle between political philosophies would be a foregone conclusion if those who oppose democracy were the only ones having potentials of education.

Merely investing the word "democracy" with an aura of emotionalism is not enough. Let us consider what can be done to teach the way of life itself. The school can introduce the child to the idea of law, and inculcate in him the right attitude to law. In school, the pupil finds himself a member of a fairly large association, with its own special structure, imposing limits on individual freedom in order that it can function smoothly. Operating under definite rules and regulations that are seen by the pupils to be necessary for the general good, and not going beyond this reasonable minimum, which is presented as something to be taken seriously and obeyed, the school can instil in the child the first article of the democratic credo: government *of* the people. The school may proceed further and enlist the co-operation of the older pupils in drawing up these rules and regulations, and in this it contributes to implementing the principles of government *by* the people.

The school can give experience and training in co-operative thinking. This is the sort of thinking that takes place in discussion at its best. The thinking is co-operative in the sense that it is directed at the solution of a shared or group problem, with each member of the group making his contribution to the solution of the common problem. Typically, the outcome does not represent the idea of any particular individual; it is the result of modification and adjustment, representing not the best idea in any absolute or abstract sense, but rather the idea that is most satisfactory to the group as a whole. To put this in another way, the individual who claims that he has the right answer, or who sees the right thing to do, must convince the others that his idea is the best; otherwise, it is simply not the answer.

Certain conditions must be fulfilled if training in this sort of co-operative or shared thinking is to be effective. The common problem must be of a sort about which the group in question has sufficient experience and knowledge in order to examine it in an intelligent manner. Extra-curricular activities, such as athletics, and production of a school magazine or a school play, and the organization of school social functions, offer the best opportunities for the purpose. This satisfies another condition of effective training: the thinking should be practical rather than theoretical; the results of it are to be implemented in practice.

The knowledge that one's thinking will be subjected to this test makes a difference, in that it tends to eliminate frivolity, caprice, contrariness, spurious cleverness, and the like. In short, this knowledge makes for *responsible* thinking. The other form of thinking may be left to the debating society, and it should be practised in moderation, because it is easy for the untrained mind to indulge in intellectual play to an extent that impairs its effectiveness for the more serious endeavor. Straight thinking rather than smart thinking, not just individualism, but responsible individualism, are the aims. It is permissible to expect that such training will have its echoes later on in serious matters, when the young person is tempted to act on individual impulse or inclination, leaving the consequences to take care of themselves, or rather to be taken care of by others.

It was with the object of providing such direct experience of democracy in action that Dewey maintained that the school should be run as a miniature society. Democracy is basically the attempt to find the right *practical* integration of what we described as the fundamental values of political or group life—liberty, equality, and co-operation or fraternity. Participation in this miniature society should foster an appreciation of liberty that is not mere individualism or license, of equality that gives opportunity and scope for the development of valuable personal talents, and of co-operation that does not mean mere conformism.

Such training in the fundamentals of the democratic way will not happen of itself, through a policy of "hands-off" on the part of the teacher. There is nothing about the democratic way of group living that justifies the assumption that pupils will in due course naturally fall into it. Indeed, political history would seem to point in the opposite direction. William Golding's story, *The Lord of the Flies*,[2] is a rather hideous reminder of what could happen to a group of children with all adult direction and control removed. The teacher's guidance is needed, but no rules can be laid down as to what form that guidance should take. All that one can say is that, while the miniature society should be, as Dewey insists, a purified and simplified version of the Great Society, it should provide a genuine preparation for that society. The danger always exists that the preparation will be distorted at the hands of the enthusiast to meet the needs of a more or less ill-considered theory.

As an example of this type of distortion, consider the principle of equality. Sentimentalists have advocated the curious idea that it is undemocratic for the school to do anything calculated to make pupils conscious of inequalities. In following this path of reasoning, they would eliminate competition in any form—the less gifted should not be made to feel "dumb," and the more gifted to feel "uppity." Apart from the fact that such a view is altogether out of line with the society for which the school is supposed to be preparing the individual, the psychology of it is mistaken. Normally, the

[2] Penguin Books: 1960.

clever person does not tend to see his cleverness as a reason for looking down on his fellows—there are always so many points at which he meets them on even, or less than even, terms. Nor does the less-gifted person usually develop any unhealthy feeling of inferiority—there is nothing unhealthy about admiration for one who can do what he himself cannot do. When the contrary happens, it is probably due to adult reactions, whether of teacher, or parent, or both. For the teacher, in particular, it is difficult not to view cleverness as something to be openly applauded, and stupidity as something to be met with impatience and even contempt.

Educational writers have dealt very fully with the above aspects of our problem, and the schools have attempted to implement these authors' ideas in practical ways. Another aspect of this question which has received less attention, if indeed it has received any, deserves our consideration. This is the matter of fostering a fundamental attitude or outlook with regard to democracy (rather than providing specific experiences), and it is of sufficient importance to merit discussion at some length.

19 *Democracy and Education: The Fundamental Outlook*

In the twentieth century, democracy has been confronted with a flat denial of its claims to be the only form of government that commends itself both to the conscience and the intelligence of men. This is not to say that democracy found practical acceptance before the twentieth century. Throughout the history of Western civilization, government rested on naked power, reinforced typically by the sanctions of custom and religion. But the idea of government by the people for the people spread both among philosophers and practical reformers, and in the French Revolution it received a spectacular expression which, though so short-lived, left behind it an ineffaceable political memory.

By the end of the nineteenth century, or, more exactly, by 1914, the future of Western civilization—in a word, progress—had become definitely identified in men's minds with the continued development of Western capitalistic democracy, represented in different manner and degree in the great Western nations, France, Germany, Great Britain, and the United States of America. Men were beginning to accept the principle that the ultimate test of government is always its impact on personality—the extent to which government provides, in its own special ways, opportunity and scope for personal development. The Western democracies still had a long way to go, but they were moving in the right direction. It is this last proposition that has been openly challenged in our day. Whatever the differences between communism and fascism, these regimes are at one in presenting this challenge. To appreciate the nature and seriousness of the challenge, let us examine it from the point of view of the more fundamental needs or motives that operate in the field of politics.

One of these basic motives is the desire for material welfare, for the necessities, amenities, and luxuries of living. Communism challenges democracy on this count. To be sure, the actual standard of living of the people as a whole may be far lower under communism than in the great democracies today, but the communists claim that this is a temporary phase of a movement, the ultimate goal of which is the economic emancipation and elevation of the masses. The communists, moreover, can always claim that the founder of their philosophy was Karl Marx, with his call to the masses to unite against a so-called democracy which was using the new technology to abase and enslave them. It is a mistake to view such ideas as mere propaganda geared to the level of understanding of backward races. On the contrary, these ideas are the firmly held credo of the fully-sophisticated Western believers in the communist regime.

Another of the basic motives that operates in the sphere of politics is the desire for power. We are not concerned here with the power motive, generally, but rather with that form of it called "political power." This is the ability to control the community by laws, by direct fiat, or by indirect manipulation in one form or another. Certain features of this motive should be noted.

First, it is not a universal motive, like the biological needs for food, sex satisfaction, shelter, and the rest. If we think of these latter as inherited appetites, the desire for power is an acquired appetite, like the need for alcohol or narcotics. This means, in effect, that it is only after experience and enjoyment of power that the desire for it is likely to develop and function as a strong drive *per se*. Power is sought in the first instance as a means to the satisfaction of other needs.

For example, power becomes connected with the interest in material needs and satisfactions, and, as with the miser's interest in gold, the means becomes the end, so that—again as with the miser —the new drive may come to dominate behavior. This is probably the truth of the matter when the ardent political reformer is said to be driven, not by any desire for the betterment of his fellows, but by a selfish desire for power. His motive is initially honest philanthropy, a passionate urge to do something to remove abuses and ameliorate the condition of his fellows. Having secured the necessary power for this purpose, however, the maintenance of his power becomes in due course an end in itself—the acquired taste grows into an imperious appetite, and he rationalizes his behavior by persuading himself that no one else can perform his function as well as he can.

Again, power becomes tied up with what the social psychologists call the "in-group," or the "we-group," feeling, the protection and maintenance of the way of living of a particular community. Particularly important is the protection of the group ways against the use of power, especially naked power or force, on the part of an outsider. This is the basis of what appears at a higher level of organization as the feeling for national liberty, and, in spite of the fact that group sentiment at this level is acquired as the result of largely direct, deliberate teaching, it can develop into one of the most lively and intense sentiments of *homo socius*. In its inception, the sentiment is negative in character, the reaction against power from without. It is thus compatible with placid acquiescence in the open use of naked power by an *insider*, one accepted as himself a member of the group.

Democracy arose out of this very issue of the exercise of power by insiders. Government by the people meant that all members of the group should share somehow in the running of the community. As a matter of political history, the issue arose at the higher, more complex levels of organization, where class divisions and class consciousness developed to the extent that particular groups came to be regarded as outsiders in so far as the masses were concerned. As outsiders, they found their authority increasingly challenged.

On the one hand, political thinkers moved, more or less gropingly, in the direction of democracy. In Western civilization, the beginnings of such practical political speculations can be discerned very clearly in the sixteenth and seventeenth centuries. Some of the thinkers (Thomas More, for example) presented—and disguised—

radical ideas in the form of utopias, while others (such as Thomas Hobbes) presented a political philosophy expressly aimed at confuting the idea of government by the people. In the eighteenth century, the movement towards a democratic political philosophy had its culmination in Rousseau's *Social Contract*. On the other hand, these underground rumblings erupted here and there in revolutionary outbursts, some of them, such as the Puritan revolution in England, the French Revolution, and the American War of Independence, leaving a permanent imprint on the political consciousness of the West.

We are not concerned here with the problem that was central for Rousseau, namely, that of the kind of political machinery best calculated to secure and maintain the sovereignty of the Sovereign People. He considered that perfect democracy was possible only in small communities, such as ancient Athens and the small Swiss cantons (of the latter he had personal experience), where the people could act directly to make and unmake laws. Rousseau had to concede that in large associations, such as the Western nations, one must have recourse to indirect or representative democracy. Our interest here is in one special aspect of representative democracy, namely, the manner in which, in spite of its defects and faults, the people who have become used to it have come to regard it as so vitally important that they will not tolerate any surrender or limitation of their rights under it.

The question is clearly not a matter of the exercise of power generating an appetite for power. The power implied in the right to vote is too vague to operate in that way. True, it is definite enough at election time, which led Rousseau to observe that under representative democracy the people are free only on that occasion. But such occasional enjoyment of the luxury of power does not account for the attitude in question. Individuals who do not take the trouble to exercise the vote would react violently to the idea of forfeiting the right to vote. In such cases, they appear to take a childish satisfaction in the mere idea that they have power if they choose to use it, an attitude akin to the ego enhancement of the little boy who dons a cowboy outfit, complete with gun and holster. Shakespeare seems to have considered this type of behavior in a similar manner, if we are to judge by one of his many sidelights on the mind of "the common people." In *Coriolanus*, for instance, the citizens take counsel together about voting for Coriolanus as consul:

> *First Citizen*: If he do require our voices, we ought not to deny him.
> *Second Citizen*: We may, sir, if we will.
> *Third Citizen*: We have power in ourselves to do it but . . .[1]

The citizens continue the fatuous discussion of their own political importance, a discussion that dissolves into silliness, and that points to the opinion, expressed frequently in Shakespeare's works, that the multitude is at bottom good-hearted, though always muddle-headed.

The story of the struggle for democracy, wherever that struggle has taken place, would seem to show, however, that the ordinary man's concern with his own *political* status is not to be thus lightly dismissed. On the contrary, it expresses a fundamental need of his nature, and it comes to be bound up with his sense of personal worth and dignity. The feeling that he is of no account in politics comes to mean—what it really is—that a very important region of his life is governed by *force*. It may take him a long time to come to see the matter in that way; custom and direct education may operate for centuries to cloud his vision. But once his feeling for political freedom is aroused, the point of no return is reached. From then onward, any regime that implies denial of the claims of awakened personality must reckon with the new factor as a continuous threat to its existence.

In less-developed societies, where the seed of democracy has not yet taken root, the way is wide open for anti-democratic regimes to establish themselves. These governments need only minister to the desire for material betterment and general security, and this they may be well fitted to do. It is thus easy to understand why the democracies may be at a disadvantage in commending their way of life to underdeveloped peoples.

The more crucial question today, however, is of another sort. What is there about the principles of communism that tends to

[1]*Coriolanus*, II, iii.

seduce individuals reared in the democratic tradition from their loyalty to that way? The evidence is already all too ample that communism possesses some element that appeals powerfully to certain people—very often to people of the educated, intellectual classes. That element is clearly something other than the desire for material betterment or for power.

The increasing dominance of science and technology on a grand scale probably plays a rôle here. Science and technology represent an orderly world, one with no place for the capricious, the unpredictable. When minds accustomed to moving about in such a tidy world turn to the world of politics, their natural impulse is to think in terms of stability, order, and control. Democracy, with its instability and seeming lack of any clear principles to give it direction, no longer makes sense to them. They are then apt to turn to a body of theories that they feel has "method" in it, and Marxism appears to them to be just such a philosophy.

These persons see in Karl Marx the Newton of political science, the one who provides a foundation on which science can build. Is this the reason, or part of the reason, for the rather shocking defection to communism in our own day of individuals of the highest scientific attainments? Is it not likely, again, that the great industrial corporations, despite their official opposition to communism, are nonetheless fostering an outlook and a spirit alien to democracy?

Another factor that penetrates even more deeply into the mind of the individual, and that is more general in its influence on him is *the need to believe*. This need tends to assert itself in all matters that are felt to be vitally important but not amenable to the definite procedure of scientific investigation. The question of how the body politic should be organized, of the individual's part in it, his rights, privileges, and duties, becomes this kind of an issue, once the social and political order sanctioned by custom and tradition has been disrupted and shorn of its old authority. It is then that men feel the need for an *ideology*.

The word "ideology" has come to possess two quite different meanings (if we ignore the loose usage of it in ordinary parlance). Karl Mannheim used the term to denote the general outlook, extending even to the world-view, or *Weltanschauung*, of a particular social class.[2] The social class to which the individual belongs, Mannheim contended, determines not only his ideas of others and his attitude towards them, but his view of life generally. We wish to use the word "ideology" in its second sense, however, the sense implied by Napoleon, when he referred contemptuously to ideologues." In this sense, an ideology is a systematically thought-out plan or pattern which the believer accepts in its entirety as right for the body politic. It is, in other words, a blueprint for society, the inspiration and direction for all efforts at social reform. For the believer, it acquires a powerful emotional appeal, functioning as a religion, with its own special orthodoxy, any deviation from which cannot be tolerated.

Marxism operates as an ideology in this sense, offering a body of definite beliefs and clear-cut answers in a region of living where matters are unstable and unpredictable. There is an element in human nature that responds to the idea of a final resting place for the questing and baffled mind. Communism can and does present itself as answer to the groping mind. Its claim, moreover, that history is on its side enhances its appeal. Democracy and communism thus appeal to two quite different needs: democracy to the need for a measure of autonomy, the need to feel that one counts in the running of the body politic, and communism to the need for something definite and final in the way of political belief. This is the essence of the cold war on the spiritual level. Furthermore, it is the theory of communism, the imaginative picture it presents, that carries the appeal. This is a clear advantage in the struggle, since it is in the nature of the communist regime that, once it has been accepted and imposed, the point of no return is reached.

Democracy can have no truck with any such detailed image of the "perfect" society. In so far as such an idea plays a part at all, it is on the purely imaginative, artistic level. The imaginative projections that have appeared in the course of our civilized history —Plato's *Republic* in the ancient world; Thomas More's *Utopia* and Francis Bacon's *Atlantis* in the Renaissance; H. G. Wells' *Men like Gods*, Edward Bellamy's *Looking Backward, 2000-1887*, together

[2]Karl Mannheim, *Ideology and Utopia.*

with Aldous Huxley's *Brave New World* and George Orwell's *1984* in modern times—have not functioned as ideologies, for an ideology is a utopia taken seriously.

There are two reasons why a democracy may not offer its believers anything in the way of an ideology. First, such an offering would imply the ability to foresee the course of historical development. The political prophets during the feudal era had no intimation of the coming of the capitalistic era. To anticipate the future in the concrete, detailed terms implied in Marxism or in any other ideology is a much more difficult matter, and today its very possibility may be discounted. A few decades ago, pacifism, in the sense of the rejection of war as a way of settling international disputes, was still an arguable matter. This is no longer so. Cuba can defy the mighty United States in a manner that was unthinkable before the menace of "the bomb" made an end of the case for war. This is but one of a number of instances that could be cited to point up the fact that it is democracy, with its non-committal attitude to the shape of things to come, that can claim to be on the side of history.

The second reason why a democracy cannot offer its believers an ideology is that an ideology, in the present sense of the word, is at variance with the very spirit of democracy, and in practice it would tend to turn democracy into some form of totalitarianism. Democracy would acquire an orthodoxy, to which its believers would become emotionally as well as intellectually committed, and that would mean the end of the flexibility which is the essence of democracy. The logic of democracy is the logic of experience, of events, as opposed to the ideologist's armchair logic.

Does this mean, then, that democracy has nothing to offer to which the believer can pin his faith? Is democracy therefore reduced to mere political opportunism? Is the belief in anything that would provide inspiration for political striving, a solid basis for enthusiasm and faith, thus discounted in advance?

The answer to all of these questions is, of course, an emphatic "no." Democracy has a credo no less binding on the believer than the articles of faith to which the ideologist must pledge himself. That credo is found in those fundamental moral values to which we have already drawn attention, values that stem from a common root, respect for personality. The final verdict on any political system is reached in terms of that standard. It is not a standard which admits of any rigid, mechanical application, but it is nonetheless valid on that account.

John Dewey, in *The Quest for Certainty*,[3] makes an impressive case for the view that obsession with the idea of certainty or finality in knowledge has been a main impediment to man's efforts to understand his environment and to come to terms with it. We can accept this thesis without committing ourselves to the general philosophy of pragmatism that Dewey advocates. The idealist or the modern realist would have no difficulty in reconciling Dewey's thesis with his own conception of the nature of truth. With respect to morals and politics, in particular, one can see the importance of putting the intelligent human being on his guard against one of the dominant drives of his nature, the desire for certainty. The argument is unanswerable as directed against fanaticism in personal morals and ideology in politics.

May we not question, however, whether *all* is uncertain, even in this uncertain field? For reasons that we have already indicated, it does not seem possible to assign the same pragmatic status to the basic moral values, to consider them in principle as provisional, tentative, and open to revision. To regard them thus is to confuse the principles themselves with their practical applications, the latter being clearly a matter of intelligent adjustment to circumstances. After all, without the acceptance, implicit or explicit, of some such guiding principles, pragmatism is blind, a matter of applying a method that works, but that works towards something we know not what. All we are saying here is that, as far as *homo socius* is concerned, the basic moral values are the core of that humanism which pragmatism makes its over-riding end.

Viewing democracy in this light, we can come to terms with a question that has reappeared from time to time in the history of ethical philosophy: Is there any valid and significant distinction between private and public morality? In other words, is the moral code for individuals in their relationships to one another equally

[3]John Dewey, *The Quest for Certainty* (New York: Minton, Balch & Company, 1929).

binding on states in their relationships to other states and to their own subjects? A totalitarian regime—communist, fascist, or other— is committed to a definite stand on this issue: the interests of the state are paramount, always. Whether these interests be defined in terms of the furtherance of an ideology or in terms of the promotion of national greatness, they automatically take precedence over the interests of the individual. This is what inevitably happens in practice, whatever the official philosophy of the regime may be.

Modern totalitarianism is thus not a matter of a double standard in morals, the political versus the personal or private standard. The double standard is of earlier origin; it arose out of regimes properly described as "political absolutisms." The regimes of the Caesars and of the kings throughout Western history who regarded their kingdoms as their personal estates were of this type. Absolutist governments in the past typically accorded their subjects a large measure of freedom in religion, custom, artistic expression, and personal morals, so long as these modes of behavior did not obviously clash with the specific interests of government. The phrase "reasons of state" had its origin in this connection, and it clearly implied a moral dichotomy or double standard.

Democracy repudiates the double standard of absolutism, and it also reverses the single standard of modern totalitarianism. In the final analysis, *homo socius* the individual takes precedence over *homo politicus* the subject. The basic moral values binding on *homo socius* are written into the commission of *homo politicus* as an overall directive, leaving him wide latitude for practical implementations. The one kind of latitude that the commission may not allow is that of using power to sacrifice individuals here and now on the plea that such use of power is only temporary, that *homo politicus* will divest himself of power once his political purpose is achieved. The democrat rejects this plea, first, on principle—it is a denial of the spirit of democracy, and second, on the practical ground that he knows full well that a power élite never has acquiesced and never will acquiesce in the surrender of its power.

To sum up, in addition to the more specific training in the way of providing experience of democratic law and of co-operative thinking and acting, the school should do what it can to foster the general, fundamental outlook that we have attempted to indicate in this chapter. What can the school do in this regard? First, it can provide training in disciplined thinking in the humanities generally. This is simply part of its proper task of providing a general education. Again, the school subject with the most direct significance in this connection is history. This should also do much to free the idea of democracy from the parochial connotations to which we referred earlier. It should, for example, dispose of the naïveté that regards democracy as a gift which a benevolent people can bestow on a backward neighbor, like a gift of up-to-date agricultural implements, with a few advisors to show how the implements work.

The one political mechanism essential to democracy is that of free, periodic elections, a criterion to be kept firmly in mind in view of the fact that the evangelists of Marxism, communism, and fascism have misused the name of democracy in their attempts to make their own regimes smell more sweetly to the masses. In history, however, the emphasis is not on democracy as a political mechanism, but on a more general concept, on democracy as a spirit that has not only managed to survive, but that has even derived fresh sustenance from, the recurring blights of tyranny and persecution. That is, after all, a more impressive argument for democracy than any specific considerations that might be adduced in support of it.

Clearly, those who insist that democracy cannot be taught are right if they mean that democracy is not just another subject to be put on the curriculum, but they are far from right if they mean that this part of the young person's education can be safely left to take care of itself.

20   *Education and the Social Sciences*

The twentieth century has seen another change which is having, and will continue to have, very far-reaching consequences for education. This is the appearance of a large and increasing number of professional students of education who have been keeping abreast of developments in psychology and the social sciences, with the express purpose of detecting facts and principles that have a bearing on education, and of inferring from them desirable changes in the educative process. This is a situation that is beyond a doubt peculiar to the present century. The interest of educationists in philosophy and psychology (the two disciplines were not clearly distinguished from one another in the past) is of course no new thing. But this interest usually meant that the educationist had accepted, more or less explicitly, a definite philosophic system, and developed his educational ideas in the spirit of it. Froebel's thinking, for example, was dominated by the philosophic system of idealism.

Philosophers, for their part, were apt to be interested in education, and some of them have made a contribution to educational thinking. This interest was, however, only incidental, and their contribution was an afterthought, having no clear connection with their philosophy. John Locke's famous *Essay Concerning Human Understanding* has, for example, no more connection with his well-known *Thoughts Concerning Education* than the fact that they were both written by the same man. Herbert Spencer's *Essay on Education* was not at all consciously inspired by his philosophy; it was written simply to challenge the dominant position of the classics in education, and to make a case for science on the curriculum. The case of Herbart, it is true, was different. Like John Dewey, in the present century, Herbart derived certain practical educational principles and procedures from his system of philosophy and psychology, and, like Dewey, his practical inferences exercised a profound influence for many years on teacher-training institutions.

But the change to which we referred is something very different from a casual liaison between education and the psychological and philosophical disciplines. It had its beginning when the universities recognized education as an academic subject in its own right. The result was a broader outlook on the subject, and particularly a tendency to link it with psychology and the social sciences. Dewey himself was a main stimulus to this movement, with his insistence that the ideas and practices of traditional education were quite out of line with the world for which education was supposed to be a preparation.

Teacher training institutions were staffed with an increasing number of students who had specialized in education, and who thus found themselves in the key position of being teachers of teachers. In the past, of course, teacher-training colleges had paid some attention to psychology and to the social sciences. In practice, such studies were never taken very seriously. The really telling impact of the professional students of education on the teacher-training institutions is a feature peculiar to this century. The impact has come from persistent effort to modify educational theory and practice in the light of established principles of psychology and social science.

Let us consider first the general problem of deducing practical applications from such principles. It is a mistake to assume that practical applications here are the straightforward matter that they are in the physical sciences. The applications of mathematics and physics to engineering, for example, are themselves a matter of exact science. Once they are worked out, there is no question of their validity. Experiment is always possible, and decisive. Clearly, this is not the case in education.

The fairer and more instructive comparison would be with the practical applications, not of the physical but of the biological sciences. Consider, for example, the applications of biology to medicine. While experiment in this field is by no means the direct, definitive matter that it is in engineering, it is nevertheless possible, and medical progress has mainly been due to it. To a certain extent, the same kind of experimentation has been available in education. The experimental animal has been used in education as in medicine, with certain conclusive results regarding the psychology of learning. In medicine, let us recall, the end or aim is clear-cut—the prevention and cure of disease—and, moreover, it is usually clear whether or not the end is being attained. Wherever there is a comparable problem in education, as is often the case in the learning of school subjects, experiment can yield results that are directly utilizable. With the broader, more general problems of education, however, the case is different.

The point that we wish to make becomes clearer when we examine a few practical examples from the fields of psychology, sociology, and general philosophy. The principles that we shall cite are in themselves sound and important; it is the practical inferences that are in question. In the discussion that follows, "principle" means sound principle, and "inference" means questionable or even wrong inferences. Let us begin with consideration of psychological principles.

Principle. In reading, one perceives the word as a whole, unitary object with a distinctive form, not as an assembly of separate letters.

Inference. Reading should be taught by the "word" method, the "look and say" method, as it used to be called. The child should learn to recognize and name a word as he learns to recognize and name any other object. The analysis of the word into letters will occur of itself in due course.

Experiment has indeed shown that the word is perceived as a whole. But the same is also true of *letters.* Each letter has a distinctive form, which is perceived directly. Learning to associate the letter forms with distinctive sounds is a much simpler task than learning to associate words with their correct names. The number of letter sounds is quite small, in English not in excess of forty. The number of words in the possession of the child, even when he begins school, has been shown to be larger than the teacher gives him credit for, and the number that he has to learn to recognize before he becomes a competent reader is very large.

To add to the child's difficulty, many words do not have very distinctive forms, and are easily confused with other words. If the child depends on the word method alone, he is going to have difficulty in getting on easy terms with the many acquaintances he will make during his school life. Today, advocates of the word method would admit this limitation and supplement it by teaching phonics, but to begin with, they were inclined to adhere strictly to a method which appeared to have the support of psychology. Here we have a case of an actually incorrect inference from a correct principle.

Principle. Learning comes easily and naturally when the individual is directly interested in what he is learning.

Inference. The school should place the emphasis on subject matter in which the pupil is directly interested, or—alternative inference—the teacher has failed to the extent to which he has come short of arousing direct interest in what he is teaching.

Our examination of this issue earlier in the book showed the fallacy of both inferences. We drew attention to forms of interest other than direct or immediate interest, and we made it clear that, because of the very nature of its task, the school must trust mainly to these other forms. What psychology does show is that interest *of some kind* must be aroused if we are to avoid a situation so unnatural as to be devoid of any true educational value.

Principle. Formal exercise of capacities such as memory, imagination, or reasoning does not result in any general development of these capacities in the manner in which exercise of a muscle results in its general strengthening. Or, in other words, "transfer of training" does not occur as a matter of course.

Inference. There is no such thing as formal training or "transfer of training," and one subject of study is as good as another for educational purposes. Our discussion of this issue pointed out how seriously misleading this inference has been in education.

Principle. Individual differences—the intellectual and emotional traits that give every personality its uniqueness — have important implications for education.

Inference. Individual differences are the most important consideration in education, and school curricula and teaching methods should be explicitly devised to minister to their expression and development.

On the contrary, education is concerned in the first instance not with the differences between individuals, but with the similarities that are the core of their common humanity. The basic traits that men have in common, in particular the traits that civilized men have in common, are the primary concern. As for individual differences, the attention that they receive will depend on two factors: their importance or value as human traits, and, again, the practical conditions under which education is carried on. Mass education will impose more or less serious limitations on what even the most conscientious teacher can do in the way of coping with individual differences.

Let us turn now to an examination of several sociological principles.

Principle. In our rapidly changing civilization, the rising generation will find itself in a world that is in many important ways very different from that of the previous generation.

Inference. The school must adjust *its* program to a rapidly changing society.

The inference here has been interpreted in different ways. Some educationists have taken it to mean that the school must try to anticipate important changes and prepare the pupil in advance to meet them. In these times it is asking too much of any institution to anticipate changes only one generation ahead; even politicians aspiring to the name of statesmen are apt to be left looking foolish when they attempt this. Apart from this fact, is the idea that the school should adapt its program to a changing society not really prompted by a tendency all too common among grown-ups, an unwillingness to leave the young to live their own lives and to learn from their own mistakes, the tendency in this case being projected into the future?

Again, the inference is taken to mean that, whatever else the school may do to the individual, it should above all teach him to be *adaptable*. Does this mean anything more than that the school should teach him to *think*? Educationists who stress the importance of this flexible, adaptable mind, and who deplore the inculcation of rigid ideas and attitudes, are beyond question right. Even with regard to basic moral principles, there must be flexibility in application, which is another way of saying that they should be applied intelligently. Is the same not true of the other basic values with which education is concerned?

To foster an appreciation of good thinking, scientific and non-scientific, here and now; to develop a preference for the higher forms of artistic enjoyment; to produce a mind that is at home in the regions of the general and the abstract; to form a will disciplined to resist distraction and to persist in the pursuit of serious purpose—these are the tasks of the school. They are its way of preparing the individual for an ever-changing, unpredictable society—and this way should be sufficient. The sociological principle that the young will face a different world from that of their elders, true though it is, does not yield any clear-cut, specific inference with respect to changes in the school.

Principle. The home today is not doing enough, if indeed it is doing anything, towards moral and religious training of the young.

Inference. This and other forms of training heretofore left to the home must now be undertaken by the school. We have already pointed out, in Chapter 8, how this inference, if taken at face value, could seriously interfere with the work which the school is expected and fitted to perform.

Next we shall choose as illustrations several principles that are philosophical rather than scientific, but that represent the same tendency towards hasty inference entailing important practical consequences. We shall cite two examples from the philosophy of pragmatism, and a third from the field of ethical theory, that is, detached from any particular school of philosophy.

Principle. Truth is ultimately relative to human needs, and is not something static which, when discovered, is discovered once for all.

Inference. The static curriculum implicitly accepted by schools in the past is in principle unsound.

The curriculum should be flexible, reflecting the changing character of the environment and the demands of adjustment. But even granting the pragmatic view of the nature of truth, does this educational inference follow? Education is concerned, after all, with the young and immature. Whichever philosophy we adopt—pragmatism or any of its rivals—is there not always a definite body of skills and knowledge that exists for the young to learn if they are going to be put *au courant* with the society into which they are born? True, knowledge and culture generally, always in a state of flux, are today changing at a greatly increased tempo, but is that a matter with any real practical implication for school children?

Principle. Action is biologically prior to knowledge, and doing to thinking. Biologically considered, the *raison d'être* of thinking is better adjustment to environment.

Inference. In education, thinking and the acquisition of knowledge should be linked to action. Hence the stress on activity programs, projects, and the like. Such programs put the young person in the rôle of active, interested discoverer, thus placing learning in its natural context.

Again we must ask whether the inference necessarily follows from the principle. Accepting the pragmatic view of the origin of thinking and the practical significance of knowledge (typically also the view of the biologist), does it follow that in the very latest product of evolution, civilized society, acquisition of knowledge should always properly occur in the context of action? To put the matter another way: Is it not reasonable to suppose that at that level it may not only be sound but actually necessary to impart knowledge directly to the young? Is it not reasonable to suppose even further that knowledge may become a matter of intrinsic interest, the satisfaction of a need which has also evolved, the need to know for the sake of knowing—curiosity, in a word?

However that may be, let it be conceded that there is this natural biological relationship between knowing and doing. Teachers should make use of it, and pupils should be given experience of it. But it is quite another matter to attach such great importance to it that teachers are left with the impression that in so far as they depart from it they are guilty of poor teaching.

Principle. The only kind of compulsion possessing ethical quality is the inner compulsion to regulate conduct in the light of standards and ideals sanctioned by the individual's own nature as a rational creature; or, more simply, the only discipline with ethical value is self-discipline.

Inference. Adults should accustom the young to self-discipline from the outset by presenting reasons for any controls they impose.

The issue here is that between authority and liberty in education, to which we have already drawn attention. The reader may recall that the matter is by no means as simple as the above inference would imply.

One could cite many other examples of the difficulty of drawing the right practical inferences from principles established by the social sciences and by general philosophy. What concerns us in this study, however, is the fact that here we seem to hit upon the underlying cause of educational tensions characteristic of the present day. These tensions find expression in the current and often acrimonious dispute between the progressives and the conservatives, or traditionalists, in education. The dispute will continue as long as professional students of education insist on trying to bring educational practice into line with advances in psychology, sociology, and the allied disciplines, and so advocate changes which clash with beliefs and practices sanctioned by tradition and seemingly supported by practical experience. Three points should be noted with respect to this basic tension.

First, the tension is permanent. Progressives, in their enthusiasm for passing on to the schools forthwith the benefit of the latest developments in psychological and social science, will tend to forget that practical application here is not the straightforward, unambiguous thing it is in the physical sciences, and conservatives, faced with innovations which they have good reason for thinking wrongheaded, will tend to repudiate the progressive and all his works, and hold to the good old way as the only safe way.

Second, the disputants are at cross purposes. The conservative directs his attack against the principles themselves, rather than the inferences from them, while the progressive, rightly believing that the principles are sound and important, attributes to the conservative a mulish adherence to the past, or, at best, a perverse effort to defend vested interests in education. This accounts for the acrimony of the dispute.

Third, the tension is an indication of vitality. Its disappearance would mean one of two things: uncritical acceptance of whatever happens to be new, or unthinking commitment to what seems to have worked well enough in the past—and the one would be as unhealthy as the other.

What of the practical teacher in this situation? Clearly, both of the opposing forces impinge directly on him. During his period of training, the predominating influence is that of the progressivist, intent on blazing new trails, an influence, moreover, to which his own young enthusiasm readily responds. When he leaves the training college for real life (which here means the classroom), he finds himself in direct contact with parents and other adults, for the most part constitutionally distrustful of change, especially in education. Moreover, in the light of the concrete realities of the classroom, what he learned about the psychology and the philosophy of education begins to appear remote, irrelevant, and unhelpful. Some of it may even appear to be positively wrong. This very practical aspect of teacher education deserves more careful consideration than it is usually afforded.

21 *Conservatism, Progressivism, and the Practical Teacher*

What practical value for the teacher have psychology, sociology, philosophy, and the philosophy of education, the subjects that have always figured more or less in his training? All teachers have asked themselves this question at some time in their careers. During their period of training, they have sought an answer from their instructors. The answer, if not evasive, was apt to be unconvincing. It seems a very natural question, when one considers the nature of these disciplines. The psychologists, for example, do not speak with one voice. They adhere to different schools of thought, such as the connection bond or stimulus and response school, the behaviorist school, the *Gestalt* or organismic school, and the psychoanalytic school.

The student no doubt finds that these schools of thought have much in common, but he also finds that they leave him with very different pictures of the mind. His instructor may point to specific cases in the teaching of school subjects where one or another of the psychological schools is distinctly helpful, and he may also add the fact that the study of psychology can make a valuable contribution to one's general culture—but even then he is not satisfactorily answering the question asked. Heretofore, the teacher probably decided that he could get along well enough without a clear answer, but today, as we indicated in the preceding chapter, he finds himself hard pressed to come to terms with the question.

The manner in which the teacher answers the question of the practical value of the subjects studied in his training will determine whether he throws his lot with the progressives or the conservatives, and that is a decision which will affect his whole professional attitude and outlook. As a practical teacher, he finds the decision far from an easy one. He encounters apparent errors and extravagances on the part of the reformers, and, as a good craftsman, he wants to have no part in such extreme views. He also meets with many instances of outmoded ideas and procedures that have been definitely discredited, and, as a liberal-minded practitioner, he is repelled by them.

In this quandary, he is not unlikely to have recourse to Mercutio's "a plague on both your houses!" He concludes, first, that he might as well forget about psychology, philosophy, and the rest in his day-to-day dealings with his pupils, and, second, in so far as his practical efficiency as a teacher is concerned, that the time that he has spent on such studies is time wasted. The object of the present chapter is to show that the first conclusion is, on the whole, right, and that the second conclusion is wrong.

In our discussion of different kinds of knowledge or ways of knowing (Chapter 3), we drew attention to a form of knowledge that we called "intuition," and we pointed out some of the different meanings that philosophers have attached to this word. Locke stated that we have an intuitive knowledge of the existence of God. Bergson used the term to denote the kind of insight manifested in instinct, a more penetrating insight than human reasoning achieves. Still other meanings have been given to this familiar term. Some philosophers have used it to denote the knowledge given in sense perception. Again, when it is inferred that if A is greater than B, and B is greater than C, then A is greater than C, the inference is said to be a matter of intuition. This seems to identify intuition with "reasoning," a use of the word which is surely confusing. Finally, the word "intuition" is used to denote a purely emotional reaction, as when we talk of an "intuitive dislike" of a particular person.

Here, as we pointed out in Chapter 3, we use the word in the sense of a judgment or conclusion that the individual believes to be right, but of the reasons for which he is not conscious, or is at the most vaguely conscious. The fact that knowledge of this sort plays a very important part in the guidance of conduct is beyond question. The learned judge accepts it when he tells the jury that it is their responsibility to decide, in the light of the whole evidence, whether the accused person is guilty or not guilty, and when he reminds them as he often does, that they have not only heard the evidence, but have had the opportunity of observing the general demeanor of the accused in court. As "twelve good men and true," they are asked to give their verdict; they will not be asked for their reasons.

There are those who would explain away intuition as basically only rapid reasoning, but this rather unconvincing interpretation stems from the fact of their thinking that intuition introduces something mysterious and unscientific into psychology, and they dislike it on that account. Intuition does nothing of the sort, unless one rejects the whole concept of the subconscious, a concept in perfectly good standing in psychological science.

Let us examine a few practical illustrations of intuition. The manner in which a good teacher deals with a particular case of insubordination depends on his awareness of the general character of the pupil involved, of the child's home background, the tone of the class as a whole, the size of the class (if he were dealing with one pupil, his treatment of the case might be very different from what he considers right when there are onlookers), and on other factors peculiar to the particular situation. The teacher's emphasis on self-discovery of knowledge as opposed to direct instruction will depend on the size of the class, the general mental calibre of it, and the amount of ground to be covered in the time available. His way of dealing with errors in language and composition, and indeed, his whole approach to that field, will be affected by what he knows of the social and home background of his pupils. His attitude to "individual differences" will be determined by the size of the class and other special circumstances. The good teacher does the right thing, "right" meaning "that which is best suited to the occasions as they arise."

But, it may be objected, does this not reduce good thinking to the exercise of plain common sense? In that case, the objector will insist, there is surely no need for any elaborate professional training; training should take the form of learning on the job. All one can do, the objector continues, is to tell the teacher to use his common sense or "mother-wit," as much of it as he has; if he has not enough of this faculty, he will never make a success of teaching. One can always, of course, put such a teacher in possession of scientifically validated methods that admit of being applied mechanically. But even with the aid of such methods, good teaching demands the frequent use of the faculty which (the objector implies) no training can cultivate—common sense.

To dispose of this argument (which carries weight for many people in and out of the profession), it is enough to point out that the way of knowing that we call "intuition" *can* be cultivated, which is the reason that we call it "intuition" rather than "common sense" or "mother-wit." Common sense implies a capacity possessed by everybody of average intelligence, and not dependent for its effective use on special knowledge or training. In point of fact, the appeal to common sense is often merely a way of belittling the importance of something that the individual is uncomfortably aware of lacking, or, again, a way of repudiating anything savoring of novelty. "Mother-wit" implies native aptitude or intelligence which likewise functions well without benefit of training. Neither term, "common sense" or "mother-wit," is a satisfactory substitute for a capacity that is dependent on training, and training, moreover, of a specific kind.

Intuition, like intelligence in any form, is, of course, affected by growth and general experience. Over and above these general factors, two factors of a more specific kind determine the level on which intuition operates: specialized knowledge and specialized interest. Let us illustrate these factors from classroom teaching.

The teacher's background knowledge of psychology, the social sciences, and philosophy makes for more accurate intuitive judgment in the complex practical situations that he meets from day to day. When he says that he is not aware of making any practical use of such studies, he is right. He is not, and ought not to be, conscious of any such practical applications. Psychology, for example, is a science, and as such is concerned with generalizations about human beings, not with the individual as such. It aims at classifying individuals in terms of general laws or principles. The same holds true for the social sciences and general philosophy. The social sciences are concerned with general laws operating in human society, not primarily with particular circumstances. Philosophy is always moving in the region of the general or abstract. These disciplines, as we have seen, are the basis of any philosophy of education.

The teacher who tries to make conscious use of a philosophy of education in the classroom is mistaken. The attempt will work against the confident, immediate reactions that make good practitioners. The teacher who discounts a philosophy of education as having no relevance to the classroom is equally mistaken; it determines his reactions in ways of which he is unaware, given that his study of it (and of the disciplines underlying it) has been governed throughout by a live professional interest.

The proviso is essential. It takes account of the second factor underlying intuitive judgment: a dominant, specialized interest. The recognition of such a judgment in the practical affairs of living is nothing new in philosophy. Aristotle, in his doctrine of the mean, gives it explicit recognition. His *phronimos*, or prudent man, is one who, by dint of reflection on happiness and the good life, and long training in making right moral choices, acquires a "habit of right judgment," so that for him the choice of the mean comes to be a matter of taste or tact, rather than of explicit thinking. The distinctive quality of the *phronimos* is common sense in moral matters, but a cultivated form of that faculty.

It is not only the teacher's professional training that raises the level of intuitive judgment in day-to-day teaching: his knowledge of the subject that he is teaching operates in the same way. The teacher who manages to keep one step ahead of his pupils in knowledge of the subject might ask what is wrong with such a method. One may feel that there is something far wrong with it, and yet be at a loss for a convincing answer. The answer is, of course, that the more extensive the teacher's knowledge of the subject, the more skilful his presentation is likely to be. It is not just that he has more knowledge to draw on; it is rather that he will draw on it to better purpose. He will, for example, exercise better judgment in deciding what he will stress and what he will pass over as unimportant for the time being. Knowledge of content or subject matter, in other words, has subtle and largely unconscious repercussions on methodology.

The reader may protest that experience belies this statement. A very learned man may be a very poor teacher of the subject in which he is so deeply versed. When this happens—and it happens often—the reason is probably not far to seek: his dominant interest has all along been the extension of his own knowledge. Imparting his knowledge to others (except of course to learned colleagues, which is quite a different matter) has never figured in his mind as an interesting and important activity on its own account. From this point of view, it would seem that there is a distinct advantage in making the teacher's preparation all of a piece, the cultural and the professional parts proceeding concurrently.

One might sum up the matter by saying that the attitude of the teacher in the actual practice of his profession is that of the artist rather than that of the scientist. The artist uses the same direct, intuitive judgment in the creation of his product. To ask the artist why he uses a certain shade of color at a particular point is to invite the simple, and for him, completely adequate answer: "Because it is right." At the same time, it would be quite erroneous to think that his experience, specialized training, and dominant interest are not determining factors. It is clear that the common distinction between the philosophy, the science, and the art of education is soundly made.

A comparison with medicine is pertinent here. The practice of medicine is to some degree (a much larger degree than in the teaching profession) a matter of the conscious, deliberate application of scientific knowledge. But, as the medical profession itself insists, there is an art as well as a science of medicine. The doctor has to rely on his intuition in numerous matters where neither science nor rule-of-thumb can help him—in deciding, for example, how much of his diagnosis and prognosis he will tell the patient.

It is true that the artist strives to produce an aesthetic experience, while the teacher (and also the doctor) seeks a result in the way of knowledge, understanding, or insight. The artist would insist, however, that he, too, contributes his special kind of insight, one not achieved through ordinary thinking. If science is to be invoked in this connection, it will be psychological science in terms of *Gestalt* psychology, with its emphasis on the role of "insight," "totality," and "the demand of the situation." Without committing oneself to the tenets of this school of psychology as a whole, one can appreciate the relevance of certain of its principles to the topic of the present chapter.

Not only in actual teaching is there need for this informed, intuitive judgment; it also plays an important rôle in curriculum-making. Educational administrators—the individuals responsible for devising the educational system, as well as for insuring its effective operation—must rely very largely on this way of thinking. They have to take account of a factor outside of the purview of the ordinary teacher, namely, the regional aspect of education. This refers to a broader milieu than the local conditions, which, as we have seen, the good teacher always keeps in mind, but there is no need for any precise distinction between the two. The region may denote a very broad milieu or a fairly narrow one.

Educational policies and programs will have realistic bearing on the values prevalent in the particular region. The milieu may be as broad as the North American continent. Operating on such a vast scale, the educational leader must be nothing less than a statesman; for the statesman's way of acting is also in the last resort a matter of using the kind of intuition that we have been describing, and he then resembles the artist more than the scientist. On the other hand, the region may be quite narrow, the "Middletown" of the Lynds' well-known studies,[1] for example. Professional training, practical experience of education, and the sociological facts reported by the Lynds, will all function to give the administrator a sense of how to adjust "the eternal verities" of education to this milieu.

It thus appears that there are two contexts in which the basic values of education should find appropriate expression. The first

[1] Robert S. Lynd and Helen Merrell Lynd, *Middletown. A Study in American Culture.* (New York: Harcourt, Brace and Company, 1929). *A Study on Cultural Conflicts.* (New York: Harcourt, Brace and Company, 1937).

of these is the time context, and we have already seen its significance in relation to the twentieth century. The second context is the space or regional. This observation recalls the permanent, fundamental tension that was mentioned in the preceding chapter, the tension traceable to a tendency, on the one hand, to concentrate on educational values in the abstract, and, on the other hand, to allow context, whether of time or place, to figure too largely in one's thinking. The conservative is disposed to err in the former way—and an error it surely is, the error of doctrinairism. In his devotion to values transmitted from the past, the conservative forgets that in the past those values did not exist merely as abstractions in the minds of philosophers, but functioned as the informing principles of a way of life, which meant that they were translated into terms of time and place. It is therefore wrong, though usual, to state that the conservative is "living in the past"; his world is neither the real past nor the living present.

The progressive, taking his cue from the advances in social science and philosophy, is talking sound doctrine when he insists that there must be a vital and vitalizing relationship between the curriculum and the community that it is designed to serve. But this adjustment to time and place may be overdone. It may result in narrowness and parochialism, the universal and timeless elements dropping out of sight altogether, and this is the myopia to which the progressive is peculiarly subject. Where it happens, history and geography become mainly a matter of events, persons, and places "in the news": democracy means what happens during local or national elections, and so forth. This form of progressivism means living in the present, but without the intellectual detachment that makes it possible to evaluate the present. Where the conservative has too little commitment or "engagement" (to borrow the existentialist s word), the progressive has too much of it.

This failing in both instances is, however, one that leans to virtue's side. The training of the practical educationist (whether teacher or administrator) should enable him to appreciate the special virtue of both the conservative and the progressive. This does not mean, however, that he should cultivate an attitude of cool, critical detachment. As a human being, pledged to the task of teaching other human beings, the practical educationist cannot escape involvement in issues that touch his mission so closely. His temperament, if not his intellect, will tend to align him with one side or the other. William James remarked about metaphysical systems that they are at bottom an expression of the particular philosopher's temperament rather than of his intellect. This may or may not be true of systems of general philosophy, but it is probably very largely true of philosophies of education. In philosophies of education, the theme is not primarily the perennial questions posed by the theoretical intelligence, but something that invites the engagement of the whole person, his emotions as well as his intellect, namely, the nature of the good life.

A professional preparation which has accustomed the teacher to think about both the "what" and the "how" of education, which has made him conversant with the best that has been said and done about these topics, and which has left him with a sobering sense of the complexity of it all, will do more than simply raise the level of his practitioner's intuition; it will go far towards preventing any partisanship—intellectual or temperamental—from interfering unduly with the realistic exercise of that capacity.

Part III:

*Notes on some Modern Philosophies
and Their Educational Bearings*

22 *Idealism*

Reference was made, in Parts I and II of this book, to the influence on education of certain schools of speculative philosophy. In this third section, we shall undertake a systematic consideration of those features in the philosophies mentioned that have had an impact on educational thought and practice. The impact might take one of two forms: it might be direct and systematic, in which case the educational philosopher deliberately sets out to deduce an educational theory from a system of philosophy; or, it might take the form of creating an atmosphere or climate of thinking that has discernible effects on education. The outstanding examples of the former type of impact have been idealism and pragmatism. In this and the following chapter, we shall consider the impacts of these two schools.

"Idealism" can be a misleading word with regard to educational philosophy, for it suggests concern for ideals, devotion to the pursuit of higher values. As used in reference to a philosophic system, the word has no immediate implication of this moral or ethical kind. It refers to the cardinal principle that reality is not material but mental in its constitution. "Ideaism" would perhaps be a better word than "idealism."

Plato produced an idealistic philosophic system, and, moreover, deduced from it what Rousseau called "the best treatise on education ever written"—surely a curious judgment from the author of the *Emile*. It is modern idealism, however, with which we are particularly concerned in our examination. This system of philosophy, which dominated philosophic thinking on both sides of the Atlantic throughout the nineteenth century, stems directly from the Irish philosopher Bishop George Berkeley (1685-1753).

Berkeley pointed out that our knowledge of the external world comes in the form of sense impressions. Some of these impressions—colors, sounds, tastes, and smells—clearly depend for their existence on a perceiving mind. If there were no perceiving minds in the world, objects would no longer possess these qualities. In other words, if everyone were color-blind, color would cease to exist. These qualities are therefore mental in character—they are "ideas," as Berkeley called them, using the terminology of his own day.

Thus far, Berkeley's reasoning is in line with that of his great predecessor, John Locke. Locke called these same qualities "secondary qualities," to distinguish them from the "primary qualities," such as size, shape, and solidity. The primary qualities, Locke maintained, inhere in the object itself, and thus have an independent status. Underlying the whole, according to Locke, there is "substance." "Substance" (*sub stans*) is that which possesses the primary qualities. This ultimate reality can never itself be known—only the primary and secondary qualities can become the object of knowledge.

Berkeley begins by asking us to reject altogether from philosophy this notion of substance, the mysterious residue which forever eludes the knowing mind. Any entity which, by definition, is unknowable can hardly have a place in a system of philosophy, Berkeley reasons. Having removed substance, he directs his attack against Locke's account of the primary qualities. Berkeley contends that these qualities, as far as dependence on a perceiving mind is concerned, are precisely in the same position as the secondary qualities. Apart from a perceiving mind, an object can no more be hard or round than it can be blue, yellow, or green. In his attempt to prove this argument, it may be noted that Berkeley made a valuable contribution to the development of psychology. The process of perception is presupposed in the existence of matter. For all objects whatsoever, their *esse* is *percipi*—their being consists in their being perceived.

Berkeley thus accomplished one of the main objects that he had in view, the refutation of materialism. From the days of Democritus onward, the materialist had periodically appeared as the *enfant terrible* of philosophy. In the seventeenth century, materialism had found notable champions, such as Thomas Hobbes in England and Pierre Cassendi (himself, like Berkeley, an ecclesiastic) in France. The traditional attitude of most philosophers and theologians to the materialist had been an essentially defensive one. Their main concern was to show that, over and above the region of matter, there exists the region of mind. The problem was to define the boundaries between the regions of mind and matter. In arguing that the independent, self-subsistent matter of the materialist is a myth, Berkeley carried the war into the enemy's camp, and the materialist found himself faced with the proposition, argued with brilliance and ingenuity, that matter cannot be real, that there can be but one reality, mind.

It may be observed in passing that materialism, in its traditional or crude form, failed to produce a satisfactory rebuttal of Berkeley's argument. By the time that the bases of the idealistic system had been weakened by destructive criticism, the advances of modern science had necessitated a new formulation of the doctrine of materialism.

Berkeley, however, was faced with an immediate difficulty in his theory. If the existence of objects is dependent on a perceiving mind, it would seem to follow that objects would drop out of existence when the perceiving mind is withdrawn, and that the objects are somehow re-created when the perceiving individual again appears on the scene. The world has thus only a purely subjective reality; Berkeley's account of our waking experience seems to rate that experience on the level of the vagaries of dreamland. The opponents of Berkeley's philosophy claim that his victory is too dearly bought, and that, in any case, the facts seem other than he imagined them. There is a regularity, order, or uniformity, an apparent stability in the world that demands explanation. The world is mental or spiritual in its inmost nature but its continuous and permanent existence must be guaranteed.

To meet this difficulty, Berkeley brought in another mind, the mind of God. Over and above the human mind, there is the mind of God, eternal, omnipresent. This is the final ground and surety of the stable order revealed in the world. Inasmuch as the objects of sense experience have a real existence which is not dependent on his mind, then, states Berkeley, "there must be some other mind wherein they exist. As sure, therefore, as the sensible world really exists, so sure is there an infinite, omnipresent spirit who contains and supports it."[1] The line of reasoning which has disposed of materialism thus leads to the solution of still another major philosophic problem, that of the existence of God.

Such, in brief, is Berkeley's statement of idealism, usually referred to as "subjective idealism." The starting point of "objective idealism" is Berkeley's fundamental proposition that the "stuff" of the world is ultimately spiritual or mental. Mind, however, as understood here, is not identical with the individual, finite mind, nor is it conceived as the mind of a Being (Berkeley's God), who somehow stands outside of the world and whose "idea" the world is. For the objective idealist, it is a cosmic, impersonal mind, of which all reality is the manifestation. The crux of the argument is that the constitution of reality and the constitution of thought are fundamentally identical, and thus when we study thought, we are discovering the nature of reality, and, conversely, in so far as we truly apprehend the world, we are penetrating to the realities of thought or mind. The cosmic mind is being revealed in the processes of world-evolution. The objective idealist considers that the human mind is part of the world-process and a manifestation of the cosmic mind.

Science, in so far as it discovers and formulates the laws of nature, is an articulation of this same universal mind. The scientist finds nature "beautiful"—"beautiful" in the sense that it is marvellously tractable to his methods. The idealist, however, sees nothing marvellous in this; the reality that the scientist is called upon to explain is itself reason or mind objectified. In Hegel's view, the real is the rational and the rational is the real. The scientist can read two implications into this apparently circular statement. He need have no qualms about the "reality," i.e. the validity, of the conclusions to which scientific reasoning leads him, and, again, he need have no fear that any piece of reality will prove intractable to the methods of human reason.

Furthermore, the history of human development, as revealed in the rise from barbarism to civilization, in the birth and evolution of

[1]George Berkeley, *Dialogues*, Vol. I, p. 424, ed. A. Campbell Frazer.

institutions, such as language, morality, and social and political forms, is but a movement towards ever clearer and more adequate articulation of the universal Reason as it operates in the human domain. The ultimate reality is variously described by terms such as "absolute mind," "thought," "reason," "spirit," and "consciousness."

This "Hegelian philosophy," as it is called after its main architect, Friedrich Hegel, developed many facets in the course of the nineteenth century. Here we need distinguish only between two of its forms, the religious and the secular. It was the religious form that dominated educational philosophy, and indeed philosophic thinking generally, during the nineteenth century. It found its way into popular philosophical thinking, as is evident from some of the novels of the period.[2]

In the religious form of the Hegelian philosophy, the absolute mind is commonly referred to as God. For the educational thinkers of the time, this interpretation provided both inspiration and direction. The inspiring thought is that of a world in time ever moving towards a more complete expression of the timeless, ultimate Spirit. Man is therefore no mere flotsam and jetsam washed up by the cosmic stream, he is part of that stream. His development is from mere "being" or "existence" to the vastly more adequate reflection of the ultimate Mind represented in the self-conscious personality. The teacher is a principal agent in directing the process to this great issue. The Hegelian system of thought thus contributes a certain nobility and even grandeur of conception to education. When educacation is conceived as the process of actualizing in the young the Reason which is the reality of "all thinking things, all objects of all thought,"[3] then education becomes in truth the noblest profession on earth.

Plato, the idealist of the ancient world, set the example for this mode of thought in his allegory of the cave.[4] Education, according to Plato, is nothing less than a complete turning round of the mind from the contemplation of shams and shadows to the dazzling vision of truth; and some fifty years of education are required to effect this change. Johann Gottlieb Fichte, one of the founders of modern

---

[2]For example, Mrs. Humphrey Ward's *Robert Elsmere* and *David Grieve.*
[3]Wordsworth: *Lines Written Above Tintern Abbey.*
[4]*The Republic.*

idealism, as well as one of its educational interpreters, formulated the mission of education in language reminiscent of the modern after-dinner speech. For the men of his era, however, Fichte's words were far from mere rhapsodizing; they were the avowal of the serious acceptance of a body of philosophic doctrine.

The religious note of idealism is strongly marked in the writings of Friedrich Froebel. His *Education of Man* and *Education by Development* abound in passages expressive of a profoundly religious outlook. These passages appear to be the expression of a simple naïve pietism, but the philosophic tenets of religious idealism are always in the background of Froebel's thinking. These same commitments to religion sophisticated by philosophy, and to philosophy humanized and personalized by religion, are reflected in the thinking of present-day proponents of idealism as an educational philosophy. Consider, for instance, H. H. Horne's well-known definition of education:

> . . . . Education is the eternal process of superior adjustment of the physically and mentally developed, free, conscious human being to God, as manifested in the intellectual, emotional and volitional environment of man.[5]

So much for inspiration. What about direction?

Idealism pointed the way to a curriculum, a curriculum with the authority of a cosmic philosophy behind it. Man's achievements in art, science, morality, and politics were considered a measure of his progress thus far in making his own mind a more adequate reflection of the absolute, objective mind. In art, man was thought to be achieving intimations of absolute beauty. Science was seen to be revealing the nature of the absolute mind as manifested in the so-called material world, the level of "petrified intelligence," as the idealist put it. Man's moral values were believed to be partial and dim reflections of absolute moral goodness.

For the idealist, the social and political institutions developed by man, from the primitive clan to the modern state, likewise represented progressive manifestations of the ideal in political relationships. History thus became an important subject of study.

[5] H. H. Horne, *Idealism in Education* (New York: Macmillan, 1927), p. 285.

Language, the tool that made all of this development possible, was regarded as an expression of reason peculiar to the self-conscious human being, and the study of it was therefore an important part of education. Fichte waxed eloquent concerning the claims of language, especially those of the mother tongue. He even rounded off his argument with the contention that the German language was the highest form of language yet evolved by man. In this contention, however, Fichte was no more dogmatic than Hegel himself, who suggested that the highest form of political development in history was that represented by the contemporary Prussian state. These were but two of the aberrations that tended to make suspect the entire philosophy of idealism.

The philosophy of idealism thus provides a content for education, for general education. The aim of the idealistic approach is to lead the pupil to possession of his spiritual heritage. For the idealist, every form of knowledge to which we have drawn attention in this study, from mere information to the highly articulated systems of philosophy and science, contributes in its own degree to the enrichment of personality by making it a more adequate manifestation of the omnipresent Divine Spirit.[6]

An account of Idealism would be incomplete without some discussion of what we have referred to as its purely secular form—a form that is usually called "absolute idealism." While this form is not as significant from the educational point of view as the religious form, it is important from the philosophical standpoint. It was dissatisfaction with the seeming implications of the secular or absolute form of idealism that resulted in criticism, and in some quarters in outright rejection, of the entire system of idealism.

According to absolute idealism, ultimate reality is timeless, complete, unchanging. We can only know ultimate reality in time as the unceasing flux of the phenomenal world. Human experience, it is true, has its roots in the nature of things; it counts somehow, but the implication of absolute idealism for human values would seem to be disturbing. Man's purposive life—his striving to over-

[6]For a well-reasoned statement in our own century of the practical implications of idealism, consult T. H. Greene, *Liberal Education Reconsidered* (Cambridge: Harvard University Press, 1953).

come imperfection, his battle against evil. his pursuit of the good and the beautiful—is carried on in time, and time is not ultimately real.

The absolute mind is timeless and complete. Hence, imperfection, evil, pain, and ugliness are but appearances after all, according to this philosophy—they are due to man's necessarily partial vision of the picture. Seen in relation to the whole picture, these parts fall into their places as contributory elements in the total perfection. This aesthetic analogy is frequently adduced by exponents of the theory of absolute idealism. It may prove satisfactory to the logical intelligence, but it commends itself less to the moral consciousness. Most disturbing of all is the seeming implication that this doctrine has for the human personality. Conceived as a mere fragment of an ultimate, impersonal mind, the personality seems to lose its status as a free, independent entity; and freedom in some real sense is the core of personality.

Consideration of this latter aspect of idealism led to a reconstruction of philosophic theory along lines that placed more positive emphasis on human personality and values. The point of view of those who favored this new position found its clearest and most vigorous expression in the philosophy of pragmatism.

23 *Pragmatism*

"Pragmatism" is the original and perhaps the most widespread designation of the philosophy that we shall examine in the present chapter. "Instrumentalism," a word popularized by John Dewey, is a term that has found favor with educationists to characterize the same philosophy. A third term, "humanism," is also used to denote this philosophy. The theory of pragmatism was first set forth in a systematic way by the American philosopher and psychologist William James. James used the theory to provide basis and justification for certain beliefs, such as the freedom of the will, immortality, and the existence of God, that did not appear to lend themselves to logical demonstration. It was John Dewey's statement of pragmatism, however, that gave the philosophy the broad currency that it enjoyed for several decades and that also developed its far-reaching implications for educational thought and practice.

Pragmatism denotes (a) a theory concerning the nature or criterion of truth, and (b) a method for discovering truth. The second meaning is implied in the first; we shall therefore consider the pragmatic view of the nature, and hence the criterion or test, of truth. The final test of truth is the practical one: how will the proposition, belief, theory, or system work out if actually put into practice? Will it advance man in his task of adjusting himself to his world? Or does it appear to be without significance for man's better adjustment, or even to be a definite hindrance to it? What practical difference does the belief or theory under consideration make for man? These are the questions that constitute the test of truth. The significance of this test will become clearer if we consider the negative aspects of the theory, the concepts that the proponents of pragmatism seek to discredit.

First, the pragmatist insists, there are no abstract logical principles which are intrinsically and eternally true, and to which all knowledge must conform. The procedure of experimental science is exactly typical of the manner in which truth is sought and tested in any field whatsoever. The scientist recognizes no *a priori* logical principles or rules of procedure; he has his technique, but there is nothing *a priori* about it. It means simply procedure which has so far vindicated itself in action, solving old problems and suggesting new ones. Should it fail to prove its worth in mastering environment, the scientist is quite prepared to discard it.[1]

According to the pragmatist philosophy, the decision rests with experiment, with the "try-out," and the same practical test holds for every field the human being is called upon to explore. In their attempts to cope with the problems of morality, men went astray, the pragmatist reasons, and they believed themselves in possession of eternal, immutable principles which should regulate their conduct. Some men have found the sources of these moral truths in pure reason, others in intuition, and still others in revelation. In every case, the individual failed to realize the true origin of moral law, that is, experience. We shall return to this word, "experience," a crucial one in the thinking of the pragmatist.

Second, the pragmatist continues, truth is not something existing in its own right, antecedent to and independent of human experience, something awaiting discovery through a proper exercise of human intelligence. Truth is not, like the continent of America, simply *there*, waiting for its Columbus to make it known. This conception of truth as something with independent, objective existence was implied in idealism, as we noted in the previous chapter. This idealistic theory represents the traditional assumption of the philosophers, and underlies, moreover, the casual philosophizing of the man in the street. The pragmatist calls this philosophy the "spectator" theory of truth, and he rejects it in favor of

[1] In *Pragmatism* (New York, Longman's Green & Co., 1907) James uses the phrase "the practical cash-value" of an idea but protests against the narrow interpretation his critics had put on the phrase.

the theory that truth is something in process of creation, with man himself the builder and maker of it. The foundations of truth are laid in man's needs; it is a monument to his success in the satisfaction of those needs.

The pragmatic theory thus implies a test of truth different from those implied in traditional philosophy, and, more specifically, from that implied in idealism. According to the traditional "correspondence" theory, truth is a body of propositions presenting a picture of reality that "corresponds" to what reality is like. Most philosophers were inclined to accept this test of correspondence. In idealism, the test is that of "consistency": reason is the reality of things, and consistency is the core of reason. A system of philosophy which claims to be true, the idealist reasons, must be internally coherent; it must not contain propositions which do not logically fit into the whole. Against the tests of correspondence and consistency, the pragmatist asserts his own test, namely, that of the meaning of the proposition or theory in terms of the satisfaction of human needs. Instead of asserting that a theory works because it is true, the pragmatist states that it is true because it works.

The pragmatist replaces traditional (Aristotelian) logic with a logic that aims at presenting a more correct picture of how the mind actually works. The essence of this logic is the principle that thought is always an instrument of adjustment. Faced with a difficulty, man may either fumble blindly like an animal trying to open a door, or he may think. In the latter case, man foresees the uselessness of certain movements and is thus saved the trouble of making those movements. The thinking that the individual undertakes consists of (a) waiting for suggestions of possible responses to the problematic situation; (b) foreseeing the consequences of any particular suggestions; and (c) accepting the suggestion that promises a solution. All thinking, whether the problem is the opening of a puzzle-box or the devising of a program of social reform, is thus, in its essential nature, instrumental. The final test is always the test of practice, of the "try-out."

The pragmatist does not mean, of course, that, for example, the only way of deciding whether euthanasia or "companionate marriage" is desirable is to institute the practice and then take note of the consequences. The practice must be *thought out* before it is tried out. But the "thinking out" is only a special form of the "trying out"—it is an economical form that eliminates wrong cues. To put this idea another way: thinking proceeds through the proper apprehension of "meanings," and a meaning is nothing other than an advance indication of a certain experience. To understand the meaning of a word is to foresee a series of events which, under certain conditions, will occur. Hence, the train of meanings of which thinking consists is a more or less complete shorthand account of the world in which we find ourselves. Actual experience is always the final test of the adequacy and correctness of our shorthand.

To understand the pragmatist's position, especially as represented by Dewey, it is always important to keep in mind what Dewey is attacking. The following excerpt from one of his later works indicates the essential object of attack:

> The doctrine that nature is inherently rational was a costly one. It entailed the idea that reason in man is an outside spectator of a rationality already complete in itself. It deprived reason in man of an active and creative office; its business was simply to copy, to represent symbolically, to view a given rational structure . . . . Its paralyzing effect on human action is seen in the part it played in the eighteenth and nineteenth century in the theory of "natural laws" in human affairs, in social matters. These natural laws were supposed to be inherently fixed; a science of social phenomena and relations was equivalent to discovery of them. Once discovered, nothing remained for man but to conform to them; they were to rule his conduct as physical laws govern physical phenomena. They were the sole standard of conduct in economic affairs; the laws of economics are the "natural" laws of all political action; other so-called laws are artificial, man-made contrivances in contrast with the normative regulations of nature itself . . .
>
> *Laisser-faire* was the logical conclusion. For organized society to attempt to regulate the course of human affairs, to bring them into the service of humanly conceived ends, was a harmful interference.[2]

This attack on the idea of nature as "inherently rational" is, of course, directed against idealism, with its doctrine that nature *is*

[2]John Dewey, *The Quest for Certainty* (New York, Minton, Balch & Co., 1929), pp. 211-212.

rationality. But the reference to natural laws shows that Dewey is thinking in particular of a point of view antedating modern idealism, and commonly expressed by thinkers of the seventeenth and eighteenth centuries. This is the idea that nature is a model of all that is good and wise. We illustrated the idea in Chapter 13 with a quotation from John Milton in the seventeenth century, and one from Alexander Pope in the eighteenth century. The whole outlook of the idealist with regard to nature is anathema to the pragmatist. Goodness and wisdom (when they appear in the picture at all) are simply descriptions of man's way of dealing with nature.

Has the pragmatist nothing to say about the nature of *ultimate* reality, the issue to which the philosophers have always addressed themselves? Some philosophers, like Democritus in the ancient world, and his later followers, have identified the ultimate reality with matter. Others, like Plato and the modern idealists, have called it "mind." Still other philosophers (Descartes, for instance) have said that ultimate reality is partly mind and partly matter, while Spinoza argued that it is neither matter nor mind, but an ultimate "something" ("substance," Spinoza called it) of which mind and matter are only two out of an infinite number of attributes, the two of which human beings can have any cognizance.

The pragmatist starts from a concept which is for him basic, experience. "Experience" means the interaction of an organism and an environment; each implies the other. An "organism" means an entity striving to further its existence in an environment, and an "environment" means the conditions impinging on an organism. As for the question of the ultimate reality underlying all of these concepts, the pragmatist says that one may speculate about this point and arrive at a reasoned metaphysic concerning it. He insists, however, that any such metaphysical system has three drawbacks: (1) There is no conceivable way of testing it. (2) It does not make any *difference* to anything or anybody. (3) It claims to be final, the last unchangeable word about the nature of things. For the pragmatist, any one of these weaknesses is sufficient of itself to discredit the system; together, they constitute decisive condemnation. In this sense it is right to say that pragmatism is not a philosophy, but a way of getting along without a philosophy.

The pragmatist is not the only philosopher who ascribes a purely practical function to the human intellect. Henri Bergson, for instance, goes part of the way with the pragmatist in limiting the intellect to an essentially practical rôle. But Bergson does not, like the pragmatist, assign such an instrumental function to the whole mind. On the contrary, Bergson's contention is that the intellect, because of this instrumental rôle, fails to impart insight into the underlying reality of things. In animals, instinct implies such direct insight into reality. In human beings, this direct insight comes from two quarters: insight provided by art, and, where morality is concerned, the insights of the great moral teachers and innovators. For the pragmatist, all such insights only signify different ways in which the organism achieves better adjustment and furthers its own development.

Let us now turn to a discussion of the educational bearings of pragmatism, as developed in Dewey's philosophy of education. For our purpose, it will suffice to do two things. First, we shall point out certain key concepts or ideas with which Dewey and his disciples have made us familiar. Critical comment will be added where it appears called for. The reader should satisfy himself that he recognizes the connection between each of those concepts and the pragmatic philosophy. He should observe that in some cases these concepts were examined in connection with the educational philosophy expounded in other parts of the present study. He should try to identify these passages and reread them. Second, we shall select one of the five concepts in question and deal with it more fully in order to make clear precisely what Dewey is attacking, and to what extent his attack is or is not justified. The reader should then attempt this procedure for himself with one or more of the other concepts. He will find that any one of them, if carefully thought through, will leave him with an overall picture of Dewey's educational philosophy as a whole.

The key concepts or ideas contained in John Dewey's philosophy of pragmatism may be stated as follows:

1. *The humanizing of knowledge and the learning process.* This idea has two aspects: (a) The basic biological function of thinking is practical—better adjustment through the overcoming of obstacles

and the solution of problems. Hence, the emphasis should be on active as opposed to passive learning, and the solution of real as opposed to merely fictitious problems. This is the basis of the so-called "activity program." (b) Learning should be related to needs, to the needs of the learner. Hence the concept of the "child-centred school."

2. *Emphasis on "shared experience," on the social content of learning.* Man is a social animal from first to last. Personal development is a matter of interaction between the individual and his fellows. Hence, learning should be a co-operative enterprise, with the school a miniature form of society.

Granting the basic importance of the social factor, to which Dewey refers here, we might ask whether there is not a form of "shared experience" which occurs apart from any actual social context. "My days among the dead are passed,"[3] says the poet Southey, as he looks round his library. Would he not claim that this, too, is "shared experience," in the company of the immortals?

3. *Emphasis on growth.* No stage of education should be a mere preparation for a later stage. Every stage has its own "needs," and growth is a matter of providing the right expression for them.

4. *False dualisms.* These are the usual distinctions between the individual and the environment, culture and vocation, work and leisure, means and end, interest and effort, subject matter and method, freedom and discipline, the individual and society. False dualisms rest at bottom on a fallacious view of education, a view that sees education as a *mechanical,* instead of an *organic* process.

The reader should be able to see for himself in what sense Dewey is right and in what sense he is mistaken in regarding these distinctions as fallacious and misleading.

5. *Education for a changing civilization and the rejection of a static curriculum.* Education is adjustment to an environment which is always changing, and changing very rapidly today. Hence the idea of a static curriculum, valid from one generation to another, is mistaken.

[3]Robert Southey: *Poems* (Houghton Mifflin Co., Boston, 1884), *Occasional Pieces.*

While Dewey was thinking here of the traditional curriculum generally, his immediate target was the kind of curriculum implied, as we have seen, in idealism. For the idealist, man's achievements to date in the arts and sciences provide education with content, with a curriculum. These achievements represent a heritage which it is the business of education to transmit to the young. Putting the young "in possession" of their heritage might suggest a misleading, indeed an actually false, analogy. It could easily be taken to mean that the task of education is to *impart* to the young as much *knowledge* about the sciences, the arts, history, economics, politics, as is possible in the time available. This leads to the "ritualistic fallacy" (as we called it earlier), which attributes mysterious educational potency to the acquisition of knowledge as such.

The idealist might make two protests at this point. He would insist, first, that knowledge merely as such is not to be discounted as lacking significance, and second, that his theory does not imply, as a worthy educational aim, any such mechanical mastery of factual knowledge. He would agree with the view advocated in this study that "appreciation" is the operative word in this connection. It is important to remember, however, that *in practice* idealism appears to have provided philosophical support for traditional procedures long regarded as highly questionable.

Idealism, again, with its concern for the different aspects of human cultural development, implies what is called a "balanced" curriculum. But this seeming merit is seen by Dewey as a defect. It means the static curriculum in another form. Dewey states:

> There is a philosophy which might well be called the check and balance theory of experience. Life presents a diversity of interests . . . an ideal education would then supply the means of meeting these separate and pigeon-holed interests. . . . The course of study must then have some civics and history politically and patriotically viewed; some utilitarian studies; some science; some art (mainly literature of course); some provision for recreation; some moral education; and so on. . . . In the multitude of educations, education is forgotten.[4]

[4]John Dewey, *Democracy and Education* (New York, the Macmillan Co., 1916), pp. 288-289.

The word "balance," as applied to a curriculum, is ambiguous.[5] It can refer to the extent to which the curriculum provides for all the important interests of life, in a word, to *breadth*. Admittedly, this may mean in practice a curriculum balanced only "on paper." Dewey's thinking turns on two further conceptions of balance. According to the first of these, the curriculum is balanced in the sense that in practice it makes provision for individual differences. The balance reflects the variety of personal aptitude and endowment, rather than the variety of cultural materials. The second conception influencing Dewey's thinking about balance is that the curriculum may be balanced or unbalanced to the degree that it does or does not reflect the contemporary world. Divorced from that context, the curriculum is static, and thus out of balance.

Dewey is right in criticizing a curriculum which is unbalanced in any of the three senses mentioned. It should be noted, however, that the attempt to produce balance in the last two of the senses referred to may also miscarry, and the result is then something artificial and educationally unsound. We have drawn attention to illustrations of this fact at various times in this study. Let us add, further, that the idealist of the present day, writing with Dewey's criticisms in mind, would concede that Dewey's strictures are sound, but would deny that they are applicable to his own educational theory.[6] These idealists could claim that Dewey's criticisms have reference to practical consequences quite unintended by the idealists themselves, a line of defence to which, as we shall see, Dewey himself found it necessary to have recourse.

As is often the case in educational writings, when the critic—in this case, Dewey—proceeds to make positive suggestions for avoiding the errors of the idealists and the traditionalists, he exposes himself to attack from both quarters. We shall confine ourselves to a general indication of the lines of the attack on Dewey's philosophy.

In the passage quoted on page 242, Dewey refers to "separate"

---

[5]For a careful examination of the ambiguities of the word "balance," the reader should consult *Year Book 1961*, National Educational Association, 1201 Sixteenth Street N.W., Washington 6, D.C.
[6]e.g. H. H. Horne and T. M. Greene.

and "pig ι-holed" interests. "Pigeon-holed" is surely a "question-begging"   but in any case, both words remind us of a principle underlying   vey's philosophy, viz. the notion of "subjects" of study as in\ 'd and educationally mischievous. It is true that the division of .   ledge into subjects can be overdone, and it is also true that   ι.d teaching will show the learner the bearing of one subject on ιnother. But it is one thing to talk about separate subjects, and quite another to talk about separate interests, or "values," as we have called them. Science consists of a number of different subjects; it represents only one basic interest or value. An appreciative understanding will not come as an incident of the study of some other interest; one must work directly for such appreciation.

Even the division into subjects is a matter of organization of the vast field of knowledge, organization indispensable not only for the learner who is trying to find his way in that field, but also for the creative thinker concerned to extend its boundaries. For example, a vocational education which brought out the social ramifications and significance of the vocation would also be general education up to a point. But how far would the device of using the vocational motive to further the ends of culture really carry us? This "cultivated vocationist," as H. H. Horne calls him, would, except perhaps in rare cases, end up with lacunae in his education serious enough to put him out of adjustment with the society in which he is living—and the pragmatist, of all people should avoid that result.

Again, is the emphasis on the self-discovery of knowledge, the testing of knowledge, and the repudiation of authority, not over-done? It leads to emphasis on scientific knowledge at the expense of other forms of knowledge, forms of knowledge which, as we have already shown, are not only implied in disciplines such as history and philosophy, but are also the kinds of knowledge by which the individual in the main regulates his ordinary living.

As for authority, surely the important thing is training in the use of the right kind of authority. Without elaborating further, it seems fair to sum up by saying that Dewey's principles are counsels of perfection, in the sense that they would be right if life, particularly the part of it devoted to formal education, were much longer than it is, and if first-class teachers, with perfect facilities and conditions, were always available. But has the *pragmatist* any right to formulate an educational philosophy in terms of a utopian situation?

It remains to add that Dewey himself, judging by his later writings, especially *Experience and Education*[7] would endorse many of the criticisms directed against practices alleged to be basic to his philosophy. He protests against what he regards as the extravagances and vagaries of practitioners of progressive education. He argues, in effect, that he presented a new philosophy of experience from which these disciples drew hasty, uncritical inferences. He deplores their assumption that "it suffices to reject the ideas and practices of the old education and go then to the opposite extreme."

At the same time, it could be said in fairness that Dewey's manner of stating his new philosophy in the first instance was responsible for much of the resulting unfavorable criticism. Dewey's earlier work, *Democracy and Education*,[8] contains all too many examples of his penchant for over-preaching his gospel. While stating a principle with the vigor and persuasiveness that is so characteristic of him, Dewey sometimes pays insufficient attention to the limitations and possible criticisms of that principle, or even brushes them aside as unimportant. An example of this weakness in Dewey's approach is his treatment of the topic of shared experience, upon which we have already commented.

In stressing the value of shared experience, Dewey says: "The use of language to convey and acquire ideas is an extension and refinement of the principle that things gain meaning by being used in a shared experience or joint action; in no sense does it contravene that principle."[9] This statement is indeed true, but might it not be that this particular "extension and refinement," where, for instance, one does the "sharing" with Aristotle and Shakespeare, is the crucial part of the educative process?

With the contrast between Dewey's earlier and later statements of his philosophy in mind, some might suggest that Dewey is inconsistent in his reasoning, and leave it at that. "Inconsistent" is an imprecise term, however, and one hesitates to apply it to a thinker

[7] John Dewey, *Experience and Education* (New York, The Macmillan Co., 1938).
[8] John Dewey, *Democracy and Education* (New York, The Macmillan Co., 1916).
[9] John Dewey, *Democracy and Education*, p. 19. (New York, The Macmillan Co., 1916).

of Dewey's calibre. In presenting his philosophy of experience, Dewy's argument is as consistent as it is vigorous. What we have here is an example of something already discussed at some length, namely, the difficulty of being sure of the practical educational inferences from philosophic or psychological premises.

This difficulty is the core of the matter. Dewey is first and foremost a critic of his times. When he wrote *Democracy and Education*, he was convinced that there was no adequate realization of the far-reaching implications of science and the scientific outlook for our industrial civilization and for democracy. Education, Dewey felt, was the point at which that lag should be dealt with and corrected. At the time of *Experience and Education*, when the spirit of change had been animating the educationists for two decades, Dewey was disturbed about some of the ideas and practices of the educational reformers, and he directed his polemic accordingly. As for consistency, there is always consistency of attitude and outlook in Dewey's writings.

One sometimes gains the impression that when the question is one of educational practice, the difference between Dewey and the idealists is small and unimportant. The idealist, for example, would say that he is at one with Dewey with respect to the importance of shared experience, co-operative thinking, pupil needs, real problems, and the rest. The idealist would merely point out the practical limits to such principles. Dewey, for his part, would not take issue with the idea that education, whatever else it may be, is always a matter of putting the individual in possession of his scientific and humane heritage. Is the difference between Dewey and the idealists then, only one of method and emphasis? Not at all. Any such practical consensus should not make us lose sight of the real educational issue that divides the pragmatist and the idealist.

For the idealist, the achievements that constitute scientific and humane knowledge are a reflection, partial and fragmentary, but nevertheless true as far as it goes, of an absolute which is the ultimate reality of the cosmos. The educationist who views the curriculum in that light is seeing it, in Spinoza's famous phrase, *sub quadam specie aeternitatis*. For the pragmatist, these same achievements only represent what man has done so far towards satisfying his needs and enriching his experience. The basic values carry no unconditional authority. They are relative, and the relativism is more than what is meant by saying that they vary with time and place; it is ultimate relativism. Without a supporting metaphysic, neither these values nor the curricula based on them are vested with any final, absolute authority. Clearly, education *means* more in the one case than in the other. Whether the individual sees good reason for accepting this further meaning is something that he must decide for himself.

24 *Realism*

The philosophy of realism was developed in the first instance as an answer to idealism. The reader will recall our comment in Chapter 23 to the effect that "ideaism" is a more accurate term than "idealism" to describe the philosophy in question, since the latter term is misleading in its suggestion of moral overtones and of a devotion to the pursuit of higher values. A similar remark is appropriate with regard to realism. The word "realism" carries the *prima facie* suggestion of a philosophy with more solid foundations than idealism; it somehow appears to be a more "real" philosophy. The reason for calling this philosophy "realism" is, however, quite a different one.

The philosophy of realism is an attempt to reinstate the ordinary man's view of the external world. According to that view, the external world exists independently of the human mind, and, moreover, is not, as the idealist would have it, mentalist in nature. In this sense, the external world is "real," and hence the term "realism." The ordinary man has always regarded the external world as real in the sense of something self-subsistent, different from mind, and operating in accordance with its own laws. Modern realism, or the "new realism," as it should be called, reasserts this view, but does so with a very important difference.

Most realists follow Berkeley in rejecting the ordinary man's picture of what the external world is actually like. But the rejection of the naïve view of things as having color, sound, taste, and smell, does not, the realists feel, justify the inference that things are mentalist in nature. Specifically, the realists argue that Berkeley confused the *process of knowing* with the *object of knowledge*. It is by way of our sensations that we come to know the external world, but this does not mean that the external world simply consists of our sensations. Having a sensation of red and cognizing a red object are not the same thing. The realists are agreed, then, that there is an external world that exists in its own right.

A second proposition on which the realists are in accord is that the human mind can know that external world, and that it can discover the nature of it, how it works. Again, they agree that in the knowing of the objects in that world, the mind contributes something; there is a subjective element in our knowledge. But this means that the mind not only knows or cognizes the object as something existing in its own right; the mind interprets the object. Such interpretation, however, does not mean creation, turning what was non-mentalist into something mentalist in nature. Finally, the realists are at one in holding that science, as far as it goes, is truly revealing the real nature of the external world.

When, however, the realists address themselves to the positive task of disentangling the subjective from the objective elements, and of describing precisely how the objective world is to be conceived, their agreement ends. A few, but only a few, have carried their realism to the point of arguing that the objective world has both the primary and the secondary qualities which the ordinary man attributes to it: things have not only the primary qualities of mass, weight, hardness, length, and breadth, but also color, taste, sound, and smell. Others give objective reality only to the primary qualities, and still others hold more sophisticated theories which we need not consider here.

The concept of time acquired a new importance in the philosophy of modern realism. The older realists pictured the external world as fundamentally static. The external world was simply there to be explored and discovered. True, some of them—Heraclitus, for example—represented the world as in a state of perpetual flux or change. But this change meant *instability*; it did not imply *development*. This latter characteristic involves change in the direction of increasingly complex forms of organization.

The notion of development as opposed to mere change began to gain currency in the early nineteenth century, and it played a part in the thinking of Hegel and his idealistic followers. But Darwinism and the theory of evolution gave specific content to the general concept of development, thus putting it on a new footing. The theory of evolution used the concept of development to account for the nature of the world—the physical world and the world of living forms—as we now find it. In this connection, the theory introduced the concept of biological time. Without that concept, the pre-modern philosophers were apt to discount time and to concentrate their interest on space. Modern philosophers, and the realists in particular, have been concerned about coming to terms with the concept of cosmic development in infinite time, as against the notion of a static universe in infinite space. S. S. Alexander's theory of emergent evolution is one important example of the philosophic attempt to present a realistic philosophy in terms of evolutionary concepts.[1]

According to this theory the evolutionary process gives rise to new forms or "emergents," by which is meant new forms which evolve out of the old forms, but which are not continuous with the old forms; they represent a higher *plane* of organization. The idea is a philosophic application of the evolutionary notion of mutations. For example, plant life is a mutation or emergent arising out of the inorganic world; animal life has the same evolutionary relationship to plant life; and the self-conscious mind as found in the human being is an emergent from animal life. Presumably the next emergent will be a form of mind as much transcending the human mind as the latter transcends the animal mind.

One cannot foresee the precise nature of this next emergent, although philosophers do speculate about this intriguing matter. Alexander makes the further and rather curious suggestion that for each emergent level the one above it is God—an interpretation of divinity which might satisfy the biologist, but which is unlikely to commend itself to the religious consciousness. Alexander's suggestion is realism carried to the point of not only denying that the external world is a form of mind, with space and time creations

[1] S. S. Alexander. *Space, Time, and Deity* (London, The Macmillan Co., 1920).

of the human mind, but of asserting that mind itself is a product of the external world, and, Alexander suggests, is "in space."

Of far greater interest to the educational philosopher, however, is the realist's view of values, especially of moral values. What is meant by a realistic view of moral values? It is not enough to say, negatively, that such a view rejects the ultimate relativism which we found to be implied in pragmatism. What is the positive teaching of realism on this issue? Moral realism can take one or both of two forms.

First, the realist may hold that moral values are inherent in the universe itself: the cosmos is a moral order. Distinctions of morally good and bad, morally right and wrong, have more than human significance; they have their ultimate basis in the nature of the universe itself. This is the typical attitude of religion to moral values, and Christianity expressly accepts it. The Hindu religion, with its doctrine of karma, according to which everyone in the end receives his deserts, likewise conceives of the cosmos as a moral order. As was pointed out in Chapter 2, one of the human needs that religion meets is that of providing such an ultimate supra-human authority for human values. The reader will recall that one form of idealism, the religious form, similarly asserts a cosmic basis for human values, though the secular form of idealism seems to carry rather a different implication.

Without committing himself to this first conception of the cosmos as a moral order, the realist can accord to moral values a reality of a different order. He may regard them as social standards possessing universal validity, and we already drew attention to what appear to be basic moral values of this nature, values which represent discoveries, in the special sense that they have become part of the value judgments of ordinary men. True, men too often flout these values in practice, but that does not mean (if the men do not present moral anomalies) that they actually repudiate these values. It is the old story of knowing the better and, under the drive of irrational motives, choosing the worse.

In the rare cases (curiously rare, if they exist at all) of primitive groups where social relations are governed by standards flagrantly at variation with these values, the explanation is probably that such groups have simply not discovered these values. In Chapter 7 we indicated what these values are, and the evidence for giving them this realistic status. In that and other parts of this essay, we also pointed out their significance for a philosophy of education.

There is yet another sense in which some realists attribute reality to moral values. In this sense, moral judgments are regarded as *sui generis*. Moral goodness (or badness) is a quality or attribute of an act which the individual perceives directly, as he perceives the color of an object. Moral goodness is not to be explained in terms of something other than itself, e.g. social approval, conformity to custom, tendency to produce pleasure or happiness, self-realization, human excellence. Goodness may entail such consequences, but these consequences do not constitute goodness. It would take us too far afield to examine this position in detail, but a further comment on realism is apropos.

Just as realism would deny the ultimate relativism of moral values, so the same philosophy would assert that aesthetic values are not, in the last analysis, a matter of time and place. *Homo socius* has discovered standards of conduct with universal validity and authority. In like manner, *homo sentiens* is in process of discovering standards of beauty which are a truer, more adequate expression of his aesthetic nature.

25 *Materialism, Scientism, and Logical Positivism*

Materialism, the oldest form of the philosophy discussed in the present chapter, received its first clear, systematic statement by the philosophers of ancient Greece, notably Democritus (ca. 400 B.C.). According to Democritus, everything consists of atoms. The atoms are conceived as small pieces of matter that are not further divisible, are infinite in number, perpetually in motion, spatially separate, and constantly colliding. Democritus viewed all reality, mental as well as physical, as a manifestation of atoms in motion. Mind is thus a form of matter, a very refined form no doubt, but matter nonetheless. To this "atomism," as Democritus' philosophy is called, another concept was added, one that was to play a key rôle in philosophical thinking. This was the concept of "determinism," by which was meant that the play of the atoms is not haphazard, but rather proceeds in a rigidly mechanical way, with no opportunity for caprice or chance.

The opposition of materialism to idealism thus began early in the history of philosophy. The great idealist of the ancient world is, of course, Plato. It is "ideas," according to Plato, that are real, not material objects; the latter possess only apparent or illusory reality. The reader will recall the opening of the gospel according to St. John: "In the beginning was the Word . . ." The "Word" is the "logos"—the mind or spirit—of Greek idealistic philosophy. Democritus would have reworded the statement of this gospel as: "In the beginning were the atoms. . . ." The opposition between the two philosophies of materialism and idealism continued throughout the centuries, with materialism retaining essentially the form given to it by Democritus.

Materialism received fresh impetus from the growth of modern science. Not that the pioneers of science openly accepted this philosophy. On the contrary, most of them were inclined to hold the position defined clearly by Descartes, himself a pioneer in both science and philosophy in the seventeenth century. This was the dualistic position according to which there are two radically different kinds of reality, mind and matter, matter being the special province of science. At the same time, the philosophic impulse always is to unify, to integrate, to make one concept serve instead of two or more. To the scientist, development in physics and chemistry seemed to point to atomism as the right philosophy for the physical world, and the tendency was to extend atomism to include the mental as well as the physical world. This situation persisted (with the same tendency apparent among the scientists) down to the nineteenth century.

It was in the later decades of the nineteenth century that materialism received the blow which made an end of it as a tenable philosophy. The blow came from the very quarter which had hitherto furnished its main support, physical science. Modern physics divided the "indivisible" atom, splitting it, moreover, not into still smaller atoms, but into entities which did not lend themselves to any such description—materialism was outmoded.

The scientists, however, retained one concept which had been part of the old materialism, and which seems indeed to have been implicit in the teaching of Democritus himself: the concept of mechanism. The mechanistic view, which left no place for caprice or chance, did not perish with the material atom. True, some of the pioneers of the new physics—Eddington, for example—suggested that the new science left room for an element of indeterminism or spontaneity, but the scientists on the whole scented danger in any departure from mechanism as a working hypothesis. So far as the physical world was concerned, there appeared no need to question this hypothesis of the uniformity of nature, as they would phrase it. But some of them (those who in the old days would have been the materialists) saw in mechanism a universal principle applicable to the mental as well as the physical world. If they did not argue for such a point of view, they assumed it. Instead of stating that everything consists of atoms, the new philosophy maintained that everything is a manifestation of rigid mechanism.

This is scientism in the strict sense of the term. The underlying assumption of this philosophy was considered in detail in Chapter 4. Contemporary scientism can take another form, however, a form that arises out of an imprecise use of the term "science." The following illustrations should clarify this second form of scientism.

In order to determine the public attitude to the question of building shelters against nuclear attack, the various organizations employ their techniques for securing representative samples of public opinion on the matter. A government that desires to obtain as correct a picture as possible of the practical consequences of nationalizing a major industry appoints a Royal Commission or a Senatorial Committee to investigate and report. A business firm that wishes to know what radio or television features are being specially favored by the public arranges to have householders phoned from time to time and asked what features they are listening to or viewing at the moment. A political party that desires to know what ordinary people are thinking about Britain's proposed entry into the European Common Market may adopt the method of so-called "mass observation" in which the party posts individuals throughout the country to report *verbatim* what particular individuals say about the matter. These literal reports are transmitted to a central agency whose business it is to interpret them. An educational administrator who wants to know how pupils are reacting to the teaching of a particular subject prepares a questionnaire and submits it to the teachers concerned. A social psychologist uses an appropriate procedure to investigate color prejudice in a particular community. The list of examples of this form of scientism is endless.

It is customary, when decribing these procedures, to use the term "scientific." But are these methods of investigation not rather illustrations of the kind or level of thinking that we called "organized," "non-scientific" thinking? The investigator's method is to procure as much evidence as possible on which to base his conclusions. He is interested in a particular kind of evidence, that based on actual observation of men and affairs, with the observation governed by as many checks and controls as his ingenuity can devise. His intention is to correct the prepossessions, prejudices, or other sources of wrong judgment to which his theorizing or "armchair" thinking is always liable. The investigator uses a procedure similar to that employed in courts of law, where all the evidence, circumstantial or other, is amassed to enable the judge and jury to decide the case before them. The historian's approach is a similar one when he insists on wading through all the available pertinent documents before he arrives at his judgment.

In this kind of thinking, some of the evidence may truly be scientific. The court may secure a ruling from a medical expert on a specific point. The historian may use the resources of science to date a document or the vestiges of a buried city. The sociologist, in his study of suburbia, may occasionally make use of science—psychological science, or statistics scientifically assembled and manipulated—but the conclusions arrived at as a whole are *not* scientific. Such conclusions represent "probable knowledge," to revert to the phrase that we borrowed from John Locke. Two investigators who had before them the same data would not necessarily draw the same conclusions from them. The fact that such conclusions are based on empirical considerations rather than on "armchair" reasoning greatly enhances the probability of their being sound, but that is another and of course a very important consideration.

"Empirical," not "scientific," is the correct term to use in reference to the kinds of investigation in question. Empiricism in philosophy denotes the attitude or point of view that distrusts *a priori*, "armchair" reasoning, and insists on making experience—the facts of life as one finds them—the starting point and the final test of one's thinking. Science is, of course, empirical; it starts from the facts and comes back to the facts. But the reader will recall from our discussion of scientific procedure that the scientist defines "fact" in a special way; a "fact" for the scientist is something objective that lends itself to being manipulated and tested in his own particular way. Empirical investigation denotes a genus of which science is only a species, though an exceedingly important species.

If we appear to have labored a distinction which ought to be sufficiently obvious, we have done so for good reason. Failure to keep this distinction in mind creates quite an exaggerated picture of the part played by science in the thinking of the civilized, educated man. In education, in particular, this confusion is all too likely to result in failure to provide the other, non-scientific kind of thinking with the training and discipline that it needs. The educationist should avoid this confusion for another reason. If he is not clear-headed and conscientious in distinguishing between what is and what is not scientific, he arouses suspicion and hostility in his academic colleagues, with the result that these and other critics will do less than justice to what he has actually accomplished in applying the scientific method to his own problems.

What, then, has been the impact of scientism on education, scientism strictly so called? It does not come within the scope of this study to answer the question in any specific manner. The reader will find the answer in any standard textbook of educational psychology. The learning process, intelligence and aptitude testing, and other areas of study provide cases in point. All that we need do here is suggest to the reader that, in consulting such sources, he should try to distinguish between two types of investigation. In the first type, the scientific method has been successfully used to solve a specific educational problem. The conclusion admits of being verified and put to practical use. In the second type (of which we have suggested examples in Chapter 22) an attempt is made to apply practically a well-established principle of psychological science, the practical implications of which, however, are not clear.

Let us turn now to the third member of the triad of philosophies that heads this chapter, logical positivism. This philosophy represents scientism in its most extreme form. For scientism, in the sense that we have discussed, a discipline such as philosophy or theology represents at best a very unreliable form of knowledge. It is a second best with which we must content ourselves until such time as science gets round to the matter in question, and that time may of course never come. The logical positivist goes still further. Disciplines such as philosophy and theology, he argues, are simply not knowledge at all.

Knowledge consists of propositions about reality. For the logical positivist, a proposition is a statement with respect to which it should be possible to describe the kind of conditions or operations which would show it to be true or false. If it is not possible to imagine such an *operational* test, then the proposition is not a real proposition at all. The proposition is, for the logical positivist, an expression of emotion or desire, in any case, of the non-cognitive part of our nature. The propositions used in ethics or aesthetics are cases in point. "It is wrong to inflict pain on a fellow-creature" really means, "I wish you would not inflict pain," or (a disguised command), "Do not inflict pain on your fellow creature!" "This picture is more beautiful than that one," is a pseudo-propositional way of saying, "I like this picture better than that one." It makes no sense to ask whether such statements are true or false.

The logical positivist's main target is the speculative systems produced by metaphysical philosophy and theology. The perennial problems of metaphysics—the existence of God, freedom of the will, immortality—are perennial because they are insoluble, and they are insoluble because they do not lend themselves to meaningful statements, that is, to statements which could conceivably be shown to be true or false. As one logical positivist put it: science deals with what we know, philosophy with what we do not know—by which he meant, cannot know.

For the purposes of this examination, it suffices to suggest one line of criticism of the logical positivist's position. Granted that these metaphysical problems are insoluble (in any sense that would satisfy the scientist), the fact that they are perennial is significant. This fact reminds us that human beings have always raised such questions and will continue to do so. The logical positivist finds himself in the position of having to say that the answers returned by ordinary, illiterate individuals, and those returned by Thomas Aquinas, Spinoza, and Kant, are exactly on a par with respect to their status as knowledge. The answers of all these individuals are equally worthless—a strange position, which it would not be unreasonable to regard as a *reductio ad absurdum* of logical positivism.

The logical positivists, however, do accord a definite rôle to philosophy. This rôle is the analysis of language, especially of the language used in science. They have indeed largely modified the original extreme stand that we outlined in favor of the position that philosophy can make a valuable contribution by way of linguistic analysis. It is an important suggestion. Friedrich Nietzsche, in one of his flashes of anticipatory insight, drew attention to the manner in which language, and in particular the grammatical structure of language, can lead philosophers astray. The logical positivists in the 1920's and 1930's made important contributions along this line. In so far as the theory has bearing on education, it is in that direction that we should seek it. At a time when electronics is enormously extending the range of influence of the spoken, as distinct from the written word, any influence that develops the analytical, critical attitude to language is all to the good.

26   *Marxism*

Karl Marx is usually regarded as the father of modern socialism. Socialistic or communistic theories of society had been projected, and in some quarters practised, long before the time of Marx—the communism of the early Christians is a case in point—but such earlier forms of socialism were in the main inspired by Christian teaching about the brotherhood of man, and in particular about the danger to man's immortal soul of the possession and pursuit of wealth. Marx put socialism on a new footing. He claimed to found it solidly on a science of society.

Marx was both a political economist and a social philosopher. His economic theory does not concern us here; his social philosophy, however, contains much that is relevant to a philosophy of education. It was, moreover, his social philosophy rather than his specifically economic doctrine that provided the lasting inspiration for his disciples. Marx's philosophy turns on two fundamental concepts, dialectical materialism and the economic interpretation of history.

Marx's concept of the "dialectic" originated with his one-time teacher, Hegel. "Dialectic" implies continuous struggle or opposition. For Hegel, this process of struggle occurs in the realm of ideas, mind, or spirit. An idea gives rise to its opposite. Out of that opposition, a further idea emerges, which in turn gives rise to its opposite, and so on, indefinitely. "Thesis, antithesis, synthesis," is Hegel's celebrated formula to describe the dialectic in the realm of the spirit, and he developed an entire system of logic setting forth the particulars of this dialectic. According to Hegelian philosophy, this spiritual dialectic is the creative, constitutive factor of all reality, including the reality of the material world.

The starting point of the Marxian dialectic is the material world and the relationship of man as a knower to that world. The relationship is not a passive one; in knowing the material world, man is actively manipulating it. He selects for attention only those features with a bearing on his needs, and he manipulates them to satisfy those needs. Hence the dialectical process: the material world presents man with an "opposite," functioning as a limitation to his efforts. He overcomes the limitation and attains a more adequate level of living. New limitations emerge at this higher level, and, with his improved equipment, man meets them—the dialectic of adjustment proceeds, for example, from the level of the digging stick to that of electronics. Man's relationship to the material world is from first to last technological, in the broadest sense of that word.

The similarity between this Marxian view of man as a knower and the view of the pragmatist is obvious. For both Marx and the pragmatist, the primary function of knowing is the betterment of action. To this extent Marx anticipates the pragmatist, and this fact accounts for the streak of sympathy for Marx apparent in the writings of other philosophers, such as John Dewey. Marxism, however, as developed by its author, is far from being a form of the pragmatic philosophy. Pragmatism would have no truck with the dogmatic certainties which are a feature of the Marxian philosophy as a whole.

In addition to the basic dialectic, an important tenet of Marxian philosophy is the bifurcation of society into two classes. The tools that man has invented, and the wealth that these tools have created, come to be possessed and controlled by a relatively small number of individuals. These few dominate the many, the Marxist reasons. Hence the appearance of two classes, the "haves" and the "have nots," "having" of course meaning "having control over the means of production and distribution," as it would be expressed at the industrial level of development. Out of this opposition develops the class struggle—the struggle of the masses—the "proletariat," as the Marxist calls them—to wrest from the few the means of economic control, and the struggle of the possessing class to retain and further that control. Marx views this struggle as the mainspring of the entire movement of history. A true philosophy of history would regard the economic factor as the basic causative factor in the historic process.

What is the rôle of the other great human interests, art, science, philosophy, and religion in the Marxian philosophy? In Marx's view, they are *superstructures* raised on the basis of the economic struggle. One must be careful not to misrepresent this aspect of Marx's philosophy. It may be taken to mean, for example, that these interests are secondary in the sense that they are relatively unimportant in human history. To see the matter in that way is to be unfair to Marx as a social philosopher.

When he regards these spiritual interests as secondary, Marx has two points in mind. First, the economic factor is primarily a question of sheer survival. Some beginning for the historic process must be found, and Marx believes it logically sound to begin with the basic biological fact of the struggle to survive. Marx's other point is that the spiritual interests are secondary, in the sense that the form they take in any particular epoch depends on the state of the economic class struggle at that time. The outlook and values of the dominant class determine what and how the artist will paint, what problems the scientist will try to solve, what ways of thinking and forms of conduct the philosopher, the moralist, and the religious leader will approve.

It is easy to point to what appears to be historical confirmation of Marx's view. In the Middle Ages, the Church was economically and politically dominant. Hence the art of the day concentrated on themes of religious character, with philosophy and religion supporting explicitly or implicitly the medieval class structure. In the realm of science, the scientist had to find a way of harmonizing his findings with the theology of the day or go under. In thus assigning the basic rôle to the material instead of the spiritual dialectic, Marx apparently reversed the Hegelian point of view. As Marx himself flippantly remarked, he took the Hegelian dialectic and "stood it on its head."

Marx's theory of economic determinism has been repudiated by his critics as an oversimplification of the historic process. In this connection, it is interesting to note the concrete case adduced by one thinker, Max Weber, to demonstrate the reverse process, the determination of economic ideas and practices by the moral standards of a particular group. In *The Protestant Ethic: The Spirit of Capitalism,* Weber argues that at a certain stage in the growth of capitalism, the Puritans were in the ascendancy, and that certain moral standards to which they attached great importance in private life were projected into their business dealings and became a feature of the capitalistic regime. For example, truthfulness and honesty in personal dealings found expression in the business world as the principle of the sanctity of contract. The Puritan condemnation of self-indulgence was reflected in their emphasis on hard work and thrift. Money, they felt, should not be spent on personal pleasures and amenities. The right thing to do with money, in their estimation, was to use it to make more money.

Again, the Puritan's conviction that one's relationship to God is directly personal, not mediated through priest or church, exerted an impact on his outlook on business. It provided justification for his intolerance of any interference with business on the part of monarchs or government—as in the old practice of monopolies, for example. The Puritan regarded business as a vocation, in the dedicated pursuit of which he was responsible to God alone.

This outline of the Puritan's process of reasoning in business serves to remind us of the fact that in human affairs the operative principle is not usually the mechanical, one-way process of cause and effect, but rather the principle of interdependence. The body politic is truly a body, in the sense that the relationship of the parts is organic, not mechanical. It is only fair to add that there is nothing to indicate that Marx would not accept this principle, on the whole. He would, however, insist that in the complex configuration of relationships that constitutes human society, the influence of the economic factor is always dominant.

The class struggle, the Marxist continues, will end when the masses wrest economic power from the ruling classes. The victory of the proletariat will come only by way of revolution. To trust to the "inevitability of gradualness" to bring about this victory is to play into the hands of the social enemy, according to the doctrine of Marx. The outcome of the revolution will be a classless society;

classless in the sense that the fundamental bifurcation based on economic power will disappear. One is left rather puzzled as to how the movement of history is to go on, with its mainspring removed.

On one point in particular Marx is explicit. The state, as we know it, will "wither away." This outcome is logically implied in Marxism, according to which the state is an institution expressly created and run by the ruling class to protect the interests of that class. In this connection, another question presents itself. What is the significance of the fact (for fact it appears to be) that in those regimes, such as Russia and China, which claim to be Marxism come true, the power of the state has been enormously extended, without any signs that this is a temporary state of things, a prelude to the "withering away"? All the signs seem to point in the opposite direction. But we need not follow up these more general issues. We are primarily interested here in the educational implications of Marxism, implications that are both interesting and important.

The negative aspects of the implications of Marxism for education were considered in Chapter 20. As an ideology, Marxism implies a general outlook that is alien to the spirit of democracy, and this point requires no further elaboration. On the other hand, the principle of dialectical materialism, and the rôle assigned to the economic factor in historic causation, carry implications of the first importance.

An interesting parallel exists between the contributions to their respective fields of Marx and Sigmund Freud. Freud put sex on the psychological map. The typical pre-Freudian textbook of psychology made at most a passing reference to sex, and in some cases the author (feeling no doubt that there was something lacking in such a casual treatment of this motive) would refer the reader to the novelists and poets for a more adequate view of the topic. This was wrong advice for the reader, since the psychologist looks for science, while the literary artist provides at most only material for science, not science itself. It was Marx who put the economic factor on the historical map with a thoroughness and impact similar to that of Freud in psychology. It might be conceded that both Freud and Marx could be criticized for overteaching their lessons, but the lessons that they taught were nevertheless unforgettable.

Through his conception of the material dialectic, Marx did more than stress the crucial rôle of technology in man's development, he put technology in the very core of man's humanity. For Marx, *homo* is in his very essence *faber*. This is an idea with which every philosophy of education must come to terms if it is not to become lopsided and inadequate. Consider, for example, the criticism that Dewey and other educational thinkers directed against the traditionally sharp distinction between cultural and vocational interests. Dewey regarded the distinction as an unfruitful legacy from the ancient Greeks, whose slave economy gave them a contempt for all forms of useful work; free men should not be concerned with such down-to-earth activities.

Developments in the twentieth century, as we have pointed out at some length in Chapter 17, have outmoded such ideas, at least to the extent that contemporary educational thinkers would have little patience with any form of educational preparation which discounted the technological context of twentieth century life. The Marxist would fully endorse this broader outlook, but he would insist that (a) educationists would have developed it long ago, had it not been for capitalism, and (b) capitalism will prevent them from giving practical effect to it in any case.

Consider, again, the non-economic, spiritual values—science, art, morality, religion. We have pointed out precisely what Marx meant by assigning these values a secondary rôle in the historic process. It would be unfair to infer that he argued for a materialistic philosophy of living. Even under capitalism, these values develop a momentum of their own. Scientists, for example, have asserted the claims of pure science, free from the shackles imposed by the economically dominant class. So, too, with the advocates of the other values.

Marx would agree that this has happened, but he would insist that (a) under capitalism, those who stand for the independence of these values are fighting a losing cause and (b) under the regime that will replace capitalism, these values will come into their own and take their rightful place in life generally, and in education particularly. It is perhaps in such a context that one ought to view Marx's dismissal of religion as "the opium of the people."[1] Religion

[1]*Communist Manifesto* (1848), Karl Marx and Friedrich Engels.

has proved a deadly weapon in the hands of the exploiters of the people. Might it not prove to be something very different, something truer to its own nature, under another regime?

From this interpretation of Marxism, which seems on the whole a fair one, it would appear to follow that there would be no substantial difference between the aim of education as presented by the Marxist and by any liberal-minded educationist of today. Hence the real issue between the two concerns the effective pursuit and attainment of the aim. Is the Marxist right when he says that under capitalism the dominant class will use its control over the financial resources of society to block essential reforms—such as the better training of teachers, the provision of adequately equipped schools, the raising of the school-leaving age, financial provision for students who are able and willing to make the most of their educational opportunities—and thus sabotage the efforts of the educationists? Or is the anti-Marxist right when he says that an ideological regime imposed by revolution will inevitably produce a new power élite, whose concern to maintain its ascendancy will make for repression of individual liberties generally, and, in particular, a surveillance over the sciences and the humanities, especially the humanities, which is incompatible with the spirit of true education? The reader may be left to ponder this question for himself, with the further problem in mind: Supposing the prognosis in both cases to be correct, which is the lesser evil?

27 *Existentialism*

Perhaps the best approach to existentialism is to regard it as a forthright rejection of ways of thinking about man that had become firmly established by the end of the nineteenth century. Two principal forms of thought were so widely accepted that they went almost unchallenged—trust in the inevitability of human progress, and belief in determinism with regard to human behavior.

Those who were convinced of the inevitability of human progress viewed the movement in the affairs of mankind as directed onward and upward. Individual human beings, they believed, may retard this movement by acting in opposition to it, or by diverting it into wrong courses, but the march of events inevitably makes for progress. The existentialists, however, do not share this faith in progress. On the contrary, they see in the present a condition of social and political deterioration, and in the future nothing but uncertainty. The optimism implicit in the former view is replaced by the overall pessimism of the latter outlook. The existentialists thus stand in opposition to the philosophic schools of both the right and the left. They reject Hegel's view—the rightist view—that progress is a matter of the further development of the social and political institutions already established. They also refuse their support to Marx's institutions. Both of these millennial ways of thinking, if we may so designate them, are equally at variance with existentialist thinking.

In one form or another, the spirit of determinism found its way into the explanation of human behavior. A fundamental philosophic form of it appears in, or could be read into, the Hegelian conception of the human mind as a fragmentary manifestation of an absolute Mind. The deterministic note was also marked in the development of psychology. Freudianism seemed to imply determinism, and so, too, did the movement of intelligence testing, with its thesis of a fixed I.Q. Indeed, the modern psychologists explicitly stated that their science, as a science, implied "psychological determinism," as they called it. Still another powerful force of determinism was the massive impact of society, with its customs, traditions, and conventions on individual behavior, an impact quite sufficient to stifle individuality.

During the nineteenth century, the more radical of the social philosophers raised their voices against the prevalent repression of individualists. In England, for example, John Stuart Mill, in his essay *On Liberty*,[1] eloquently appealed to the individual to be himself and to shake off the forces of conformism pressing on him from every side. In Russia, literary artists were preoccupied with the same theme. Fyodor Dostoievski was interested in, and for a time even obsessed by, the doctrine of the so-called "nihilists." If the teachings of the "nihilists" amounted to little more than the extolling of sheer emotional caprice, they were, nevertheless, in Dostoievski's opinion, closer to his concept of what life ought to be than any attempts to regulate conduct by cold and bloodless rational principles.

The existentialists disposed of the whole issue of man and his behavior in a manner that was for them definitive. They *defined* the human being as a creature possessed of the power of free choice. Freedom, for the existentialists, is the essence of man's humanity. Animals live on the plane of perception, in an objective world, of which they are themselves a part, and in which there is no place for freedom. The world of the human being is twofold, however, consisting of the objective world of perception and the subjective world of imagination. By virtue of this special situation, the human being's entire reaction is different: it is the reaction of

---

[1] *On Liberty* (The Harvard Classics, 1909), V. 25.

an individual free to choose. He is not only an individual—the animal is also that—but he is a *human* individual, and that, for the existentialist, makes all the difference between determinism and freedom.

Out of this common code of belief various types of existentialism developed along different lines. One of the earlier expressions of existentialism took a theological form. Sören Kierkegaard, a Danish theologian and philosopher, used the existentialist principles of freedom of the will as a basis for the reconstruction of theology. Martin Heidegger and Jean-Paul Sartre presented existentialism as a philosophy of atheism—pessimistic atheism. Karl Jaspers and Gabriel Marcel were existentialist theists; their point of view included a belief in the existence of God. In their writings, all of these thinkers concerned themselves, in varying degrees, with the metaphysical underpinnings of existentialism. The scope of our study is limited, however, to existentialism as a philosophy of conduct, as an ethical philosophy.

The human being's freedom of choice differs from caprice in a very important way. As he is confronted by one situation after another, the manner in which the individual chooses entails a crucial consequence, in that it determines the kind of human being he will become. Instead of viewing his decisions as arising out of certain traits that constitute his nature, the existentialist thinks of man's nature as the result of his decisions. Hence the name "existentialism," with the principle that existence precedes essence. According to traditional modes of thought, choices or decisions are the result of a pre-existing "essence"—the essentials of human nature. Existentialism reverses this viewpoint and sees "essence" as the outcome of a pre-existing, freely-choosing individual.

This observation brings us to another principle that figures prominently in the existentialist ethic—personal responsibility. The individual as such is confronted with unique situations, and in his attempts to cope with these situations, he is not able to learn directly from the experience of others. He is, in other words, thrown on his own resources. The phrase "experience of others" includes what is usually called the "lessons of history." Human beings can look for no real guidance from this quarter, the existentialist claims, since history, far from "repeating itself," is itself a non-recurring series of unique situations and events. The individual cannot even evade responsibility by refusing to make a choice, by deciding to do nothing, and thus letting events take their course, for such an action of not-choosing is itself a choice, entailing its own consequences. The existentialist cannot turn to anyone whom he may think wiser than himself, for the wisdom of another individual, precisely because he is another individual, is not applicable to his own personal situation. The existentialist is thus alone, and the idea of "aloneness" recurs often in the existentialist mode of thought. Sartre, for example, makes frequent allusions to it in his literary, as well as in his philosophical writings.

The idea of isolation is related to another idea to which the existentialist gives prominence—that of tension. The freedom of the human being is regarded by the existentialist as a "dreadful freedom," and he pays for it in the coin of inescapable tension. This is what the existentialist has in mind when he calls his philosophy a philosophy of "anguish." Man's freedom is thus both the crown he wears and the cross he must carry as marks of his humanity. Life is one free choice after another, every choice fraught with unpredictable consequences.

The more pessimistic existentialists give prominence to another note, the note of tragedy. In their view, one fact casts its dark shadow over life and turns all the tension and seriousness of it into futility, into meaninglessness. This is the stark certainty and finality of death.

Another important tenet of the existentialist philosophy is the principle of engagement or commitment. There are two aspects to this principle. First, it represents a form of knowing or insight that comes from active participation or involvement in life, as opposed to reflection on life. The mode of commitment is the "feeling" way of knowing, as opposed to the "cognitive" way. The man who has spent his life immersed in practical politics "knows" politics in one way, the way of engagement; the social scientist "knows" politics in another way, the way of rational reflection.

A second aspect of the principle of engagement results from the belief that interaction with other selves in the decisions and actions of real life is the way to a knowledge both of oneself and of others.

This interaction discovers what Sartre calls "the world of inter-subjectivity." Here Sartre seems to have in mind what has been called the "dialectic of personal growth": knowledge of self and knowledge of other selves develop *pari passu.*

It is usually held that the French version of existentialism was profoundly influenced, if not directly inspired, by the conditions of life in the French underground resistance movement during the Second World War. Sartre had personal experience of the *maquis,* and certain aspects of his existentialism would seem to be a reflection of that experience. The member of the *maquis* lived in a world from which all the old stability had been removed. He had to cope with quite unpredictable situations, and the consequences of his actions were also unpredictable. Life was filled with menace, and, though part of an organization, he was, for good reason, kept without knowledge of the particulars of that organization. The member of the *maquis* was thus alone. Existentialism may indeed have been an exaltation and elaboration of that way of living. This particular illustrative situation, life in the *maquis,* would not, however, account for the reception accorded to existentialism as a general ethical philosophy. We have already pointed to another and probably more telling factor in this matter, namely, the need for a reassertion of the principle of free will. Existentialism appeared as a "new deal" for freedom.

It is not our purpose here to examine in detail the reasoning on which the existentialist view of freedom is based. In any case, the principle of freedom is presented as the basic presupposition of the entire philosophy, and may therefore claim immunity from criticism. Criticism would be more properly directed against the resulting philosophy as a whole. In this connection, we need only observe that it is still unclear whether existentialism belongs to the mainstream of philosophical thinking, or whether it is but a side issue. Has the "new deal" in human freedom resulted in new insights or emphases which will make a difference to subsequent philosophical thinking, or does it merely stand as a passing protest against the older ways of thinking?

In more specific terms, it is not as yet clear how far the existentialist means to carry his distinction between the way of knowing represented in engagement or commitment and that resulting from rational reflection. The question also arises as to how serious he is in suggesting that the wisdom arising out of rational reflection is illusory, something without value for the guidance of conduct. If the existentialist means to offer engagement as the right way of living, he exposes himself to an objection that is very relevant to our purpose here. Few would deny that at least one trait, and probably a basic trait, of the educated mind is the power of detachment from the hurly-burly of living, the ability, as it were, to stand farther away from the picture and get a better view of it. To use existentialist language, "the world of inter-subjectivity" is seen from time to time in a way which brings an element of objectivity to it; and such objectivity is the starting point and the terminus of rational reflection. Indeed, is this not precisely what the existentialist or any other philosopher is doing when he undertakes the task of constructing a philosophy?

In the more practical sphere, there is one aspect of existentialism that is of special interest to the educational philosopher. This is the emphasis on *responsibility*. There is something refreshing and invigorating about the existentialist view of man as a free and responsible creature in his inmost nature. While he cannot claim to be "master of his fate," he is always "captain of his soul." Apart altogether from the question of the philosophic defensibility of this view, may we not submit that, from an educational standpoint, it should be accepted as sound doctrine?

Should not the young be trained to see their freedom, which they will in due course insist on asserting, as related to personal responsibility? In our discussion of the "peer group," we saw how the adolescent in particular is apt to go through a phase in which, in the name of freedom, he rejects adult standards and accepts the more or less flighty standards of his group. These standards may bear on very serious matters, such as staying in school or leaving it, marrying now or later. He no doubt finds it exhilarating to see himself a free agent in such important matters, but his heady feeling of freedom should be tempered with a sobering sense of personal responsibility.

Freedom without responsibility is, after all, sophisticated infantilism—which is not a contradiction in terms. By whatever means available, adults should impress on the young person the idea that *responsible* individualism, not just individualism, is the thing that matters. Freedom is exciting, but it is not fun. That is good existentialism. Is it not also good education?

References for Further Reading

(Most of the references are more or less relevant to all three parts of the text. The grouping is intended to indicate emphasis only.)

Part I

Bagley, W. C. *Education and Emergent Man* (New York, Thomas Nelson and Sons, 1934)

Barzun, J. *The House of Intellect* (New York, Harper and Row, 1959)

Chisholm, G. B. *Can People Learn to Learn?* (New York, Harper and Row, 1958)

Cook, Lloyd A. and Cook, Elaine F. *A Sociological Approach to Education* (New York, McGraw-Hill Book Co., 1950)

Cunningham, W. F. *The Pivotal Problems of Education* (New York, The Macmillan Co., 1940)

Demiaskivich, M. J. *An Introduction to the Philosophy of Education* (New York, American Book Company, 1935)

Harvard Report. *General Education in a Free Society* (Harvard University Press, 1945)

Horne, H. H. *The Philosophy of Education* (New York, The Macmillan Co., 1904)

Hook, S. *Education for Modern Man* (New York, Alfred A. Knopf, 1963)

Hutchins, R. M. *Higher Learning in America* (Yale University Press, 1936)

Hutchins, R. M. *Education for Freedom* (Louisiana University Press, 1944)

Irving, J. A. *Science and Values* (Toronto, Ryerson Press, 1952)

Livingstone, R. *On Education* (New York, The Macmillan Co., 1944)

Macdonald, J. *Mind, School, and Civilization* (Chicago University Press, 1952)

Maritain, J. *Education at the Cross-roads* (Yale University Press, 1944)

Maritain, J. *Man and the State* (Toronto, W. J. Gage, 1951)

Meiklejohn, A. *Education Between Two Worlds* (University of Chicago, 1942)

Neatby, Hilda. *So Little for the Mind* (Toronto, Clarke Irwin, 1953)

Park, J. *Bertrand Russell on Education* (Columbus, Ohio State University Press, 1963)

Popper, K. R. *Conjectures and Refutations* (New York, Basic Books, 1963)

Price, Kingsley. *Education and Philosophical Thought* (Boston, Allyn and Bacon, 1962)

Redden, J. D. and Ryan, F. A. *A Catholic Philosophy of Education* (St. Paul, Minn., Bruce Publishing Co., 1955)

Russell, Bertrand. *Education and the Good Life* (New York, Boni Liveright, 1926)

Russell, Bertrand. *Education and the Social Order* (London, Allen and Unwin, 1961)

Whitehead, A. N. *The Aims of Education* (New York, The Macmillan Co., 1953)

Ulich, R. *Philosophy of Education* (New York, American Book Co., 1961)

Ulich, R. *The Human Career* (New York, Harper, 1955)

Part II

Broudy, H. S. *Building a Philosophy of Education* (New York, Prentice-Hall, 1954)

Bode, B. H. *Progressive Education at the Cross-roads* (New York, Newson and Co., 1948)

Brubacher, J. S. *Modern Philosophies of Education* (New York, McGraw-Hill, 1950)

Brameld, T. *Towards a Reconstructed Philosophy of Education* (New York, Dryden Press, 1956)

Childs, J. L. *Education and Morals* (New York, Appleton-Century-Crofts, 1950)

Childs, J. *American Pragmatism and Education* (New York, Holt, 1956)

Conant, J. B. *Education in a Divided World* (Harvard University Press, 1949)

Conant, J. B. *The American High School Today* (New York, McGraw-Hill, 1959)

Cornelius, D. K. and St. Vincent, E. *Cultures in Conflict* (Chicago, Scott, Foresman & Co., 1964)

Dewey, John. *Democracy and Education* (New York, The Macmillan Co., 1916)

Dewey, John. *Experience and Education* (New York, The Macmillan Co., 1938)

Finney, R. L. *Sociological Philosophy of Education* (New York, The Macmillan Co., 1928)

Hansen, K. H. *Philosophy for American Education* (New York, Prentice-Hall, 1960)

Hardy, C. D. *Truth and Fallacy in Educational Theory* (New York, Columbia University Teachers' College, 1962)

Kandel, I. *Conflicting Theories of Education* (New York, The Macmillan Co., 1938)

Kandel, I. *The Cult of Uncertainty* (New York, The Macmillan Co., 1943)

Kilpatrick, W. H. *Education for a Changing Civilization* (New York, The Macmillan Co., 1951)

Kilpatrick, W. H. *Philosophy of Education* (New York, The Macmillan Co., 1951)

Lamont, C. *Humanism as a Philosophy* (New York, Philosophical Library, 1949)

Mayer, F. *Philosophy of Education for Our Times* (New York, Odyssey Press, 1958)

MacKinnon, Frank. *The Politics of Education* (University of Toronto Press, 1960)

Morris, Van Cleve. *Philosophy and the American School* (Boston, Houghton Mifflin Co., 1961)

Popper, K. R. *The Open Society and Its Enemies* (London, Routledge, 1945)

Snow, C. P. *The Two Cultures* (New York, Cambridge Press, 1959)

Stanley, W. O. *Education and Social Integration* (Teachers' College, Columbia, 1953)

Woodring, P. *A Fourth of a Nation* (New York, McGraw-Hill, 1957)

Wynne, J. P. *Philosophies of Education* (New York, Prentice-Hall, 1947)

Part III

Barzun, J. *The House of Intellect* (New York, Harper, 1959)

Breed, F. S. *Education and the New Realism* (New York, The Macmillan Co., 1939)

Brinton, C. *Ideas and Men* (New York, Prentice-Hall, 1959)

Burns, H. W. and Brauner, C. I. *Philosophy of Education* (New York, Ronald Press Co., 1962)

Bruner, J. S. *The Process of Education* (Harvard University Press, 1950)

Butler, J. D. *Four Philosophies and Their Practice in Education and Religion* (New York, Harper, 1951)

Greene, T. *Liberal Education Reconsidered* (Harvard University Press, 1953)

Horne, H. H. *The Philosophy of Education* (New York, The Macmillan Co., 1927)

Judges, A. V. *Education and the Philosophic Mind* (London, Methuen, 1927)

Kneller, G. F. *Foundations of Education* (New York, John Wiley & Sons, 1963)

Lieberman, M. *Education as a Profession* (New York, Prentice-Hall, 1956)

Lodge, R. C. *The Philosophy of Education* (New York, Harper, 1957)

Michelson, C. (Edit.) *Christianity and the Existentialists* (New York, Charles Scribner's Sons, 1956)

O'Connor, P. J. *Introduction to the Philosophy of Education* (London, Routledge and Kegan Paul, 1957)

Park, J. (Edit.) *Selected Readings in the Philosophy of Education* (New York, The Macmillan Co., 1958)

Phenix, P. H. *Philosophy of Education* (New York, John Wiley & Sons, 1961)

Rusk, R. R. *Philosophical Bases of Education* (New York, Houghton Mifflin Co., 1938)

Scheffler, J. *Philosophy and Education* (Boston, Allyn and Bacon, 1958)

Scheffler, J. *The Language of Education* (Springfield, Ill., Thomas, 1960)

Smith, B. O. and Ennis, R. H. *Language and Concepts in Education* (Chicago, Rand, McNally, 1961)

Torrance, E. P. *Talent and Education* (University of Minnesota Press, 1960)

Hunt, R. N. *The Theory and Practice of Communism* (Harper, 1950)

Katz, J. (Edit.) *Canadian Education Today* (Toronto, McGraw-Hill Co. of Canada, 1956)

Further Recommended Reading (Historical-Philosophical)

Brauner, C. J. *American Educational Theory* (New York, Prentice-Hall, 1964)

Brubacher, J. S. *A History of the Problems of Education* (New York, McGraw-Hill, 1955)

Butts, R. *A Cultural History of Western Education* (New York, McGraw-Hill, 1955)

Cole, L. *A History of Education from Socrates to Montessori* (New York, Rinehart, 1950)

Mayer, A. E. *The Development of Education in the Twentieth Century* (New York, Prentice-Hall, 1949)

Phillips, C. *The Development of Education in Canada* (Toronto, W. J. Gage, 1957)

Randal, J. *Making of the Modern Mind* (New York, Houghton Mifflin Co., 1940)

Rusk, R. R. *The Doctrines of the Great Educators* (New York, The Macmillan Co., 1957)

Ulich, R. *Three Thousand Years of Educational Thought* (Harvard University Press, 1947)

Ulich, R. *History of Educational Thought* (New York, American Book Co., 1950)

42nd NSSE Yearbook, Part I.

54th NSSE Yearbook, Part II.

Index

Date Due